LIMITING OMNIPOTENCE

The Consequences of Calvinism

*A Study of Crucial Issues
in Reformed and Dispensational Theology*

DAVID DUNLAP

GOSPEL FOLIO PRESS
304 Killaly Street West, Port Colborne, ON L3K 6A6, Canada

Copyright ©2004
David Dunlap
All rights reserved

Published by GOSPEL FOLIO PRESS
304 Killaly Street West
Port Colborne, ON L3K 6A6
Canada

ISBN 1-897117-00-0

Cover design by Daveen Lidstone

ORDERING INFORMATION:
Gospel Folio Press
Phone: 1-800-952-2382
E-mail: orders@gospelfolio.com

Printed in the United States of America

Endorsements

David Dunlap has thoroughly explored the tenets of Hyper-Calvinism as bolstered by Covenant Theology from both an historical and scriptural perspective. His frequent use of quotes from reputable sources gives both validity and completeness to his work. When all "boiled down" his analysis sufficiently demonstrates that Calvinism, in its raw form, is a "fear based" and "works based" dogma that actually restricts God in His attributes and character. The writing style is thought provoking, but gracious and respectful. He does not resort to demeaning tactics or slander those with opposing views, but simply allows his arguments to rest on the inerrancy of Scripture.

—*Warren Henderson*
Rockford, IL

I believe this work makes a valuable contribution to one's library. I am conservative and careful as to what books I keep on my shelf but this one when published, will certainly have a place there. In these days it will provide a handy reference work for those who desire to learn more about Calvinism. Thank you for it and for the privilege of being of some small help in its production.

—*Colin Anderson*
Stratford, ON, Canada

I found this book especially helpful to me because it explained the full dimensions of Reformed theology that have become so prevalent today in evangelical circles. It carefully explains how imbalance of the truth of God's Word can lead to a misrepresentation of God and His character. It should be carefully read and digested.

—Robert Gessner
Allentown, PA

David Dunlap has skillfully exposed many of the errors of Reformed theology in a clear, and concise manner. His desire in dealing with these important issues is only to ask the most important question: "What saith the Scripture?" (Rom. 4:3). Especially helpful is his chapter on the "vicarious law keeping" view held by many today. May the Lord deal with each of our hearts that we might learn, unlearn, and relearn!

—George Zeller
Middletown Bible Church
Middletown, CT.

Atonement

What means a universal call
If there be not enough for all?
As if the Savior passed some by
While He for others' sins did die,
And that, though all are told to come,
Or that, in some mysterious way,
The Scriptures mean not what they say.
The mighty work of Jesus scan—
He "tasted death for every man."
He "died for all" that they who live
Back to Himself that life should give.
He has for "all" Atonement made—
For all mankind the ransom paid.
God loved the world; and when He gave
His Son, it was the world to save.
And though He knew some would not take
Of the provision He would make,
The foreseen choice of self-willed man
Changed not Heaven's universal plan,
As in the love that moved His heart,
All in The Atonement had a part.
If not, He only mocks their fate
Who presses all, "ere 'tis too late,"
To trust a work not for them done,
To take a pardon while there's none,
To fly from hell without a way,
Or perish if they disobey.

They never can the sinner reach
Who thus a crippled Gospel preach.
'Tis He who knows of food for all
That only can afford to call
A hungry world to come and feed—
All others would but mock their need.
O tell the tidings all around,
That every soul may hear the sound—
Th' Atoning work embraces all
Who were enveloped in the Fall.
To earth's remotest regions go,
And preach to every child of woe,
Impartial who or what they be-
The rich, the poor, the bond, the free,
That Christ on their behalf has died,
That God with Him is satisfied,
And now is ready to forgive—
The simple terms, "Believe and live."

—William Blaine,
"Lays of Life and Hope"
Bagster, London, 1938

Contents

Endorsements 3
Forward 9
Preface 11
1. The History and Importance of Calvinism 15
2. Reformed Theology and the Character of God 39
3. Reformed Theology and the Origin of Sin 49
4. The Sin Nature, Total Depravity, and Choice 61
5. Election, Salvation and Blessing 75
6. Reformed Theology and Limited Atonement 101
7. Reformed Theology and Regeneration 121
8. Reformed Theology and Eternal Security 137
9. The Sovereignty of God 157
10. Reformed Theology and Romans 9 175
11. Is Faith the Gift of God? 195
12. Reformed Theology, the Law, and the Rule of Life 205
13. Reformed Theology and the Christian's Standing 221
14. Reformed Theology and "One-Naturism" 233
15. Reformed Theology and the Righteousness of Christ . 255
16. Reformed Theology and Antinomianism 269
Bibliography 287

Forward

Thomas Newberry translates 1 Timothy 1:11 in his marginal notes this way, 'according to the gospel of the glory of the blessed God...' The character of the gospel and the character of God cannot be separated. What is true of one, is true of the other. It is precisely this theme that David Dunlap takes up with clarity and fullness.

There has been sloppy and dangerous thinking among popular evangelicals when it comes to the truth of the gospel and the character of our God. Relying heavily on some of the thinking of spiritual giants of the past, there has been a failure to compare what they said and what God said. The result has been we have moved to 'another gospel' (Gal. 1:6). This 'other' gospel has weakened our witness and robbed us of power.

We have lost the vision of the limitless nature of God's grace and mercy, the boundless character of His love, the wideness of His invitation, His generosity, His unrestrained, even prodigal heart that throws open the doors of heaven to, as the old hymn put it, 'that grand word 'whosoever''.

Quotations of popular modern day evangelicals together with worthies of the past are faithful. That is they are fair representations of what the author intended to say and no open-minded reader will be able to charge the writer with taking these out of context. David also freely acknowledges that many other things said and written by these well known men are faithful to the scriptures. It is their errors and its implications he takes issue with.

Everyone interested in communicating the gospel will benefit from reading this book. Each chapter will require thinking. This is not a work for the careless. The abundance of scripture references enables all of us to be "Bereans" in our reading. The author welcomes that. This will cure us from *Limiting Omnipotence*.

—*Brian Gunning*
September 2004

Preface

After preaching one evening, C. H. Spurgeon was approached by a young man. This man in laboring to reconcile the apparent conflict between the sovereignty of God and human freedom became more and more confused and confounded. He decided that Mr. Spurgeon might be a help to him. So he asked, "Sir, how do you reconcile the sovereignty of God with the free will of man?" Mr. Spurgeon with a sparkle in his eye replied, "My good man, I never try to reconcile good friends."[1]

These pages are a humble attempt to put into biblical perspective many of the questions I have been asked concerning the doctrine of election. This is a doctrine that has been the source of angry debate and division among Christians. Divine election and human responsibility are both equally and forcefully taught in the Word of God. But extreme Calvinism and Arminianism have stressed one aspect of this doctrine over the other. This led Mr. C. H. Macintosh to call Calvinism a "bird with one wing," a lopsided presentation of this important doctrine. The same could be said of Arminianism. Since many of the questions that are posed are directed at Calvinism, these pages will be for the most part directed at that particular teaching.

At the outset, I must tell you that I am not a "Calvinist" or an "Arminian" and that my understanding of what the Bible teaches concerning this theme will be my guide in the pages that follow. I make no apologies for my opposition to any doctrine that is not supported by the Word of God; my desire is that this book will not engender more strife but will be a help to the people of God. I do appreciate some of what "Calvinists" affirm and teach. Undoubtedly, we find some of its tenets taught in Scripture: such as the sovereignty of God, justification through faith alone, etc. However, there is also much in it that Scripture does not teach, and we will examine many of these doctrines. These teachings have proven to be harmful to many Christians in undermining their confidence in the justice and righteousness of God. They have also been the source of divisions in local assemblies. My conviction is that Calvinism limits the glory of God by limiting His love, mercy, and grace, and by compromising His justice, righteousness, and holiness.

Another has well summarized this tendency within Calvinism by writing, "Calvinism makes God the author of sin and reduces man to a poor puppet of destiny. It robs Christianity of all morality and deprives heaven of holiness. It takes away the guilt of sin and lifts the blame of hell from the souls of men and lays it at the feet of God. According to this view the mass of men are dead—dead and damned through no fault of their own. They never had a chance. They were sinful before they had sinned. They never will have a chance. To preach the gospel to such is not only useless, but cruel. It is an insult to the helpless dead, a mocking of the lifeless lips with offers of the Bread of Life. Remember you who are called to be 'Guardians of the faith' that almost all the heterodoxy and a full half of the infidelity of today, is the recoil of men's minds and hearts and consciences from such teaching as this."[2]

PREFACE

Calvinists will rarely concede that their view compromises the very character and attributes of God but in a chapter entitled *God, Freedom and Evil in Calvinist Thinking*, the Calvinist theologian, Dr. John Feinberg, admits,

> "Sometimes it would be easier not to be a Calvinist. An intellectual price tag comes with any conceptual scheme, but the one that comes with Calvinism seems beyond the resources of human intelligence to pay. Calvinists hold views that appear at very least counterintuitive. This is especially so with respect to Calvinist accounts of God's sovereign control in relation to human freedom and moral responsibility for evil.
>
> If Calvinists are right about divine sovereignty, there seems to be little room for human freedom. If freedom goes, so does human moral responsibility for sin. Worst of all, if Calvinists are right, it appears that God decides that there will be sin and evil in our world, maybe even brings it about that there is such evil, and yet, according to Calvinists, is not morally responsible for any of it. We are.
>
> If this is Calvinism's God, Calvinism seems not only intellectually bankrupt but also religiously bankrupt. Who could worship this God? Moreover, if atheists understand this portrait of God as paradigmatic of traditional Christianity, no wonder they are repulsed by Christianity. Although committed atheists will not likely abandon their atheism for any concept of God, at least the Arminian portrayal of God seems more attractive than the Calvinist portrayal."[3]

I would like to express thanks to a number of friends who helpfully read, commented on, and critiqued earlier versions of this work. Among these were Michael Attwood, Warren Henderson, James McCarthy, Edwin Bills, William MacDonald, and Jabe Nicholson of Uplook Ministries. Thanks to my beloved wife, Faith, for her sacrificial labor in proofreading. Sincere thanks goes to Colin Anderson, of Stratford, Canada, who labored in proofreading this work and made numerous helpful suggestions and corrections.

Endnotes

[1] C. H. Spurgeon, *The Treasury of the New Testament*, vol. 2, (Grand Rapids, MI, 1950), p. 355
[2] Robert McClurkin, Election, (St. Catharines, Ontario: Clarion Press, 1978), p. 2
[3] Thomas R. Schreiner, Bruce Ware (edited), *The Grace of God, the Bondage of the Will*, vol. 2, (Grand Rapids, MI: Baker Books), Chapter 20, John Feinberg, p. 459

- 1 -
The History and Importance of Calvinism

Few can disagree with the view that Calvinism is one of the most important theological movements in the history of the Christian church. Whether one is a Calvinist or a non-Calvinist, all must acknowledge that Calvinism has claimed an important and influential role in molding and shaping the church for the last five hundred years. Calvinism's theological and philosophical perspective has influenced and colored nearly every aspect of the church. Calvinism can determine one's views on politics, government, the Christian life, the study of eschatology, the nature of God, the character of man; the list is endless. A study of Calvinism is so important that every serious Christian should know something of what it teaches: its major tenets, its flaws, and its strengths. To form a firm understanding of Calvinism, it is important to understand its place in history and its early beginnings. Allow us to begin at the beginning or even prior to the beginning of system of doctrine called Calvinism. The theological framework of what we call Calvinism was virtually unknown for the first three hundred years of the Christian church. Of all the writings that have survived from the early church, not one major Orthodox Church leader taught what may be called Calvinism. Nearly every important early church leader, such as Clement of Alexandria (150-215 AD), Justin Martyr (100-165 AD), Origen (185-254 AD), Cyril of Jerusalem (312-386 AD), Jerome (347-420 AD), taught the doctrinal perspective we call "free will," Roger Forster and Paul Marston, in their thoughtful work *God's Strategy in Human History*, write:

> "The doctrine of 'free will' seems to have been universally accepted in the early church. There does not seem to have been a single church figure in the first 300 years who rejected the doctrine, and most of them stated it clearly in works, which we still have. We find it taught by great leaders in places as different as Alexandria, Antioch, Athens, Carthage, Jerusalem, Lycia, Nyssa, Rome, and Sicca. We find it taught by the leaders of all the main theological schools. The only ones to reject it were heretics like the Gnostics, Maricon, Valentinus, and the Manichees."[1]

Who was the first to introduce to the church the teaching that is called Calvinism? To discover the roots of Calvinism, we must look at the later life and writings of Augustine (354-430), the Bishop of Hippo, in North Africa.

AUGUSTINE

Aurelius Augustine was born in 354 AD at Thagaste, which is modern-day Algeria. He was named after two of Rome's leading emperors; as they would lead in political battles, he would lead the Church through theological battles. Augustine studied philosophy, mathematics, Latin, and speech, and was a professor of Rhetoric at the University of Milan. While Augustine is considered by many to be one of the greatest minds and most powerful orators of the church, he lived the first 32 years of his life in the pursuit of sensual pleasure and wealth. After his conversion in Milan, Italy, in 386 AD, his life evidenced a decisive and dramatic change. The man who was once devoted to pleasure and learning, was now devoted to God and His church. In 391, Augustine was ordained as a priest, and then later installed as the Bishop of Hippo in North Africa. It was at this time that Augustine would have his greatest impact.

In 390, a British monk, named Pelagius, came to Rome and had an immediate impact on the church through his teaching and the character of his life. Pelagius impressed church leaders by his righteous life, and soon, by his teaching. Pelagius reasoned that if God commanded us to live moral and upright lives, then He must also give us the ability to obey. Pelagius denied the sin nature in man. He believed that the sinfulness of man came from man living in a sinful world. It was the influence of the world that developed sinful habits in man. Pelagius argued that unregenerate man is capable of living sinlessly by simply exercising his will for the good. God gave this ability to him. Pelagius wrote:

> "A man (unregenerated) can be without sin and keep the commandments of God, if he wishes, for this ability has been given to him by God."[2]

Augustine was outraged at the doctrine of Pelagius. And so began the 25 year crusade of Augustine against the teaching of Pelagius. Historians know very little about Pelagius; the information that has survived comes from the writing of Augustine and others who opposed Pelagius. However, we can be assured that the teaching of Pelagius was unorthodox, and the church is indebted to Augustine for his efforts in refuting this error.

Nevertheless, we cannot assume that the doctrine of Augustine was fully orthodox and Biblically sound. Augustine taught that salvation came only through the Roman Catholic Church. He accepted the books of the Apocrypha as equally inspired as other books of Scripture. He interpreted Scripture using the allegorical method, popularized by Origen (185-254) and the Alexandrian school. Augustine tried to harmonize Scripture with the philosophy of Plato. He also taught the erroneous doctrines of infant baptism and baptismal regeneration. In refuting Pelagius, Augustine endorsed the unbiblical practice of infant baptism. He wrote:

> "Man is born condemned for Adam's sin and is incapable of not sinning. A man's will avails for nothing except to sin. Only the supernatural power of God's grace, imparted through (infant) baptism, could heal the deadly wound of sin upon the human soul."[3]

Nevertheless, Augustine possessed a great theological mind and his views on the Scriptures would exert a lasting impact upon the church. Augustine's greatest contribution would come through his application of the sovereignty of God to salvation. Augustine was the first church leader to teach the doctrines of predestination and unconditional election. His thinking in this area would greatly influence the Reformers. Augustine argued that God was sovereign, and by this sovereignty, all that comes to pass is ordained and decreed by God. He taught that man does not have a free will, but a will that is in bondage and enslaved to sin. Augustine taught that only the power of God's grace could restore, in some measure, the free will lost in the fall of Adam. However, this grace cannot be received by an act of the human will, or the exercise of faith, it must be given as a gift of God. Augustine wrote:

> "The Spirit of grace therefore causes us to have faith, in order that through faith we may, upon praying for it, obtain the ability to do what we are commanded."[4]

He taught the Calvinistic doctrine of double predestination. He argued that God predestinated some to eternal salvation while others are predestinated to eternal punishment. Roger Olsen, writing in Christian History magazine, comments on Augustine's book, *On the Predestination of Saints*. This Augustine scholar writes:

> "God simply chooses some persons out of the mass of fallen humanity to save and leaves others to their deserved condemnation. The reason some are so graced and others passed over lies only in "the hidden determinations of God."[5]

Augustine may very well be called the father of modern day Calvinism. He is equally considered to be the father of the modern Catholic Church. The Catholic Church, however, has largely passed over his doctrine of predestination. Prior to the Reformation, Augustinian theology had fallen into disfavor in the Roman Catholic Church. If not for the Reformation and its leaders, Augustinian theology may have been only a footnote in the annals of church history. The influence of Augustine on the Reformers is incalculable. Calvin and Luther both confessed that his writings greatly contributed to their theology. John Calvin, expressing his indebtedness to Augustine, once candidly admitted:

"Augustine is so completely of our persuasion, that if I should have to make written profession, it would be quite enough to present a composition made up entirely of excerpts from his writings."[6]

THE CONTRIBUTION OF MEDIEVAL SCHOLASTICISM

Augustine once commented that he burned with desire for the writings of Latin and Greek authors such as Seneca, Plato, Plotinus. For this reason, with his Christian Platonism, he was considered the foremost authority and greatest influence upon the Scholasticism movement. Scholasticism is the medieval practice of interpreting Scripture according to the philosophic ideas of Aristotle and Plato. In addition to Augustine, Catholic theologian Thomas Aquinas (1225-1274) influenced many with his scholastic work *Summa Theologica*, where, using the entire work of Aristotle, he attempted to harmonize Greek philosophy with the Christian theology of revelation. These Scholastic writers greatly influenced the Reformers, thereby introducing the philosophies of Aristotle (384-322 BC) and Plato into Calvinistic theology. Luther was an unashamed admirer of the Scholastic writers, and this philosophic-theological thinking influenced his theology. Theologian Reinhold Seeburg explains:

"Luther, it is well known, had pursued a thorough course of Scholastic study, making himself familiar particularly with Lombard, Occam, D'Alli and Biel. The influence of these studies was a permanent one. He had imbibed the outline and organization of the theological ideas of Scholasticism, and they remained as the points of connection in his theological thinking."[7]

John Calvin was also thoroughly versed in the theology of Plato and Aristotle, as well as the Scholastic writers who attempted to harmonize philosophy and Scripture. He was most affected by the Neo-Platonism of Augustine. Dr. Laurence Vance sets forth the influence of Neo-Platonism on the thinking of John Calvin:

> "Calvin was familiar with the Scholastic authors as well, especially Anselm (1033-1109), Lombard (1100-1160), Aquinas (1225-1277), and Bernard (1090-1153). He also freely quoted ancient Greek and Latin authors. And although Calvin knew the church fathers extremely well, as no one else in the century, he regarded Augustine as the best and most reliable witness of all antiquity."[8]

Scholasticism introduced a rigid deterministic philosophy into the theology of the Reformers. The doctrine of the sovereignty of God was now understood to mean that everything that comes to pass in the world is decreed and determined by God. This would include unconditional election to salvation, reprobation (the idea that God elects some to eternal punishment), and the belief that God is the author of sin, and that every sin committed is decreed by God. Reformed theologian Dr. James Daane laments this strong Scholastic influence on Reformed theology, writing:

> "It is no accident that in Scholastic Reformed theology God's sovereignty has increasingly been disassociated from his grace and associated instead with His determination of all things...Aristotle said that philosophy

began when men began to wonder. But when philosophic rationalism (determinism) has done its work, the wonder evaporates from Christianity and the mystery departs. If God and His decree, and in consequence, the world and its history no less, are exhaustively rational (determined), the gospel need not be preached, for there would be nothing for preaching to accomplish, since everything would remain rational (determined), whether men respond in faith or unbelief."[9]

JOHN CALVIN

John Calvin (1509-1564), as Augustine before him, was the most significant and important theological thinker of his generation. John Calvin was born in 1509, in Noyon, France, about 25 years after the birth of Martin Luther. Calvin was a second-generation Reformer, building on the work of those before him. The great burden of the first generation of Reformers was justification by faith and grace; the emphasis of the second generation of Reformers was the sovereignty of God and unconditional election. John Calvin was well trained to be the most influential second-generation Reformer. At the age of 12, he began his theological training by studying Latin in Paris; later he entered the University of Paris to study literature, philosophy, and language. After earning a master's degree, he entered the University of Orleans to study law. Sometime between 1529 and 1534, John Calvin was converted after reading the Scriptures and the writings of Martin Luther, and personally witnessing the burning of a Protestant martyr in France. Following his conversion, he fled Paris and sought refuge in the Protestant city of Basel, Switzerland. In 1535, at the age of 27, John Calvin wrote the most important work of the Reformation, *The Institutes of*

Christian Religion. This work, although written just a few years after Luther's *The Bondage of the Will*, is considered to be the most thorough Protestant examination of Roman Catholicism and the doctrine of justification by faith alone. In later editions of The Institutes, beginning with the 1539 edition, Calvin systematically sets forth for the first time his views on the doctrines of election, predestination, and the sovereignty of God. In 1535, he moved to Geneva. After living there for only 18 months, he moved to the free-city of Strasbourg, where he met Reformers Martin Bucer and Heinrich Bullinger. Under the tutelage of Martin Bucer, John Calvin became one of the leading voices in Reformation Europe.

Throughout his life, John Calvin's pen would not rest. He was a prolific writer. He wrote commentaries on the books of the Bible, and numerous works on theology, church government, ethics, and philosophy. Calvin's contributions to sound theology were enormous. He defended the three-fold call of the Reformation: Solo Scriptura, Solo gratis, Solo fide, that is salvation by Scripture alone, grace alone, and faith alone. He expounded eloquently upon the doctrine of justification. He wrote ably on the person of Christ, the death of Christ, and the doctrine of God. By the end of his life he had written over 11,000 pages of correspondence, commentaries on every book in the Bible, and numerous volumes on theology and related subjects.

In his writings Calvin returned time and again to the subjects of predestination and election. One reason that he focused on these doctrines was that he was called to defend them. Not everyone was pleased with his writing and theological reasoning. One Dutch theologian, Albert Pighius (1490-1542), issued a response to Calvin, entitled Ten Books on Human Free Choice and Divine Grace. Although Albert Pighius died soon after he wrote his treatise, Calvin issued a response in 1552, defending his doctrines in a book called *Concerning Eternal Predestination*. A number of years later, another theologian Sebastian Castellio (1515-1563), published an examination of Calvin's work. Calvin responded with another book called *A Defense of the Secret Providence of God*. The teachings of Calvin stirred the passions of many on both sides of the controversy. In 1551, the Calvinist city of Bern, Switzerland, sent a request to Geneva for "a cessation of discussion of the predestination issue for the sake of the tranquility and peace of the church." On another occasion, fellow Reformer Heinrich Bullinger wrote to Calvin, "Believe me, many are displeased with what you say in your Institutes about predestination." Calvin's doctrine on election and predestination stressed:

1. Theological Determinism	God decrees or ordains all events that come to pass.
2. Total depravity	The interpretation that Adam's fall resulted in the absolute inability of man to exercise faith in Christ.
3. Double Predestination	The teaching that God pre-destines some to eternal life and that He predestines others to eternal punishment.
4. Irresistible Grace	The doctrine that God regenerates the elect alone and gives to them alone the gift of faith.

JACOB ARMINIUS

Four years prior to the death of John Calvin in Genevea, Switzerland, Jacob Arminius (1560-1609) was born in Oudewater, Holland. This man of humble beginnings was destined to have a theological impact equal to or greater than that of John Calvin or Martin Luther. Arminius' father died when he was very young, and he was raised in the home of Theodorus Aemilius who taught him Latin, Greek, and theology. When he was 15 years old, he was enrolled at the University of Marburg in Germany. Marburg was Germany's first Protestant university, founded by Lutheran theologian Philip Melanchthon in 1527. Later, Arminius distinguished himself at the University of Leiden, where he studied for five years. He was granted a scholarship to the university in Geneva, Switzerland, where he studied under the teaching of Theodor Beza. He attended the University of Basel, where, upon graduation, he was offered a professorship, but refused on the grounds of his youth. Arminius was a brilliant student, an accomplished theologian of the highest order, an eloquent orator, and a respected Calvinist churchman. Upon his return to Holland, he accepted an offer to be the minister in a Reformed church in Amsterdam. He served there for fifteen years and was a church leader among the Reformed churches in Amsterdam. In 1603, he was asked to take a professorship at the University of Leiden, where he continued until his death in 1609. It was at the University of Leiden that he clashed with ultra-Calvinist theologian Francis Gomarus. This encounter soon drew leading political figures into the theological fray. Arminius' ideas quickly won the support of Grand Pensionary (highest-ranking government officer) Johan van Oldenbarneveldt (1547-1619); the attorney general of the provinces of Holland, Zeeland and Friesland, Hugo Grotius

(1583-1645); and many other leading officals in the regions of Holland, Delft, and Utrecht. Soon after the death of Arminius in 1609, these political and theological struggles threatened to divide the nation.

The time of Jacob Arminius's labors, was also a time of religious war and political upheaval in Europe. Spain was at war with Holland, and the Dutch Calvinists were leaders in the revolt against Spain. In 1573, William of Orange, the military victor in Holland's battles against King Philip of Spain and his brutal general, the Duke of Alva, publicly declared himself to be a Calvinist. In 1581, the Reformed faith was declared to be the state religion. The friction between the Calvinists and the Arminians in Holland was religious as well as political. Religiously, the Calvinists argued that salvation was entirely God's decree; the Arminians defended the doctrine of free agency. In politics, the Calvinists were for centralized political authority; the Arminians supported states' rights.

Although it is impossible to separate the political from the religious, there were serious and important theological issues at stake. These theological issues are still hotly debated today. It is noteworthy that Arminius was a respected Calvinist until his death, and that he resisted and fought against the seeds of division in the Calvinist movement that would ultimately come. In 1603, Arminius was appointed Professor of Theology at the University of Leiden, where he was quickly thrust into controversy with the hyper-calvinist views of Francis Gomarus (1563-1641). Extreme Calvinists, such as Gomarus and Beza, used the ideas of the philosopher Aristotle in their interpretation of Scripture. These Calvinist theologians applied the logic and syllogisms of Aristotle, and that of Scholasticism, to arrive at their theological conclusions. Arminius, from the earliest days when he studied under Beza in Geneva, refused this method. Arminius read the writings of Peter Ramus (1515-1572), a strong critic of the views of Aristotle. Arminius argued that Bible doctrine should be learned inductively and not deductively. That is, scriptural knowledge should be learned as one compares Scripture with Scripture, and not by reading theological views into Scripture based upon philosophical logic. John Parkinson frames the importance of this issue when he quotes theologian Alister McGrath:

> "For Arminius, the Bezan approach to theology via predestination is the result of the application of a deductive and synthetic method; the correct theological method, he argues is inductive and analytic...Under Beza, Aristotelian syllogistic logic became an essential component of the curriculum of the Genevan Academy."[10]

Arminius also clashed with the "high Calvinists" in the area of the decrees of God. The extreme Calvinists based their view of election and predestination upon the content and the order of the decrees of God. Their view was called the "Supralapsarian" position of the decrees, which held that even the fall of man was foreordained by God. Arminius refused to interpret election and predestination based upon this unorthodox view of the decrees, but rather upon the revealed Word of God. The high Calvinists wanted all Reformed ministers to sign a Calvinist Statement of Faith, based upon the Calvinist creeds and the Supralapsarian view. The debate soon turned on what would be the Reformed churches' final authority: the creeds or the Scriptures? Arminius rejected the Supralapsarian view of the decrees because:

- It was not supported by Scripture.
- It had not been held by Christian scholars in 1500 years and had never been accepted in any church council.
- It made God the author of sin.
- It made the decree of election refer to uncreated man.

Arminius taught that election must be understood to be centered in Christ. The question that he proposed was: Do we believe because we are elect, or are we elect because we believe? Arminius argued that Christ, not the decrees, is the source and cause of salvation. Arminus feared that Gomarus and other Supralapsarian interpreters of Calvin were in danger of making Christ a mere instrument, or means of carrying out a decree. He argued that election was according to foreknowledge; that is, God elects to salvation all those who, according to His divine foreknowledge, would one day believe on Christ.

THE IMPACT OF THE SYNOD OF DORT

Historical documents reveal that Jacob Arminius' life and service for God were marked by devotion to God, a love for the Scriptures, and a toleration of others. Throughout his entire life, he was considered an orthodox Calvinist theologian. He differed from the more extreme Calvinists on the underlying basis of Scripture interpretation and the interpretation and content of the divine decrees. Arminius did not seek to change the Reformed church or condemn others because of differing views. The famed lawyer Hugo Grotius (1583-1645) once said of Arminius: "Condemned by others, he condemned none." However, after the death of Jacob Arminius, there was increasing political pressure from the extreme Calvinists upon the Arminians. The Arminian view concerning "states' rights" was seized upon by the Calvinists. The Arminians were a relatively small minority and weak politically in Holland. The hyper-Calvinists, who were more powerful, wanted to rid Holland of the political and spiritual influence of the Arminians. The synod of Dort was the vehicle designed to accomplish this end. The Calvinist government took great interest in the proceedings. Government officials were present at all the sessions and the government of Holland assumed all the expenses connected to the proceedings. The synod of Dort was convened in Dordrecht, Holland, on November 13, 1618, and concluded in May of 1619. This particular gathering is significant because it was there that the famed "five points of Calvinism" were hammered out. The teaching of Calvin, Luther, and later, Beza had spread throughout Europe during the previous sixty-five years. But not everyone was content with the teaching, and there were important pockets of resistance to this system of doctrine in Holland. Those who opposed Calvinism were called the "Remonstrance," or later the "Arminians." These Christians agreed with the tenets of moderate Calvinist Jacob Arminius, who had died suddenly in 1609. The Remonstrance movement in Holland was led by John Uytenbogaert (1557-1644), Simon Episcopius (1583-1643), and Hugo Grotius. The Remonstrance (Arminians) argued the following points:

(1) God has decreed to save those who shall believe on Jesus Christ and persevere in faith.
(2) Jesus Christ died for all men, providing redemption for those who believe.
(3) Man is in a state of sin, unable to save himself or do anything truly good.

(4) Man cannot, without the grace of God, accomplish any good deeds; but this grace can be resisted.
(5) Believers have the power to persevere, but as to whether they can fall away, that must be determined from the Scriptures.

The Calvinists in Holland issued what was called the "Counter-Remonstrance." In this statement they argued the following seven points:

(1) Because the whole race has fallen in Adam and become corrupt and powerless to believe, God draws out of condemnation those whom He has chosen unto salvation, passing by others.
(2) The children of believers, as long as they do not manifest the contrary, are to be reckoned among the elect.
(3) God has decreed to bestow faith and perseverance, and thus save those whom He has chosen to salvation.
(4) God delivered up His Son, Jesus Christ, to die on the cross to save only the elect.
(5) The Holy Spirit, externally through the preaching of the Gospel, works a special grace internally in the hearts of the elect, giving them power to believe.
(6) Those whom God has decreed to save are supported and preserved by the Holy Spirit, so that they cannot finally lose their faith.
(7) True believers do not carelessly pursue the lusts of the flesh, but work out their own salvation in the fear of God.[11]

The Synod of Dort consisted of 154 sessions, where 102 Calvinist leaders were official members of the conference, together with 28 delegates from France, (Arminians) was barred from any participation, except for a one-month period, at the twenty-second session, when they appeared as defendants. This small party of thirteen was led by Simon Episcopius, who presented their defense. After their defense they were brusquely ordered out of the proceeding. As a result, the five points of Calvinism were unanimously declared to be the official position of the states of Holland, and the Remonstrant position was declared heretical. At the adjournment of the Synod in May of 1619, the thirteen Arminian defendants were called before the States-General of Holland and asked to recant or cease teaching their doctrines, or suffer banishment from the country. Because of their refusal, over 200 Arminian ministers were deposed from their pulpits and many were banished from the country. At the conclusion of the Synod of Dort, the Canons of Dort were issued. These canons formed the five points of Calvinism:

1. Total Depravity
2. Unconditional Election
3. Limited Atonement
4. Irresistible Grace
5. Perseverance of the Saints

What was the effect of this synod upon Protestant Europe? How did other Calvinist leaders react to the decisions of Dort? The civil and religious leaders at the Synod of Dort were undoubtedly surprised to learn of the disapproval of many of their peers. Historian T. C. Gratton details the consequences of the Synod of Dort in the Netherlands and in wider Europe. He writes:

"Theology was mystified; religion disgraced; Christianity outraged. And after six months' display of ferocity and fraud, the solemn mockery was closed by the declaration of its president that its miraculous labors made hell tremble. Proscriptions, banishments, and death were the natural consequences of this synod. The divisions which it had professed to extinguish were rendered a thousand times more violent than before. Its decrees did incalculable ill to the cause they were meant to promote. The Anglican Church was the first to reject the canons of Dort with horror and contempt. The Protestants of France and Germany, and even Geneva, the nurse and guardian of Calvinism, were shocked and disgusted, and unanimously softened down the rigor of their respective creeds."[12]

THE INFLUENCE OF THE WESTMINSTER CONFESSION

Twenty years after the Synod of Dort, the controversy that swirled in Holland had soon spread to England. A nation that was once solidly Roman Catholic was now becoming strongly Calvinistic. The English reformation was different than the reformation in Europe. The reformation in England was energized primarily by the development of the English Bible. However, there were also a growing number of those who were sympathetic to the views of the Arminians. The Arminian view was gaining support among political leaders because it insisted that no temporal leader could be the head of the church. In 1643, an assembly was called by Parliament, at the Westminster Abbey in London, with the purpose of providing the government with a document that might be used to establish Calvinism in England. The Westminster Assembly consisted of 151 members:

121 Calvinist church leaders, 10 members of the House of Lords, and 20 members of the House of Commons. The assembly lasted about 6 years, beginning in 1643 and continuing until 1649, consisting of 1,163 numbered sessions. At the conclusion of the Assembly, the Westminster Standards were drawn up, the most well-known being the *Westminster Confession* and the *Longer and Shorter Catechisms*. The Longer Catechism contains 196 questions and answers, while the Shorter Catechism has 107 questions and answers. The Westminster Confession is considered by Calvinists to be the most complete and accurate statement of Christian doctrine ever developed. Calvinist author Kenneth Good explains the reason for this conviction:

> "The Westminster Confession represents a culmination or perfection of the 'Reformed Faith' after it had been tested by and reacted to Romanism, Lutheranism, Arminianism, Anglicanism, and Anabaptism. It speaks with the precision and depth of Puritanism, and it incorporates the full-grown flower of a developed covenant theology."[13]

The Westminster Confession of Faith has become the standard of Calvinist thought in Reform churches throughout the world. In many Reformed seminaries, students are required to memorize the Shorter Catechism of the Westminster Confession. Many leading Calvinists look to the Westminster Confession, more than any other document, as the standard and authority for all doctrine and practice.

CALVINISM TODAY

The Calvinism of Augustine, Calvin, the Synod of Dort, and the Westminster Confession tended to represent Calvinism in its more theological extreme. These great Christian minds and councils hammered out their theological positions amid controversy and doctrinal rancor, causing their positions to be more extreme than they otherwise might have been. These theological opinions tended to swing as far as possible away from their opponents, instead of setting forth a balanced and fair treatment of Scripture. One wonders what might have been written by these same men during a time of relative theological calm. As time has progressed, many Calvinists have moderated and have incorporated many typically non-Calvinist concepts into Reformed theology. Some Calvinists have offered more moderate views concerning Theological Determinism, Unconditional Election, Limited Atonement and Irresistible Grace. Reformed theologian James Daane, the former editor of The Reformation Journal, has proposed radical changes in many of these areas in his book, *The Freedom of God*.[14] The use of gospel invitations was once thought to be the sole property of the non-Calvinist, but this practice was effectively used in the evangelistic preaching of George Whitefield and C. H. Spurgeon. This practice continues to be used today by some Reformed churches. The Wesleyan teaching of the Baptism of the Holy Spirit, or "Second Blessing," was once soundly rejected by the Reformed church. However, the respected Calvinist preacher Dr. Martin Lloyd-Jones (1903-1984) of London incorporated this doctrine into his teaching ministry. He set forth this view in his commentary entitled, Romans 8:5-17-The Sons of God.[15] As regarding the doctrine of Limited Atonement, many Calvinists are abandoning the Reformers' more extreme view, and opting for the "unlimited" view, as once suggested by Jacob Arminius. Calvinist pastor R. T. Kendall, of Westminster Chapel in London, has surprised many of his Calvinist friends with his more moderate view of the Perseverance of the Saints. He has argued for a view that is more similar to that of Dispensationalism than Calvinism in his book *Once Saved, Always Saved*.[16] However, some Reformed leaders have been resisting these changes. They are suggesting a return to and defense of the Calvinism defined by the Synod of Dort and the Westminster Confession. Some Reformed writers are becoming more and more extreme in their views and aggressive in their opposition to Dispensational and Evangelical theology.[17] This strong emphasis by some Reformed theologians has, unfortunately, sparked a divisive and polarizing attitude among conservative evangelicals.

"NON-CALVINISM " TODAY

In the Calvinism debate, it is assumed by many that there are only two possible viewpoints: Calvinism and Arminianism. At times, these two schools contend with each other as if there was no other Scriptural perspective. To many Christians, neither of these two viewpoints are satisfying, nor do they appear to be fully true to Scripture. Their convictions are expressed in the words of Richard Montagu (1577-1641), when he asserted that he was "neither Arminian, nor a Calvinist, nor a Lutheran, but a Christian," What do these Christians believe? They believe that man has been fully corrupted by the fall of Adam, but that the fall has not resulted in an inability to exercise faith. They believe that election is according to divine foreknowledge, "elect according to the foreknowledge of God…" (1 Pt. 1:2). They believe in the infinite drawing and convicting power of the Holy Spirit unto salvation. They believe that salvation is entirely of God (Jon. 2:9). They believe that a Christian cannot lose his salvation, for he is kept to the uttermost by the power of God (1 Pt. 1:5, Heb. 7:25). They reject theological labels that serve more to categorize believers than to fully express the truth of God. They look to the Scriptures as their divine compass and standard, and studiously resist any theology that would go beyond the bounds of Scripture. They echo the thoughts of C. H. Mackintosh (1820-1896) who wrote:

> "A disciple of the high school of doctrine will not hear of a world-wide gospel of God's love to the world, of glad tidings to every creature under Heaven. He has only gotten a gospel for the elect. On the other hand, a disciple of the low or Arminian school will not hear of the eternal security of God's people. Their salvation depends partly upon Christ, and partly upon themselves. All this dishonors God, and robs the Christian of true peace...it leads a person to pride himself on having the truth of God when, in reality, he has only laid hold of a one-sided system of man."[18]

THE FOCUS OF THIS BOOK

Throughout these pages, the reader will notice the frequent use of the term "non-Calvinist," This term is used to indicate a view, we trust, that is neither Calvinist nor Arminian, but one supported by Scripture. The term is not used to disparage the Calvinist or Arminian, but to simply suggest a biblical alternative. At times the reader will be convinced that the author is a Calvinist, and at other times that he is an Arminian. It is our hope that he is neither, but only faithful to the Word of God.

THE HISTORY AND IMPORTANCE OF CALVINISM

The purpose of this book is to provide a greater understanding of what is called Reformed, or Calvinstic, theology. The aim is not to be overly critical, but hopefully gracious and fair to their views. Nevertheless, due to differences in points of theology, doctrinal criticism will necessarily appear. This work is designed to be an aid to the serious Christian, but not necessarily to the theologian and scholar. There has been the attempt to footnote quotations as much as possible, but not exhaustively so, as in more technical works. The goal is to produce a work that is as readable and helpful as possible, without being too technical and obtuse. The structure of this work is to consider the Five-Points of Calvinism, otherwise known by the acronym TULIP: Total Depravity, Unconditional Election, Limited Atonement, Irresistible Grace, and Perseverance of the Saints. In addition to this emphasis, the book will also consider the practical consequences of Reformed theology by examining more closely Reformed doctrines such as "One-Naturism," the sovereignty of God, Romans chapter nine, the "rule of life" of the believer, the character of God, and the gift of faith. The reader will soon notice the absence of any discussion on the prophetic aspects of Reformed theology such as Amillennialism and Covenant theology. It has been our desire to keep this work reasonably brief, noting that others have ably and thoroughly written on this subject.[19]

It is our conviction that a study on the subject of Calvinism and its implications is important and necessary. May this study, in a small way, introduce some to the subject and thereby, be a resource in the understanding of Holy Scripture, enabling us to increase in knowledge and devotion for the Lord Jesus Christ.

Endnotes

[1] Roger Forster, Paul Marston, *God's Strategy in Human History*, (Bromley, England: STL Books, 1974), p. 198
[2] Christian History, Augustine, Issue 67, 2000, p. 30
[3] Ibid, p. 30
[4] Ibid, p. 30
[5] Ibid, p. 31
[6] Ibid, p. 31
[7] Reinhold Seeburg, *The History of Doctrine*, (Grand Rapids, MI: Baker, 1997), p. 223
[8] Laurence Vance, *The Other Side of Calvinism*, (Pensacola, FL: Vance Publications, 1999), p.103
[9] James Daane, *The Freedom of God*, (Grand Rapids, MI : Eerdmans, 1973), p. 163
[10] John Parkinson, *The Faith of God's Elect*, (Glasgow, Scotland: Gospel Tract Publications, 1999), p. 53
[11] John T. McNeill, *The History and Character of Calvinism*, (New York, NY: Oxford University Press, 1967), 264-265
[12] T. C. Gratton, quoted in *The Historian's History of the World*, (New York: T. S. Williams, 1905), p. 564
[13] Kenneth H. Good, *Are Baptists Reformed?*, (Lorain, OH: Regular Baptist Heritage Fellowship, 1986), p. 86
[14] James Daane, The Freedom of God, (Grand Rapids, MI: Eerdmans, 1973)
[15] D. Martyn Lloyd-Jones, *Romans 8:5-17- The Sons of God*, (Grand Rapids, MI: Zondervan, 1980), p. 233-369
[16] R. T. Kendall, *Once Saved, Always Saved*, (Chicago, IL: Moody Press, 1983)
[17] John Gerstner, *Dispensationalism: Wrongly Dividing the Word of God*, (Brentwood, TN:Wolgemuth and Wyatt, 1991), Keith Mathison, *Dispensationalism: Wrongly Divinging the People of God*, (Phillipsburg, NJ : P & R Publishers, 1995)
[18] C. H. Mackintosh, *Treasury; One Sided Theology*, (Neptune, NJ: Loizeaux, 1983), p. 604-605
[19] Dwight Pentecost, *Things to Come*, (Grand Rapids: Zondervan), Charles Ryrie, *Dispensationalism Today*, (Chicago, IL: Moody Press, 1999), Renald Showers, *There Really is a Difference*, (Bellmawr, NJ: Friends of Israel, 1990)

- 2 -
Reformed Theology and the Character of God

Dr. A. C. Gaebelein, member of the editorial committee of the 1909 Scofield Reference Bible was once asked what he thought about the Calvinist book The Sovereignty of God written by Arthur W. Pink. He responded,

> "Mr. Pink used to be a contributor to our magazine. His articles on Genesis are good, and we had them printed in book form. But when he began to teach his frightful doctrines that make the love of God a monster, we broke fellowship. The book is totally unscriptural. It is akin to blasphemy. It presents God as a Being of injustice and maligns His holy character. It denies that our blessed Lord died for the ungodly. According to Pink's perversions, Christ died for the elect only. It is just this kind of teaching that makes atheists."[1]

Our interpretation of the sovereignty of God will, to a large degree, influence our understanding of the character of God. The doctrines concerning God's very nature and His attributes are at stake. The Calvinist lays great weight upon the power and decrees of God, often to the expense of the surpassing greatness of His holiness, justice, love, and grace. The Scriptures reveal that the ultimate purpose of the doctrine of God's sovereignty is certainly to display the multi-faceted glory of God. The redemptive plan of God will, in a future day, showcase to all those in heaven and upon earth God's unrivaled greatness. Both the Calvinist and the non-Calvinist will grant this point. However, they both come at it from very different points of view. The Westminster Confession states,

> "By the decree of God, for the manifestation of His glory, some men are predestinated unto everlasting life, and others foreordained unto everlasting death."[2]

In another place the Westminster Confession states how God further manifests his glory:

> "The rest of mankind, God was pleased, according to the unsearchable counsel of His own will, whereby He extendeth or withholdeth mercy as He pleaseth, for the glory of His sovereign power over His creatures, to pass by, and ordain them to dishonor and wrath for their sin, to the praise of His glorious justice."[3]

According to this teaching, in some inexplicable way, the richness of God's glory is displayed in predestinating the non-elect to everlasting wrath, suffering the second death in the lake of fire. We must respectfully disagree with this point of view, for it compromises and does violence to the holy character of God.

SOVEREIGNTY AND THE GRACE OF GOD

The non-Calvinist, while granting fully the majestic sovereignty of God, lays stress to the fullness and wonder of the grace of God that has appeared unto all. It is through grace that

God makes man what he is. It was grace that formed man out of the dust of the earth and created him in God's image. It was this same grace that brought Christ down to man. This grace is unlimited in its sufficiency (Ps. 49:7-8), unlimited in its scope (Tit. 2:11), unlimited in its efficiency (Rom. 1:16), unlimited racially (both Jew and Gentile), and unlimited culturally (Col. 3:11).

Redemptively, grace is the full and unmerited favor by which God, in the Lord Jesus Christ, provides salvation for an unworthy world. Man has no ability and no will apart from God's enabling grace and the work of the Holy Spirit. Moreover, grace is the act of God in reaching down to man in his weakness and sin. Concerning this connection between grace and redemption, Dr. Vernon Grounds, the former president of Conservative Baptist Seminary in Denver, writes:

> "More than simply unmerited favor, grace is the omnipotent help which God in His freedom chooses to give through Jesus Christ and by His Spirit, liberating man from his self-incurred bondage and misery, reestablishing a right relationship with Himself."[4]

The non-Calvinist celebrates the limitless grace of God, while the Calvinist on the other hand places unwarranted limitations on the grace of God. To his credit, the Calvinist rightly stresses the sufficiency of God, but then limits the efficiency of grace to the elect alone. The late Herman Hoekema, former professor at Calvin College in Michigan, is representative of this point of view:

"God loves the elect because they are righteous in Christ; he hates the reprobate because they are sinners. The elect alone are the objects of grace; for them alone is the gospel good news. For the reprobate God has no blessing at all, but only an eternal hatred. Rain and sunshine, the hearing of the gospel, the sacrament of baptism (if administered to a person as an infant) all are curses *heaped upon the reprobate by God.*"[5] (italics mine)

In great contrast to this, the Scriptures express the fullness of grace to "all" with great emphasis. Notice with care the small but important word "all," indicating that God's grace is not just for the elect, but for all the lost of the world. "For God hath concluded them all in unbelief, that He might have mercy upon all" (Rom. 11:32). "All we like sheep have gone astray, we have turned every one to his own way and the Lord hath laid upon Him the iniquity of us all" (Isa. 53:6). "But we believe that through the grace of the Lord Jesus Christ we shall be saved even as they" (Acts 15:11). "For the grace of God that bringeth salvation hath appeared to all men" (Tit. 2:11). "The Lord is not willing that any should perish but that all should come to repentance" (2 Pet. 3:9). With firm resolve the Word of God affirms the grace of God is available to all men, and that grace is sufficient to save us from sin of the deepest dye, and is efficient to save all who trust in Christ for salvation.

SOVEREIGNTY AND THE LOVE OF GOD

Just as God's grace reaches down to all men, so in like manner, the incomparable love of God reaches out to all mankind. The love of God for a world that has turned its back in unbelief and scorn is one of the most sublime themes of all the Word of

God. The words and truth of John 3:16 have been the means of comfort and salvation to thousands, "For God so loved the world that He gave His only begotten Son that whosoever believeth on Him should not perish but have everlasting life." Yet there are some who would question if God truly loves all equally. Some insist that God's love extends to the elect alone and on the non-elect God bestows His hatred. The hyper-Calvinist author A. W. Pink writes:

> "To tell the Christ-rejector that God loves him is to cauterize his conscience, as well as afford him a sense of security in his sins. The fact is that the love of God is a truth for Saints only."[6]

If the love of John 3:16 was for the world of the elect alone, why did the Lord use it in His address to Nicodemus, an unbeliever? Moreover, why did the Lord say of the rich young ruler, "Then Jesus, beholding him loved him..." (Mk. 10:21)? In this case an example of an unbeliever, who loved his riches more than Christ. Nevertheless, many Calvinists will argue that the overall tenor of the Bible supports their position. Romans nine is frequently pointed to in support of the teaching that God hates the non-elect. There Paul says, "Jacob have I loved but Esau have I hated" (Rom. 9:13). Concerning this verse, it should be noted that Paul is referring to the seed of Abraham nationally. This reference is to Jacob and Esau as nations one thousand years after they were born. This is clearly seen in Paul's reference to Malachi 1:2-3, which states the context as "his heritage," This is not an instance of God's hatred of Esau, as an individual, as one of the non-elect, before he was born.

The Calvinist's restriction of the love of God to the elect alone reveals a serious error concerning the very nature of God's love. He contends that because the non-elect have rejected Christ and continue in sin, therefore God's love is not upon them. However, we all were at one time in that position. God loves us because He loves us. God's love is unconditional. It is all of God. God's love is not because He saw anything in us deserving of love, for there was no merit. "For when we were without strength, in due time Christ died for the ungodly...But God commendeth his love toward us, in that, while we were yet sinners, Christ died for us" (Rom. 5:6, 8). Does God's love extend to only those who were more worthy, more lovable, or more deserving? No. God's love was extended to all persons. This affirms His very nature for God is love.

SOVEREIGNTY OF GOD AND RIGHTEOUSNESS

The righteousness of God is often spoken of as one of the moral attributes of God. Righteousness is the aspect of His character, which is seen in God's treatment of man. God's justice leads Him to treat all persons alike, and bestow no special favors in regard to salvation. Both the Calvinist and the non-Calvinist agree that God is just and righteous. Needless to say, they both look at it from a very different perspective.

The Calvinist sees God bestowing special blessings and favors upon the elect, favors that He withholds from the non-elect. According to Calvinism, it is the elect alone whom He loves and to whom He gives the gift of faith, grants regeneration, provides redemption, and draws with irresistible grace. Yet the Bible says, "For there is no respect of persons with God" (Rom 2:11), and "The righteousness of God which is through faith in Jesus Christ to all and on all them that believe. For there is no difference; for all have sinned and fall short of the glory of God" (Rom. 3:22-23 NKJV). Later in Romans, Paul states that God has "...concluded them all in unbelief, that He might have mercy upon all" (Rom. 11:31). All have sinned, are in unbelief, and therefore are lost.

But before we leave this facet of the justice of God, there is another aspect we would like to explore, namely, the position of Calvinism in regard to the destiny of children that die in infancy. Many Bible expositors teach that in the event of death, infants will go to heaven. They stress that the redemptive work of Christ upon the cross was sufficient for the sin nature that we receive from Adam, and now we are only responsible for sins committed. Did not John the Baptist say, "Behold the Lamb of God who takes away the sin of the world" (Jn. 1:29)? He does not say "the 'sins' of the world" but rather "the sin of the world;" the word is singular, indicating that Christ's death dealt judicially with original sin. In the book of Romans the apostle Paul also makes this theological distinction. In Romans 3:21-5:12 he speaks of sins, that is the sins that we have committed. Then in Romans 6:1-7: 25 he writes of sin, referring to our sin nature. This distinction is emphasized again by John, the apostle, in 1 John chapter 1. In verse 8, he writes, "If we say we have not sin, we deceive ourselves, and the truth is not in us," Here he is referring to the sin nature that we all possess. But then in verse 10, he teaches that we all commit sin when he writes, "If we say we have not sinned, we make him a liar..." Surely, Christ died for the individual sins of each person, but also for our sin nature (Jn. 1:29). It was at the cross that our sin nature was judged. Therefore, at the Great White Throne judgment of unbelievers the Word of God says, "...and the dead (unsaved) were judged out of those things written in the books, according to their *works*" (Rev. 20:13). Notice that the unbeliever is judged according to his "works," not his sin nature. Therefore, infants who die will not be judged for the sin nature, but for sins. Upon this point J. Albrecht Bengel, (1687-1752) the respected Lutheran theologian and Greek scholar, comments:

> "Infants are objects of Divine care, not because they have not been under the curse like others, but because they have been rescued from it. The human race was one mass of perdition, in which infants are included, on account of original sin, and concerning this sin the whole of it has been redeemed."[7]

J. A. Bengel was not teaching a veiled form of universal salvation for all men, but rather, laying emphasis upon the fact that the redemptive work of Christ judged sin, that is the guilt of original sin. Sinful man is not punished in hell because he is guilty of possessing a sinful nature, but rather for his sinful deeds. Infants who die will not face the eternal torments of hell due to the guilt of original sin. The punishment for that sin has been born already by Christ. Nevertheless, we still suffer from the power of indwelling sin because, although its guilt was judged by Christ at the cross, it has not been removed from the believer. Moreover, King David comforted himself in the truth that original sin would not keep infants from heaven. Upon the death of his own child he wrote, "But now he is dead, wherefore should I fast? Can I bring him back again? I shall go to him, but he shall not return to me" (2 Sam. 12:23).

John Calvin rejected this truth at the expense of the holy character of God. He taught that non-elect infants, upon death, would be judged for the guilt of original sin. He thereby does violence to the justice of God concerning infants. John Calvin writes:

> "Original guilt is sufficient to condemn men...and those infant children who are taken from this life before they could display any works of faith because of their age...some born in Jerusalem pass thence to a better life, while those of Sodom to the forecourt of hell..."[8]

This and other such comments have served as fodder for fervent Calvinists to teach that thousands of non-elect infants will suffer eternal torment in hell. One such teacher is Harold Camping, "Family Radio" commentator based in Oakland, CA. Thankfully, moderate Calvinists reject this unbiblical notion. This view does grievous damage to the justice of God, and must be rejected by every sincere Christian.

The Calvinistic view of God's sovereignty has been found to impugn the holy character of God. It places unwarranted and unbiblical limitations upon the grace, justice, love, and mercy of God. These aspects of God's character extend to the non-believer as well as to the believer. It turns the biblical doctrine of God on its head. The love of God becomes hatred for the non-elect. The death of Christ for all men becomes the death of Christ for a chosen few. A just God becomes unjust. The God of the Calvinist is not the God described by the Word of God, thus undermining and making a mockery of the Christian's object of worship, his comfort in trial, and the hope of eternal salvation. Christians must jealously guard against every subtle attack upon the holy nature and character of God, even though couched in high-sounding theological words.

Endnotes

[1] Arno Gaebelein, <u>Our Hope,</u> Vol. 37, No. 11, May 1931, p. 684
[2] *Westminster Confession*, Reformed Presbyterian Church, Pittsburgh, PA, 1989
[3] Ibid
[4] Vernon Grounds, *Grace Unlimited*, (Minneapolis, MN, Bethany Pub., 1986), p. 23
[5] James Daane, *The Freedom of God*, (Grand Rapids, MI , Eerdmans, 1973) p. 24
[6] A. W. Pink, *The Sovereignty of God*, (Grand Rapids, Baker , 1992), p. 200
[7] J. A. Bengel, *Gnomon of the New Testament*, (Scotland, T & T Clark, 1957), p. 346
[8] John Calvin, *Concerning Eternal Predestination*, (London, Clarke Pub., 1961), p. 84

- 3 -
Reformed Theology and the Origin of Sin

The origin of sin has perplexed Christians throughout the history of the church. Many have asked, since God is supremely good and untainted by sin and infinitely sovereign over His created universe, how is it that sin entered the world which God declared to be "very good?" It has been pointed out that God could have created the angels and Adam and Eve in a state of holy perfection, so it would have been impossible for them to sin. However, this would have resulted in reducing God's noblest creation to mere machine-like figures, void of free choice. God desires man to respond to Him through choice. God, in His sovereignty, gave to man a will as an integral part of his nature. God will not oppose His own will nor violate the nature He designed for man. However, Scripture reveals that man's choice is not always God's will. How did sin enter the world? It was through disobedience to God's revealed will on the part of the first man and woman. For we read, "By one man sin entered the world and death by sin"(Rom. 5:12). God did not ordain it, but allowed it. It has been rightly said that man's freedom of will comes at a high price. The price of this freedom has been war, crime, rebellion, and sin. Sovereignly, God determined this freedom of choice given to man to be worth the price. This being said, we must never infer that the freedom of choice in man can thwart God's ultimate will. This perfect will is the eternal purpose of God, founded upon His all-wise and eternal counsel, which is settled, ordained, and unalterable (Eph. 3:11).

In wrestling with this solemn question, some have sadly concluded that God Himself is the author of sin. Overzealous followers of John Calvin, seeking to validate his theology, set this doctrine forth. To their credit it must be said that John Calvin and many moderate Calvinists did not hold to this teaching. Nevertheless, its foundations are rooted in the writing and thinking of John Calvin. Calvin rightly believed in God's sovereignty over His created universe, but then he took this important doctrine an unfortunate step further.

THE CALVINIST DOCTRINE OF DETERMINISM

John Calvin taught that God decrees all things which come to pass; this teaching is called "Determinism," According to determinism, there is no event, no act, and no decision of man that God does not ordain to happen exactly as it occurs. This includes war, natural disaster, injustice, immorality, and sin. In his most important theological work, *The Institutes of Christian Religion*, which formed the thinking of his followers, John Calvin wrote:

> "By predestination we mean the eternal decree of God, by which He determined with Himself whatever He wished to happen with regard to every man. All are not created on equal terms, but some are preordained to eternal life, others to eternal damnation; and accordingly, as each has been created for one or other of those ends, we say that he has been predestined to life or death."[1]

Joining him, the intrepid reformer Martin Luther, in his classic work, On the Bondage of the Will, defended the view that God decrees all things, including the sinful acts of man and Satan:

> "...We do everything by God's will alone, and by a necessity that is laid upon us...so that all things still happen by necessity, as it respects us...since then God moves and actuates all things in all things, it cannot be but that He also moves and acts in Satan and in the wicked...(the wicked) hurried along by this impulse of divine omnipotency...Hence it arises, that the wicked man cannot but go astray and commit sin continually; inasmuch as being seized and urged by the power of God, he is not allowed to remain idle; but wills, desires, acts just to what he is."[2]

This theological perspective continues to be taught in our present day. A. W. Pink, the hyper-Calvinist author who died in 1952, writes:

> "Nothing ever comes to pass except what He decreed."[3]

The next logical step in this teaching of "determinism" is to declare that God is the originator of sin. After the death of John Calvin in 1564, Theodor Beza, the professor of theology at the University of Geneva, became the leading proponent of this particular error of Calvinism. Through his far-reaching influence, this error became accepted as orthodoxy, and spread rapidly throughout Europe.

THE COORNHERT "HERESY?"

In 1579, an educated Dutchman and the Secretary of State, Dirck Coornhert (1522-1590), kindled a theological firestorm by his scholarly lectures and writings in refutation of Beza's teaching. Coornhert argued that if, as Beza said, God causes sin, then in reality He is the author of sin. The Bible, he said, did not teach such a monstrous thing. Coornhert was attracting such a large hearing and arguing so brilliantly that great fear was awakened, lest the whole structure of Calvinism in the Low countries be undermined. At the same time two Calvinist ministers, Arent Corneliszoon and Reynier Donteklok wrote a book, critical of the views of Beza, called *An Answer to Some of the Arguments Adduced by Beza and Calvin*. No minister seemed to be able to refute these men, and so Jacob Arminius was commissioned by the Reformed church to do so. Arminius had studied under Beza in Geneva, and had also distinguished himself at the University of Leyden. At the time of the controversy, he enjoyed acclaim as a preacher and Bible exegete in the Reformed church in Amsterdam. Arminius set himself to the task of answering Coornheert. He began a serious review of predestination from the Bible itself and particularly from the book of Romans. The deeper Arminius went into his study of Romans, the more he became convinced that what Paul was teaching was a refutation of Beza's concept of predestination. Arminius' scholarly mind was now challenged to explore the subject more thoroughly. He read the church fathers. In his research he discovered that no church father had ever taught Beza's view. Needless to say, the refutation of the Coornheert "heresy" was never issued.[4]

THE CALVINIST DOCTRINE: GOD IS THE AUTHOR OF SIN

Unfortunately this doctrine, that God is the source of sin, continues to be taught by Calvinists down to the present day. This is the inevitable conclusion of the teaching that God decrees and determines everything that comes to pass. If one is to be a consistent "determinist," he must believe that the God that decrees eternal salvation for the elect, must also decree the more repulsive acts that have occurred down through the pages of world history. This, according to many Calvinist writers, must also include the entrance of sin into the world. The earnest Christian must recoil and reject the blasphemy of this God-dishonoring doctrine. One can hardly imagine that Christians would publicly teach such a doctrine, but sadly it is true. Mark the words of Calvinist professor Dr. John Feinberg of Trinity Evangelical Divinity School:

> "I hold that all things are causally determined...God having made the choice, He created Adam as sinning."[5]

This seems to imply that God not only created Adam and Eve, but that God was involved in the act of Adam's and Eve's sin. This quotation is not written in isolation; its author is one of many Calvinists who have taught that sin is a result of God decreeing it in man. The popular author, A. W. Pink, presses this doctrine on his readers when he asserts confidently:

> "Clearly it was the divine will that sin should enter this world, or it would not have done so. God had the power to prevent it. Nothing ever comes to pass except what He decreed...God's decree that sin should enter this world was a secret hid in Himself."[6]

Respected Calvinist writer and executive secretary of the NIV Translation Committee, Edwin H. Palmer, in his book *The Five Points of Calvinism* boldly states:

> "To emphasize the sovereignty of God even more, it is necessary to point out that everything is foreordained by God...It is even biblical to say that God has foreordained sin. If sin was outside the plan of God, then not a single important affair of life would be ruled by God. For what action of man is perfectly good? Thus once again, we confess with full force the absolute sovereignty of God. He predestines, elects, and foreordains."[7]

The popular radio pastor Dr. John MacArthur, a noted Calvinist, writes:

> "Sin is something God meant to happen. He planned for it, ordained it—or in the words of the Westminster Confession, He decreed it. Evil and all its consequences were included in God's eternal decree before the foundation of the world."[8]

The popular Calvinist theologian and author R. C. Sproul, Jr. argues along the same line of reasoning as many other Calvinist writers, but he takes it one step further. Sproul argues that because God determines all things that come to pass, then God must be the creator of sin.

> "Every Bible-believing Christian must conclude at least that God in some sense desired that man would fall into sin...God wills all things that come to pass. It is in His

power to stop whatever might come to pass. It is within His omniscience to imagine every possible turn of events and to choose that chain of events which most pleases Him...But wait a minute...Isn't it impossible for God to do evil? He can't sin. I am not accusing God of sinning; I am suggesting that He created sin."[9]

It must be stated, in the strongest of terms, that not all Christians believe that it pleased God for sin to enter the world! Is it not abundantly clear that not all things that come to pass please God? Israel in the wilderness displeased God, Jonah displeased God, Judas displeased God, Lucifer displeased God, Adam displeased God. Did it please God to create sin? God forbid! God deliver us from the twisted sophistry that would in any way attribute the first sin of Adam, and every sin since, to God. This doctrine may be the most insidious and God-dishonoring doctrine ever proposed.

The Calvinist well realizes that to ascribe the origin of sin to God is biblically untenable and contradictory. For he is well aware that God is infinitely holy and by His very nature is unable to be even associated with sin. When the Calvinist is pressed to explain himself, frequently the appeal is made to the mystery of God. That is to say, yes, God is the author of sin, however, we cannot explain the apparent biblical contradiction. Dr. Norman Geisler recounts a conversation he had with the late Calvinist Professor Dr. John Gerstner:

Years ago when the late John Gerstner and I taught together at the same institution, I invited him into one of my classes to discuss free will. Being what I have called an extreme Calvinist, he defended Jonathan Edwards' view that the human will is moved by the strongest desire. I will never forget how he responded when I pushed the logic all the way back to Lucifer. I was stunned to hear an otherwise very rational man respond to my question "Who gave Lucifer the desire to rebel against God?" by throwing up his hands and crying, "Mystery, mystery, a great mystery!" I answered, "No, it is not a great mystery; it is a grave contradiction,"[10]

The Calvinist mistakenly believes that since man does not have a self-determined free will, then by necessity, God must be the author of sin. This position is in opposition to all logic and biblical revelation, which in the final analysis, pits God in rebellion against God. This belief is an affront to a holy God and is a biblical and logical impossibility.

THE BIBLICAL ORIGIN OF SIN

Is this what the Bible teaches? How did sin enter the world? In using the Holy Scriptures as our divine compass in our search for an answer, we find they clearly teach that God is not the author of sin, nor will He entice man to sin. For the New Testament states, "Let no man say when he is tempted, I am tempted of God: for God cannot be tempted with evil, neither tempteth He any man" (Jas. 1:13). In another place we read, "Thou art of purer eyes than to behold evil, and canst not look on iniquity" (Hab. 1:13). Again, "For all that is in the world, the lust of the flesh, and the lust of the eyes, and the pride of life, is not of the Father" (1 Jn. 2:16). The careful student of Scripture will conclude that God has never caused anyone to sin, for sin is always the result of either Satan or man in rebellion to God. "From whence come wars and fighting among you? Come they not hence, even of your lusts that war in your members?" (James 4:1) Beyond a doubt, God is sovereign, holy, faithful, just, good, unchanging, all-powerful, unequalled and above all. Therefore, to ascribe, surmise, or to insinuate in any way that God is the author of sin is to besmirch and malign the surpassing greatness of His Name. In setting forth the seriousness of this error, Bible teacher Harold Mackay passionately writes:

> "Does God foreknow all things? Absolutely! Does God permit all things? Yes! Did God decree all things? No! There is no question but that all God's eternal plans and purposes will be ultimately and completely fulfilled. But this is not to say that God decreed all the intervening happenings in the history of mankind. To infer that all the crimes, corruptions, atrocities, tragedies and wars that have stained the pages of human history were according to God's eternal decree is too horrible a thought to entertain for one moment."[11]

How then does Scripture reconcile God's sovereignty with the entrance of sin? We find that God certainly, by virtue of His foreknowledge and omnipotence, has the power to know all things and ordain all things; yet the Bible teaches that He allows certain events and decrees others, but does not decree all things. Though Scripture plainly teaches that man can oppose both the will and plan of God (Lk. 7:30, Mt. 23:37), mortal man cannot hinder or thwart God's sovereign and ultimate plan for this world.

However, individually, man can decide not to have a part in it. Our Savior God wills for all men to be saved, and to come unto the knowledge of the truth (1 Tim. 2:4)-this is His sovereign plan; but some may choose not to have any part in it. The Scriptures repeatedly state that man can exercise a will given to him by God, and with that will, reject the desires, blessings, and privileges that God has for him.

Psalm 25 reveals to us something more of the eternal ways of God. The psalmist states, "Good and upright is the Lord; therefore He will teach sinners. The meek will He guide in justice; and the meek will He teach his way...The secret of the Lord is with them that fear him" (25:8-9, 14). These verses may suggest to us that God in His sovereignty does not want unwilling followers. On the contrary, He wants those who will freely accept His instruction and counsel. He wants relationships with His people that are based on mutual affection and love, not on coercion and force. The words that the Psalms use are "teach" and "guide," God could force unbelievers and irresistibly cause their hearts and wills to do as He pleases. However, it would result in bringing to pass a people without wills of their own, the very thing God does not desire. God desires men to believe in Him unconstrainedly through the use of the freedom of the will, which He has given to them.

Why is it that sin entered the world? It is the same reason that some men perish and others believe in Christ unto eternal life: the decision of man to act in rebellious disregard to God's will. We must set aside the notion that sin entered the world by any desire of God; and in like manner, the notion that God does not desire to save all, for Scripture tells us that He does (2 Pt. 3:9). But man can and does reject God's will and plan for him. God, in His sovereignty, designed man with a free will and, despite the fall and ruin of sin, His divine purpose will not be frustrated. He will not force men to believe, but desires all men to freely come to faith in Christ.

Endnotes

[1] John Calvin, *Institutes, Vol. 2,* (Grand Rapids, MI, Eerdmans, 1952), p. 206
[2] Quoted by G. H. Lang, *World Chaos,* (London, Paternoster Press, 1950,) p. 60, 61
[3] A. W. Pink, *Gleanings from the Scriptures,* (Chicago, IL, Moody Press, 1964), p. 206
[4] M. Wynkoop, *Foundations of Wesleyan-Arminian Theology,* (Kansas City, MO: Beacon Hill, 1967), p.48
[5] John S. Feinberg, *Predestination and Free Will,* (Downers Grove, IL, Inter-Varsity Press, 1986), p. 24
[6] A. W. Pink, *Gleanings from the Scriptures,* (Chicago, IL, Moody Press, 1964), p. 207
[7] Edwin H. Palmer, *The Five Points of Calvinism,* (Grand Rapids, MI, Baker Books, 1979), p. 82-83
[8] John MacArthur, *Vanishing Conscience,* (Waco, TX, WordPublishing, 1995), p.113
[9] R. C. Sproul, Jr. *Almighty Over All,* (Grand Rapids, MI , Baker Books, 1999), p. 53-54
[10] Norman Geisler, *Chosen But Free,* (Minneapolis, MN, Bethany House, 1999), p.133
[11] Harold Mackay, *Biblical Balance,* (Port Colborne, Everyday Publications, 1978), p. 55

- 4 -
The Sin Nature, Total Depravity and Choice

At Noyon, France, there were born two brothers, John and Charles Calvin. John from his earliest days was thoughtful, studious, and reverent. At age 27, he wrote one of the Christian church's most influential books, The Institutes of Christian Religion. When he died in Geneva in 1564, he left the world principles that would guide thousands of Christians. The other brother, Charles, pursued a course of self-indulgent living. Charles' life was as worthless and infamous as John's was noble and honorable. How do you explain the difference between those men? Not heredity, not environment; both enjoyed the same home, the same early influences. The difference is to be explained in choice.

Throughout the Word of God, the ability of unregenerated man to choose or to place faith in the Savior is evident. This ability is exercised within the prescribed boundaries and is ultimately subject to the sovereign will and purpose of God. It must be equally stressed that man, in his trespasses and sin, cannot in and of himself do anything to merit salvation. Salvation, of course, is through God and of God, and except for the grace of the Lord Jesus Christ; the unbeliever would be lost forever. Yet we must never say that man is unable to place his faith in the Lord Jesus Christ because of his sinful nature or his total depravity. The sin nature has corrupted and marred what God had perfectly created in Adam, and it has polluted the world through immorality, perverseness, and every conceivable sinful act. Yet man is not so ruined by sin as to be unable to believe in the Savior when drawn by the surpassing grace of God and convicted by the indomitable Holy Spirit of God. We might reason in this way. A man's body and mind may be so ravaged by disease that he is mentally tormented and physically crippled; yet he is still able to know that he must seek a capable physician. Man is sick and ravaged with sin, yet he can come to the Savior by faith. Concerning this point J. Boyd Nicholson, Sr., has well said:

> "That God is sovereign is fundamental to the faith. That God in His sovereignty gave to man a will to exercise freely is fundamental to our nature. God will not oppose His own will nor violate the nature He Himself designed. He will not conscript the unwilling into heaven nor consign the unable into hell."[1]

However, on the other hand, some would maintain that the non-elect cannot place faith in the Lord Jesus Christ, for they are dead in their trespasses and sins and unable to believe. It is further asserted that faith is a gift of God and this gift is given exclusively to the elect.

TOTAL DEPRAVITY OR ABILITY

The crux of the matter is to what extent an unbeliever is ruined by sin. The non-Calvinist would maintain that the sin of Adam has, in a deep and profound way, devastated God's original creation. The fall has created enmity with God, separation from God, corruption, and ruin in man. However, the fall has not produced an inability in man to respond to the promptings

THE SIN NATURE, TOTAL DEPRAVITY AND CHOICE

of sovereign grace. For the writer of Hebrews, speaking of those who come to God, states, "He that cometh to God must believe that He is, and that He is a rewarder of them that diligently seek him" (Heb. 11:6). Does this not suggest that man has some ability to come to God and seek Him, despite the corruption of sin? In explaining what depravity is and is not, Augustus H. Strong, the former President of Rochester Theological Seminary, writes in his *Systematic Theology:*

> "Yet there is a certain remnant of freedom left to man. The sinner can (a) avoid the sin against the Holy Ghost; (b) choose the less sin rather than the greater; (c) refuse altogether to yield to certain temptations; (d) do outward good acts, though with imperfect motives; (e) seek God from motives of self-interest...The sinner can do one very important thing—give attention to divine truth."[2]

The Calvinist would state that man is "dead," Spiritual death means inability to believe, understand, or respond. A dead man is just that—dead, unable to respond. A. W. Pink, defending this point of view, writes:

> "What can a lifeless man do, and man by nature is dead in his trespasses and sins. A dead man is utterly incapable of willing anything."[3]

Calvinist writers David N. Thomas and Curtis C. Steele in their book, *The Five Points of Calvinism,* add these words:

"Adam's offspring are born with sinful natures; they do not have the ability to choose spiritual good over evil. Consequently, man's will is no longer free."[4]

DOES THE BIBLICAL WORD "DEAD" MEAN INABILITY?

What do the Scriptures say? Indeed, the Word of God does say that unsaved man is "dead" (Eph. 2:1). But what does the Bible mean when it speaks of "spiritual death?" Does it mean that man is incapable of faith? Or is he unable to respond, even as a dead man is lifeless and is unable to respond? Notice the way the word "dead" is used concerning our position in Christ in Romans 6. There the Christian is "Dead to sin" (6:2), yet believers are exhorted not to yield themselves as instruments of unrighteousness unto sin" (Rom. 6:13). If "dead" means inability to respond and lifelessness, this cannot be the meaning here—for the "dead-to-sin" Christian feels the pull of sin and is told not to yield to it.

In another place, John 5:25, we read these words, "Verily, verily, I say unto you, 'The hour is coming, and now is, when the dead shall hear the voice of the Son of God: and they that hear shall live.'" Here again we read of those who are "dead," in this case unbelievers, and the exhortation is to "hear" the Lord Jesus Christ. Unbelievers, of whom we would be led to believe are unable to respond, are lifeless, and whose "will" is in bondage and cannot respond. These are not just the elect, but also all the dead, all the lost, all unbelievers. The words of Christ are "...the dead shall hear the voice of the Son of God," This is the first remarkable thing that "the dead" and "lifeless ones" hear! The dead are able to respond and are invited to believe. Additionally, we find that incumbent upon hearing is faith; because we read that those who "heard" lived. This life is spiritual and eternal in the Lord Jesus Christ, for everlasting life is spoken of in the previous verse. The "spiritually dead" here can hear and can believe unto eternal life. No less than the eminent expositor William Kelly concludes:

> "His voice goes forth 'to every creature' in the gospel; 'and those who hear shall live.' Such are the means and conditions for life. It is of faith that it might be by grace. Those then that hear shall live. Never does a sinner trust God for eternal life till grace makes him see his sins and distrust himself utterly."[5]

In a similar way, evangelical Bible teacher Warren Wiersbe writes these words:

> "The lost sinner is helpless to save himself and he certainly cannot give himself life. How are dead sinners raised from the dead? By hearing God's Word and believing on God's Son. His word is living and powerful and can raise sinners from spiritual death."[6]

Expositor C. H. Mackintosh, author of *Notes on the Pentateuch,* cuts to the very root of the issue when he writes:

> "There is life-giving power in the Christ whom the Word reveals, and in the Word, which reveals Him. The Lord Christ can make dead souls, as well as dead bodies, hear His quickening voice. It is by His mighty voice that life can be communicated to either body or soul."[7]

To answer the question can those dead in trespasses and sin place non-meritorious faith in Christ unto salvation? The answer is, of course, yes! Can he respond apart from Christ and his Word? No. Can he respond apart from the work of the Holy Spirit? Again the answer is no, for salvation is entirely of God.

THE MEANING OF THE WORD "DEAD" IN SCRIPTURE

If, as we have shown, the word "dead" does not indicate the inability to respond to God, what then does "dead" mean? There are seven different "deaths" in Scripture, and in each case, the primary meaning is separation. At "spiritual death" there is the separation of spirit and soul from God. In Genesis two, God spoke to Adam concerning the tree of the knowledge of good and evil, "For in the day that thou eatest thereof thou shalt surely die" (Gen 2:17). When Adam ate of the tree he died spiritually. It is obvious from the text that he did not die physically. It is also clear that the "death" here was not the inability to respond to God, for Adam could hear God speaking and hid himself. The "death" spoken of here was *separation from a relationship with God* because of sin. Likewise, in each of the other cases of death in Scripture, the primary meaning is also separation. In "eternal death" there is separation from God forever (Matt. 25:46). In "physical death" it is separation of human life (soul and spirit) from the body. These seven deaths and seven separations of Scripture are shown in chart form on page 67.

THE SIN NATURE, TOTAL DEPRAVITY AND CHOICE

SPIRITUAL DEATH	At conception	Born in Adam	Separation of your soul and spirit from God	Gen. 2:17 Eph. 2:1	Salvation; being "born again"
PHYSICAL DEATH	When you die	Fall, curse and being in Adam	Separation of your soul and spirit from your body	Heb. 9:27	For the believer, it is "sleep," then resurrection
ETERNAL DEATH	Begins when you die and lasts forever	Physical death apart from faith in Christ	Separation of your body, soul and spirit from God forever	Rev. 20:14 Matt. 25:46	Salvation and eternal life
POSITION DEATH	At salvation, new birth	Born in Christ; Identified with Christ	Separation Old life, a man in Adam under the dominion of sin	Rom. 6:3-6 Gal. 2:20	Positionally dead but alive and risen in Christ
FELLOWSHIP DEATH	During your life after salvation	Personal sin of a believer	Separation From right fellowship with God	1 Jn. 1:9 Jn. 13:8 Jas. 1:15	Confession of sin and yielding to God
FAITH DEATH	During the life of the religious but unsaved	Living in an unsaved condition	Separation from faith which saves	Jas. 2:17 Heb. 6:2	Salvation in the Lord Jesus Christ
CHILD BEARING DEATH	During old age	Physical limitation	Separation from child-bearing health	Rom. 4:17-19	Miracle from God

TESTIMONY OF SCRIPTURE

The large number of Scriptures, which charge the unbeliever with the responsibility to respond to the Word of God, evidences that he is enabled to do so by grace. "Whosoever believeth on the Lord Jesus Christ shall not perish..." (Jn. 3:16). "And him that cometh to Me I will in no wise cast out"(Jn. 6:37). "And I, if I be lifted up from the earth, will draw all men unto Me" (Jn. 12:32). "But if the wicked shall turn from his sins that he hath committed...he shall surely live..."(Ezek. 18:21). This has long been a thorn in the side of many Calvinistic writers. Unsure on which side of the question to come down, some have even said that the offers to believe by God are real, but then again, God never really expects the non-elect to ever come and respond. This, of course, would be an affront to the very justice and truthfulness of God. It would touch on His character, and undermine His divine attributes, which constitute His very nature and essence.

F. W. Grant summarizes well the teaching of all of Scripture concerning the ability to believe and respond when he writes:

> "God's love to the world is manifested on the cross. It is not allowable to narrow this down to a love simply to the elect, as has been only too often done. God 'willeth not the death of a sinner,' but on the contrary He 'will have all men to be saved, and to come to the knowledge of the truth.' These testimonies are simple, and they deny that there can be any contrary decree of God hindering the salvation of any. The Redeemer's words as He wept over Jerusalem assure us that it is man's contrary will that resists God's will — 'How often would I

have gathered your children together, even as a hen gathered her brood under her wings, and ye would not!' But this is the will of man itself, what shall we make of it? Is there not after all in it, define it as we may, some mysterious power which, spite of the fall, spite of the corruption of nature, should yet respond to these invitations, these pleadings of divine grace?"[8]

Not only is there biblical evidence that man can respond to the promptings and pleadings of divine grace, but man can also resist them.

GOD'S WILL CAN BE RESISTED

Is God's will always done? To many the answer is, of course, No. Seeing there are horrific crimes in the inner cities, brutal and indiscriminate bloodshed in wars between nations, and rampant immorality we must conclude that this is not God's will, and His will is not done. Yet as we have shown already, the Calvinist maintains a "determinist" perspective; that is, God's will in every detail and event of life is decreed by Him and consequently must come to pass. Many say in the realm of salvation that man cannot restrain the "irresistible grace" of God; consequently they must believe unto salvation. Therefore, His will is always done in the world. What does the Word of God teach? In a survey of Scripture we discover that man can oppose and reject both the will and plan of God. At the outset, we see man can reject the counsel of God. Luke 7:30 says, "But the Pharisees and the lawyers rejected for themselves the counsel of God, being not baptized of him…" Mortal man cannot hinder or thwart God's sovereign and ultimate plan for this world. But as an individual, man can decide to have no part in it. The Lord Jesus Christ will come again to rapture the church; this is His sovereign plan, but some will choose not to have any part in it. The Pharisees rejected the "counsel of God," but this did not hinder God from achieving His ultimate sovereign purposes. However, they did fail to enter into God's blessing and privilege for their lives. W. E. Vine carefully distinguishes between the will of God that can be resisted and the sovereign purposes of God that cannot be altered. He writes:

> "'For who withstands His will?'(Rom. 9:19) The word rendered 'will' is boulema, which signifies a deliberate purpose and is to be distinguished from the more frequent and general word thelema, which, frequently has the meaning of a desire, or spontaneous will. Man is able to resist the will, the thelema, of God, but whatever takes place, God's determinate counsel, boulema, is never prevented from fulfillment."[9]

The Scriptures repeatedly state that man can exercise a will given to him by God and, with that will, reject many desires, blessings, and privileges that God wills for him. We see this in texts such as:

- Matthew 23:37, "How often would I have gathered your children together, even as a hen gathers her chickens under her wings and you would not."

- Acts 7:51, "Ye stiff-necked people and uncircumcised in heart and ears, ye do always resist the Holy Spirit: as your fathers did, so do ye."

- 1 Timothy 2:4, "God..who will have all men to be saved, andto come unto the knowledge of the truth."

From these verses and many others, we see that not all men do God's will. We see man may resist the Holy Spirit and God's will concerning their salvation and that men may also resist the plan and will of God for their lives. Many Calvinists would reply that men may resist it at a certain point in their lives, but later they will receive the "irresistible" grace of God. It must be pointed out from these verses that resistance to the Holy Spirit and God's plan for their lives was permanent.

In response to these thoughts, Isaiah 46:10 is often used as support of the Calvinist view. This verse reads, "My counsel shall stand, I will do My good pleasure." If we were to take this verse as teaching that God determines each and every detail of life, then much of Scripture would not be in agreement. Therefore, we must take God's counsel and pleasure in Isaiah to be the broad outline of His ultimate sovereign purposes. These purposes will stand unhindered by any ability of man. These counsels of which Isaiah speaks are not the individual will of man, but the divine acts of a sovereign God. For Isaiah in another place states, "...Because when I called, you did not answer; when I spoke, you did not hear; but did evil before Mine eyes, and did choose that wherein I delighted not"(Isa. 65:12).

GOD'S COUNSEL AND FREEDOM OF THE WILL

Finally, we read in Psalm 32, "I will instruct you in the way that you should go: I will counsel you with my eye upon you. Be you not as a horse or as mule, which has no understanding: whose mouth must be held in with bit and bridle, lest they will not come near unto you" (32:8-9). Why does God say these things from the mouth of David, whose life illustrated the blessedness of obedience and the agony of disobedience? It may suggest to us that God in His sovereignty does not want mule-like followers who must be "irresistibly" forced to obey with bit and bridle. On the contrary, He wants those who will freely accept His instruction and counsel. He wants relationships with His people that are based on mutual affection and love, not based on coercion and force. Psalm 32 reveals to us something of the heart and ways of God. He could, figuratively speaking, "bridle" unbelievers and irresistibly cause their hearts and wills to do as He pleases. However, it would result in bringing to pass "bridled mules," robots if you please, without wills of their own, the very thing God does not desire. God desires men to believe unconstrainedly through the use of the freedom of the will which He has given to them. Why is it that some men perish and others believe in Christ unto eternal life? It is not that God does not desire to save them, because Scripture tells us that He does. But men can and do reject God's will and plan. In His sovereignty God designed man with freedom to the will, and despite the fall and ruin of sin, this divine purpose will not be frustrated. He will not force men to believe, but wills that all men will repent and enter into a free mutual love relationship. He does not want bridled mules but men who freely will come to faith in Christ.

Endnotes
[1] J. B. Nicholson, What The Bible Teaches, 1 Peter,(Scotland:Ritchie, 1986), p. 42
[2] A. H. Strong, Systematic Theology, (Philadelphia, Judson, 1907), p.640
[3] A. W. Pink, The Sovereignty of God, (Grand Rapids, Baker Books, 1992,) p. 140

[4] Steele, Thomas, Five Points of Calvinism, (Phillipsburg, NJ: Presbyterian and Reformed, 1963), p. 25
[5] W. Kelly, Gospel of John, (Denver, CO. : Wilson Foundation, 1966), p. 114
[6] Warren Wiersbe, Bible Exposition Comm., John, (Wheaton, IL:Victor, 1989) p. 306
[7] C. H. Mackintosh, Treasury, (Neptune: Loizeaux, 1976), p. 618
[8] F. W. Grant, Sovereignty of God in Salvation, (NY:Loizeaux Brothers, ND), p. 153
[9] W. E. Vine, Romans, (London, GB: Oliphants LTD, 1948), p.146

- 5 -
Election, Salvation and Blessing

Since the Reformation era, no doctrine has been more fiercely debated or more theologically maligned than the doctrine of divine election. Indeed, to many Christians the doctrine of election is not considered to be founded upon Scripture at all. This, however, is very unfortunate, since the doctrine is, in fact, very biblical and, when rightly understood, one of great blessing to the believer. For it elevates to its very zenith the majesty, grace, wisdom, and faithfulness of God. Moreover, the whole counsel of God is not proclaimed when this important doctrine is neglected.

Election is a sovereign act, made possible through the infinite grace of God bestowed upon believers alone for special spiritual blessings and service. God chose them in Christ before the foundation of the world (Eph. 1:3). The phrase "in Christ" indicates that all of God's purposes, to those in spiritual union with Him, are brought to pass through the worth and work of the Lord Jesus Christ. The doctrine of election, indeed, allows God to be God, in all His greatness and majesty.

The New Testament words that are especially important in this discussion are the words "prooridzo," meaning, "to predestine, to determine beforehand;" and "eklogomai," meaning, "to elect, to choose, to select," Related terms are the adjective "eklektos," meaning "elect" or "chosen;" and the noun "ekloge," meaning "the election," The Scriptures indicate that the doctrine of election is used also in reference to Israel in the Old Testament, and to Christ, the Church, the Apostles, and numerous other individuals in the New Testament.

THE ELECTION OF CHRIST

The Lord Jesus Christ is called the "Elect" or the "Chosen" in both the New and Old Testaments. Isaiah announces, "Behold My Servant, whom I uphold; Mine Elect, in whom My soul delighteth…" (Isa. 42:1) In Matthew, the gospel writer quotes the prophet, "Behold My Servant, in whom I have chosen; My Beloved, in whom My soul is well pleased…" (Matt. 12:18). The Greek word "elect" that is used here of Christ is the same word that is used of believers throughout the New Testament. A proper understanding of Christ's election will serve us well in understanding the biblical doctrine of election. It hardly needs to be said that the election of Christ does not in any way relate to Him being chosen for salvation. What then, does Scripture mean when it speaks of Christ as "elect?" Christ's election beautifully sets forth His pre-eminence, worth, belovedness, and His humble servanthood to the Father.

Christ's election conveys the deep love and value the Father has for the Son. The Scriptures reveal that the words "elect" or "chosen" and the word "beloved" are so closely related that it may be said that they are interchangeable. This idea is beautifully seen in the three-fold declaration of pleasure of Christ by the Father. In Matthew 17:5 we read, "This is my beloved Son in whom I am well pleased; hear ye Him;" and then in Mark 9:7 again we read, "…a voice came out of the cloud, saying, 'This is My Beloved Son: hear Him.' In these accounts in both Matthew and Mark, the word "beloved" is used of Christ; but when we come to the parallel passage in Luke, we read, "And a voice came out of the cloud, saying, This is My Son, My Chosen One; listen to Him (Luke 9:35 NASV)! The Greek word here "eklelegmenos" is used 17 times in the New Testament. It is translated in each case by either the words "elect" or "chosen," We may say, therefore, that one meaning of the word "chosen" or "elect" as regarding Christ and believers is the idea of value and preciousness. The main thought is not selection, but rather value. Peter underscores this beautifully when he writes of Christ, "To whom coming, as unto a living stone, disallowed indeed of men, but chosen of God, and precious;" again, a few verses later, "Wherefore it is contained in Scripture, 'Behold, I lay in Sion a chief corner stone, elect, precious...'" (1 Pet. 2:4, 6).

Christ's election does not only denote preciousness, but also pre-eminence, belovedness, and holy service to God. Regarding the role of Christ's service, the prophet Isaiah explains, "I have put My Spirit upon Him: He shall bring forth judgment to the Gentiles...He shall bring forth judgment unto truth. He shall not fail nor be discouraged, till He have set judgment in the earth: and the isles shall wait for his law" (Isa. 42:1-4). Our Lord Jesus Christ was commissioned by the Father to a specific task. His service would involve redemption, teaching, judgment, and in a coming day, to rule and to reign on the earth. In His first coming, this mission was primarily redemptive. He testified, "But the Son of Man came not to be ministered unto, but to minister, and give His life a ransom for many" (Mk. 10:45). But in His second coming, His primary work will be judgment and rule, "...Bring forth judgment to the Gentiles...till he have set judgment in the earth: and the isles shall wait for His law," The mission and work of God's Elect will be finished when "He shall have delivered up the kingdom to God, even the Father...that God may be all and in all" (1 Cor. 15:24).

Therefore, the election of Christ, briefly stated, is an announcement of His infinite value to the Father and His commission in the world to holy service. John Parkinson has well summarized this meaning of the election of Christ when he writes:

> "The meaning and usage of Christ as elect has to do with pre-eminence (chief-cornerstone 1 Pt. 2:6); service (Behold my servant, Matt. 12:18); Preciousness (precious, 1 Pt. 2:4); choseness (Chosen of God, 1 Pt. 2:4); and belovedness (My beloved, Matt. 12:18)."[1]

THE ELECTION OF ISRAEL

Without question, one of the most significant themes in the Old Testament and in much of the New Testament is the election of Israel. In Genesis chapter 12, we read of the foundation of Israel's election, "...I will make of thee a great nation, and I will bless thee, and make thy name great; and thou shall be a blessing: And I will bless them that bless thee, and curse him that curseth thee: and in thee shalt all the families of the earth be blessed" (Gen. 12:2-3). In the Pentateuch we read, "For thou art an holy people unto the Lord thy God: the Lord thy God hath chosen thee to be a peculiar people unto Himself above all peoples that are on the face of the earth" (Deut. 7:6). Later in the Psalms, "For the Lord hath chosen Jacob unto Himself, and Israel for His peculiar treasure" (Ps. 135:4). In the Prophets, "But thou Israel, My servant, Jacob whom I have chosen, the seed of Abraham My friend; whom I have taken hold of from the ends of the earth and called thee from the corners thereof, and said unto thee, 'Thou art My servant, I have chosen thee and not cast thee away'" (Isa. 41:8-9). Election is always seen as an act of mercy and an expression of the love of God for Israel. It is for this reason that He redeemed them from bondage and made provision for the forgiveness of sin. Israel has been chosen not merely for her own sake, but as an instrument of blessing in the hand of God to the benefit of other nations (Gen. 12:3, Isa. 65:18-20).

What was God's sovereign purpose in the election of Israel? Was Israel chosen so she might receive eternal salvation? Are all those in Israel saved? What do the Scriptures teach in regard to Israel's election? At the outset, we must say that Israel's election does not denote her eternal salvation. If this were true then all those of other nations would be eternally lost, because they are not elect. This is obviously not true. One might readily think of Ruth, Melchizedek, and the city of Nineveh, as well as others who were saved. What then is the purpose of Israel's election?

When Abraham was called, God said He would make of him a great nation. God promised to his seed a land in which they would be blessed with fruitful harvests, deliverance from their enemies, and blessings upon their families, if they would be obedient to His commands. "The Lord shall make thee plenteous in goods, in the fruit of thy body, in the fruit of thy cattle, and in the fruit of thy ground, in the land which the Lord swore unto thy fathers to give thee...The Lord shall open unto thee His good treasure, the heaven to give the rain unto thy land in His season, and to bless all the work of thine hand: and thou shalt lend unto many nations, and thou shalt not borrow" (Deut. 28:11-12). National Israel was chosen by God to be His people, to be a light to the nations, and to occupy a privileged position on earth. Every Israelite was part of the elect nation, but not every Israelite was saved. Paul tells us in 1 Corinthians 10 that though all passed through the Red Sea and came into the wilderness, many perished because of sin. "But with many of them God was not well pleased: for they were overthrown in the wilderness" (1 Cor. 10:5). Israel's election was based on birth, circumcision, and God's sovereign choice. One could have a proper standing as being among elect Israel and still be lost eternally. The Dutch Bible scholar W. J. Ouweneel explains:

> "Israel's election was merely an outward election on the basis of birth and circumcision; if one did not believe, but flouted God's words, he would be lost—yet, nevertheless, he was a part of God's chosen people! This election had to do with a person's outward temporal position upon the earth, not with his eternal destiny."[2]

How did one become part of elect Israel in the Old Testament? Were some of the descendants of Abraham, Isaac, and Jacob chosen to become members of the elect nation while others were passed by? No, individual Jews were elect because they were born as national Israelites. A child born of Jewish parents immediately entered Israel's election. A much smaller number entered into Israel's election because they chose to be part of the nation. Ruth did not enter Israel by birth, but she chose to do so. She said to Naomi, "Your people shall be my people, and your God my God" (Ruth 1:16). Those people who were born into Israel or chose the nation as their own came into its national election. In the New Testament Paul tells us that among national Israel there were also those who believed on Christ unto eternal salvation. This remnant of faithful Israel Paul calls "the elect according to grace" (Rom. 11:5-7). Paul argues that an individual enters Israel's election by either birth or choice, but an individual obtains a right standing with God only by faith (Rom. 11:7, 23).

Israel was chosen by God from the foundation of the world to fulfill an eternal purpose. "Come ye blessed of my father, inherit the kingdom prepared for you from the foundation of the world" (Matt. 25:34). God desired, first of all, for Israel to be His people and that He might be their God. Secondly, He desired Israel to be a witness and a light to the heathen nations; and thirdly, He desired her to occupy the land promised to Abraham, wherein she could receive material, temporal blessings. Israel's election was unearned and unmerited, but with this privilege there was also solemn responsibility. Her failure to live according to God's commands would lead to the loss of blessing. We have seen, thus far, that election does not mean the sovereign decree of God from eternity past to select some to eternal salvation, while passing over others.

ELECTION IN THE CHURCH DISPENSATION

Even as the election of Christ and the election of Israel do not denote election unto eternal salvation so too election in this present dispensation does not refer to salvation from sin. The Bible teaches that just as Christ and Israel were elect, so too the church is elect. This is a major theme of the writers of the New Testament. We read, "But ye are a chosen generation, a royal priesthood, an holy nation...that ye should show forth the praises of Him who called you out of darkness into his marvelous light" (1 Pt. 2:9); and in Romans "He that spared not His own Son, but delivered Him up for us all...who shall lay anything to the charge of God's elect" (Rom. 8:32-33). A study of the Old Testament reveals that God chose Abraham and his seed to be His chosen people. Likewise, in this dispensation God chose Christ and those "in Him," both Jew and Gentile, to be His people. God, through His sovereign will and electing grace has selected His "Chosen One" to fulfill His purposes and the church is chosen in Him to be His elect people.

At once we see beautiful similarities and marked differences between the election of the church and the election of Israel. Israel and the church were both chosen to do a work. Israel was to be a light to the Gentiles, and the church was to show forth the unsearchable riches of Christ. The entrance into both Israel's and the church's election was through birth and choice. Those people who were physically born into Israel or personally chose the nation as their own, came into its national election. Likewise, those who are born again spiritually through faith in Christ, come into the election of the church. In both cases, when a person becomes a vital part of either elect Israel or the elect church, he at the same time shares in its election. But there are differences, too. Israel's election was earthly and material, while the church's election is heavenly and spiritual. Israel's election was from the foundation of the earth (Matt. 25:34). The Church's election is from before the foundation of the world (Eph. 1:3). The chart below contrasts the election of Israel with the church.

	Israel	**Church**
Election	Chosen in Abraham	Chosen in Christ
Task	Light to the Gentiles	To preach the unsearchable riches of Christ
Entrance	Physical birth	Spiritual new birth
Blessings	Earthly and material	Heavenly and spiritual
Origin	From the foundation of the earth (Mt. 25:34)	From before the foundation of the world (Eph. 1:3)

WHAT IS ELECTION?

Election is the sovereign choosing by God, before the foundation of the world, of those who are in Christ to receive spiritual blessings and a call to a divine work. These high and spiritual blessings were purposed by God from eternity past for those who are elect in Christ. When a person places faith in Christ, he is numbered with the elect in Christ. He is not elected to be put in Christ, but he is elect because he is in Christ by faith. Paul expresses it this way, "Blessed be the God and Father of our Lord Jesus Christ, who hath blessed us with all spiritual blessings in heavenly places in Christ: According as He hath chosen us *in Him* before the foundation of the world, that we should be holy and without blame before Him in love" (Eph. 1:3-4).

Leading Bible teachers have suggested that this passage in Ephesians contains one of the most important keys in understanding divine election. This passage clearly tells us that election is: (a) "in Christ;" (b) before the foundation of the world; and (c) unto heavenly blessings. The subject of election in this passage turns on the phrase "in Christ" (1:4). G. C. Berkhouwer, a leading Calvinist scholar explains:

> "...The history of the doctrine of election may be interpreted as an effort to understand the meaning of these words...there is election only in Christ...God's election is an election in Christ."[3]

Therefore, we may be permitted to assume that our election "in Christ" is a crucial element in understanding the doctrine of election. What then does Scripture mean when it teaches that election is "in Christ?" Many careful Bible students have concluded that since Christ is the Elect One based on Isaiah 42:1, therefore our election is "in Him," In other words, when an individual comes to faith in Christ, he also, at the same time, shares in the election of Christ because of that vital relationship the Bible calls "in Christ." Christ's election becomes the election of the church. British Bible scholar Dr. Alan Richardson explains:

> "If Christians are 'the elect,' it is because they are 'in Christ,' because they are baptized into the person who alone may be truly called the Elect of God."[4]

Dr. William W. Klein, the chairman of the New Testament Department at Denver Seminary, Colorado, adds:

> "Christ is the principle elected One, and God has chosen a corporate body to be included in Him. Election is the corporate choice of the church 'in Christ.' Before the foundation of the world God made His choice: those in Christ would be His people. Paul posits the goal of this election: in Christ the chosen ones would become holy and blameless. Election exists to produce a holy people."[5]

If the church is elect, by virtue of the fact that the church is "in Christ," God's elect One, we may be justified in concluding that God has chosen this people to accomplish His purposes on earth. Election is unto service and a divine task. This chosen people, the church, would bear the imprint of heaven by displaying to a lost world the character of Christ, while accomplishing His purposes. Paul states this same truth in another way, "Put on therefore, as the elect of God, holy and beloved, bowels of mercy, kindness, humbleness of mind, meekness... forgiving one another...even as Christ forgave you..." (Col. 3:12-13). Hereby, the character of the primary "elect One" defines and sets forth the spiritual character of the church in her service. Furthermore, by virtue of this "in-Christ-election," Christ's calling becomes the church's calling, Christ's resources become the church's resources, and Christ's work in the world becomes the church's work in the world. His election is our election. What is the goal and purpose of the election of the church? What was the eternal purpose before the foundation of the world of our election in Him? Christ's election was to a task. Israel's election was to earthly blessings and a task. So, too, the church's election is to heavenly blessing, but also to a task. What tasks are the elect to accomplish? As Christ came to seek and to save those who were lost (Lk. 19:11), so too the church is to take up this same mission and preach Christ in Jerusalem, Samaria, and the uttermost parts of the earth (Acts 1:8). The church, as a royal priesthood, is to fulfill the task of worship and praise; she is to "show forth the praises of Him who called you out of darkness into his marvelous light " (1 Pt. 2:9). God has chosen the church to display to angels the multi-faceted grace of God (Eph. 3:10).

Moreover, God has also chosen the church to be the recipient of the heavenly blessings. God has seated the elect church in the heavenlies and, in that position, has blessed her with all spiritual blessings. Among these divine and heavenly blessings are: holiness, adoption, sonship, and conformity to Christ. F. B. Hole, the careful Bible commentator writes:

"Before the foundation of the world He chose us in Christ. Let the two words "in Him" be noted, for again and again they, or their equivalent, occur in this chapter. As a matter of history we each were in Adam before we were in Christ, but before Adam was created, God saw us in Christ, and on that basis we were chosen. What was in view in His choice was that we might be holy and blameless before Himself in love."

William Kelly (1820-1906), the distinguished Greek scholar, expands on the thought of election to blessing in Ephesians 1:4-5 stating that the election of the church is to "heavenly blessedness:"

"The choice of saints for heavenly blessedness was before the creation of the universe, before the foundation of the world."[7]

THE BLESSINGS OF ELECTION

This brings us to consider the meaning of the terms "election" and "predestination." The two are closely linked in the Bible. Predestination is used only four times in the New Testament; the word election and its related words are used twenty-seven times. In their most basic meanings, election means to "choose," and predestination means to "mark out beforehand." However, there are subtle differences. We may well define election as the sovereign act of God in grace, whereby He chose, in eternity past in Christ, believers for heavenly blessings. On the other hand, predestination is the purpose, goal, or end result that God desires for a believer. In every case where these words are found, they never relate to a "choosing out for salvation," but rather denote a "choosing" or "a marking out beforehand" of believers for heavenly and eternal blessing. H. A. Ironside (1876-1951), the respected commentator and Bible expositor, clarifies the meaning of predestination and its blessings:

> "There are two things that are absolutely clear in Scripture—one is that God by His foreknowledge has predestinated all who believe in the Lord Jesus Christ 'to be conformed to the image of His Son' (Rom. 8:29). Predestination is never to heaven nor yet to hell; but always to special privilege in and with Christ. All who believe in Him were chosen in Christ "before the foundation of the world."[8]

BLESSING OF HOLINESS AND BLAMELESSNESS — Paul describes the goal of God's choosing in Ephesians chapter one, "that we might be holy and blameless before Him in love" (Eph. 1:4). God, before the foundation of the world, has chosen believers in Christ to bear the very stamp of heaven. God's plan is for believers to share in God's attributes of holiness and blamelessness. God has chosen believers in the church to possess higher blessings than Adam ever enjoyed on earth. Careful Bible students suggest that Adam could never be described as holy, but rather as innocent, for he never knew what sin was until he fell. Our Lord, on the other hand, was holy, for He understood the depth of sin but did not yield to it. In divine election, God is choosing believers to bear His very character while living in a fallen world. Lastly, we read in Ephesians chapter one, that believers might dwell in His very presence, "before Him in love," It seems that God's purpose is to have a people before

Him, who are not only characterized by His attributes of holiness and blamelessness, but who enjoy the riches of His eternal and boundless love.

BLESSING OF SONSHIP — Paul's second reference to the blessings of election in Ephesians chapter one is more elevated than his first. The first blessing links believers with the very character of God, holiness and blamelessness. The second blessing raises up the believer and links him to God Himself in sonship. "Having predestinated us unto the adoption of children by Jesus Christ to Himself, according to the good pleasure of His will" (Eph. 1:5). The phrase "adoption of children" is drawn from the Greek word "huiothesia," meaning, "placing as a son," This doctrine tells us that we are more than children of God. The term "child of God" relates to spiritual birth, but the term "son" of God relates to family standing. We are born again as children of God, but as sons, we have been placed as adult sons in God's family. Through sonship, the believer can immediately draw on all of the riches of the Father's wealth and the spiritual blessings of heaven.

BLESSING OF CONFORMITY TO THE IMAGE OF HIS SON — The third spiritual blessing of predestination/election is conformity to the image of Christ. Paul writes in Romans chapter eight, "For whom He did foreknow He also did predestinate to be conformed to the image of His Son, that He might be the firstborn among many brethren" (Rom. 8:29). The word "conformed" is the Greek word "summorphos," which conveys the thought of the moral character of Christ and not merely His external physical appearance.

Although these words were crafted with the utmost simplicity, they contain the matchless grace of an incomparable God. Believers are to be conformed to the very image of the lovely Son of God. The One in whom was all the Father's delight! Christ, He who was full of grace and truth; Christ, the obedient servant; Christ, that impeccable sacrifice—we are to be conformed to His image—nothing lacking, nothing short! The One who was full of grace, mercy, humility, beauty, and glory; we shall be like Him. Paul said it in another way, "When Christ, who is our life, shall be manifested, then shall ye also appear with Him in glory" (Col. 3:4)! William MacDonald captures much of its meaning, when he writes:

> "That ungodly sinners shall one day be transformed into the image of Christ by a miracle of grace is one of the most astounding truths of divine revelation. The point is not, of course, that we will ever have the attributes of deity, or even that we will have Christ's facial resemblance, but that we will be morally like Him, absolutely free from sin, and will have glorified bodies like His."[9]

THE BLESSING OF BELOVEDNESS AND VALUE — The term the "elect" throughout the Bible conveys the idea of love, nearness, and preciousness to God. Therefore, in the New Testament the idea of election suggests much more than the irresistible choosing for salvation; the term elect is, firstly, an elevated term, which sets forth the dignity and value of the elect to God. Three times we read that the elect are beloved by God: "Put on therefore, as the elect of God, holy and beloved…" (Col. 3:12); "knowing brethren, beloved of God, your election, how that…"

(1 Thess. 1:4); "we are bound to give thanks to God always for you, brethren beloved of the Lord, for God chose you..." (2 Thess. 2:13). Additionally, we read of Rufus, "chosen in the Lord" (Rom. 16:13). Here, the word "chosen" is a unique and special word denoting "eminence," Concerning this verse, the outstanding Greek authority W. E. Vine states that it signifies "...the sense of eminent,"[10]

ELECTION REFERS TO CHRISTIANS ALONE

The term "elect" is never used of the unsaved in the Bible; it is a term that always refers to those who are already saved. Time and time again, careful study shows that election is a doctrine that is written to and refers to Christians only. In Ephesians, Romans, 1 Peter, Titus, and other passages, the message of election is to Christians and for Christians. Colossians 3:12 reads, "Put on therefore, as the elect of God, holy and beloved, bowels of mercy, kindness, humbleness of mind, meekness and long-suffering..." In this verse the elect are described as "holy" and "beloved," descriptive and suggestive words which can only characterize believers. It would be contrary to the tenor of Scripture to look at unsaved people in the world and wonder if they are some of God's elect. The unsaved, the Bible teaches, are those "who have their understanding darkened, being alienated from the life of God through the ignorance that is in them because of the blindness of their heart: who being past feeling, have given themselves over unto lasciviousness, to work all uncleanness with greediness" (Eph. 4:18-19). This can never be descriptive of the elect. The unsaved are never numbered among the elect, for the term "elect" is a term that refers only to believers.

Paul writes to the church of the Thessalonians, saying, "Knowing, brethren beloved, your election of God..." (1 Thess. 1:4). This is an important verse for both Calvinists and non-Calvinists to consider. A number of questions might be raised; first, how did Paul know that all the believers in this assembly were elect? How could Paul know who were and were not the elect of God? Is not election a secret hid in God alone? It seems clear that he calls them all elect because they had already placed faith in Christ and were in active fellowship in a local church. Paul writes earlier in Thessalonians 1:1 "...unto the church of the Thessalonians which is in God the Father and in the Lord Jesus Christ. The believers at Thessalonica are noted by Paul to be "in Christ" and "in God the Father," which denotes salvation and the unique privilege of the believer. The term "in Christ" is a wonderful theological phrase that teaches that the believer is placed in a marvelous union with Christ. One who joins himself to the Lord is one spirit with Him (1 Cor. 6:17 NASV). Christ's riches are our riches, His power is our power, His resources are our resources, and His position is our position. To be "in Christ" is to share in the very life of God through Jesus Christ (Eph. 1:3). The biblical term "in Christ" and the truth of divine election both express the high privilege and position of the believer. In the New Testament, when the term "elect" refers to the Christian, it is a collective term of endearment, dignity, and the high position the believer has in Christ. We read, "Who shall lay any thing to the charge of God's elect?" (Rom. 8:33). This verse dispels the popular notion that election is a mysterious and secret doctrine that is hid in God alone. Paul knew who the elect were and could freely speak of them as elect. Samuel Fisk, a Baptist theologian, unfolds this aspect of the New Testament's teaching of election:

"Predestination and election do not refer to certain people of the world becoming saved or lost, but they relate to those who are already children of God in respect to certain privileges or positions out ahead; they look forward to what God will work in those who have become His own."[11]

Paul could speak freely of those who were God's elect because of their personal faith. The unbeliever cannot be among the elect, for the most important of reasons, he does not possess faith. The emphasis of the apostle in his letter to Titus is that the most foundational characteristic of the elect of God is their faith. Paul writes to Titus, "Paul, a servant of God, and an apostle of Jesus Christ, according to the faith of God's elect, and acknowledging of the truth which is after godliness" (Tit. 1:1). Paul stresses two important points about the faith of God's elect. Firstly, the elect are God's elect! The elect possess the marks that set them apart as God's own people. They have godliness. They have truth. They know and own God as their Sovereign and Lord. The unbeliever does not do this. Our Lord Jesus Christ told the unbelieving Jews "you are not of God" (Jn. 8:47). Secondly, the elect of God have faith. There are no unbelievers among the elect. The "faith of God's elect" refers to the body of truth, or the doctrines, to which all subscribe. Foremost of these is faith in the finished work of the Lord Jesus Christ upon Calvary's cross for salvation. The doctrine of election does not refer to unbelievers, or the choosing of some to salvation while passing others by; rather, it speaks of the uniqueness and dignity of the believer's position in Christ. Sir Robert Anderson (1841-1918), the Old Testament scholar and theologian, sets forth the very heart of the term "election" when he writes:

"First, the Scriptural expression 'God's Elect' is not the mere statement of fact, or even of a privilege, but like first-born, it is a title of dignity and privilege, applicable exclusively to the Christian. And secondly, the prominent thought in election, especially in this dispensation of the Church, is rank and privilege, and not deliverance from perdition."[12]

In this chapter we have tried to show that the doctrine of sovereign election has more to do with the blessings of salvation than with salvation from sins; more to do with service to God than with an irresistible decree; and more to do with those "in Christ" than with the choosing of some to salvation while passing over others. However, the serious Christian is often troubled by so-called "election-to-salvation" proof texts. These texts are often the source of much rancor and debate. In theological discussion many have found that these texts are theological bullets that extreme Calvinists like to fire. Nevertheless, these texts are extremely important and are central to any understanding of the doctrine of election. Therefore as we close this Chapter allow us to spend some time reviewing these texts and suggesting a viewpoint that may be more in line with the immediate context and the tenor of New Testament theology.

ELECTION PROOF TEXTS

2 THESSALONIANS 2:13 — "But we are bound to give thanks always to God for you, brethren beloved of the Lord, because God from the beginning hath chosen you to salvation through sanctification of the Spirit and belief of the truth."

This verse contains two words that seem to thrill the Calvinist and unsettle the non-Calvinist—those being, "chosen" and "salvation." However, good interpreters of Scripture first seek to understand biblical words in their context. With this in mind, let us look more closely at the word "salvation" in Paul's writing. Paul writes, "For God hath not appointed us to wrath, but to obtain salvation by our Lord Jesus Christ" (1 Thess. 5:9); and later, "Therefore I endure all things for the elects' sakes, that they may obtain salvation which is in Christ Jesus with eternal glory" (2 Tim. 2:10). In both of these verses the context is physical deliverance (through Christ's coming for the church) from the judgment and wrath that will fall upon this world. The word "salvation" in 1 and 2 Thessalonians and 1 and 2 Timothy may be best understood in light of the coming of Christ to deliver or "save" believers from future judgment.

We might suggest that Paul is setting forth a promise of end-times tribulation deliverance in this verse. The believers at Thessalonica are not in danger of persecution from the "man of sin…the son of perdition" (2:3) because the Lord will deliver them from judgment before that time. Additionally, God will also keep them through the trials and persecutions of this life (1 Thess 1:6) through their ongoing growth in sanctification and belief in the truth.

When would this salvation or deliverance work of God begin in their lives? The words "from the beginning" are two words in the Greek New Testament, "ap arches." These words have been translated by many New Testament scholars as "first fruits, or new converts" (F. F. Bruce, Jamison, Fausett, Brown). *The Revised Standard Version* of the Bible suggests that the verse should be read, "God chose you as the first converts…" If this is indeed the proper translation, we might suggest that God has chosen to deliver the believers of this early church from the judgment and the wrath to come, as well as from trials in this life through sanctification and belief in the truth.

ACTS 13:48 — "And when the Gentiles heard this, they were glad, and glorified the Word of the Lord: and as many were ordained to eternal life believed."(KJV)

Paul and Barnabas had begun their preaching ministry in Pisidian Antioch in Acts 13:14-52. Many Gentiles were ready to believe the truth and approached the gospel messengers. "The Gentiles besought that these words might be preached to them the next Sabbath" (13:42). On the other hand, while some Jews believed, the majority were moved with envy and "spoke against those things which were spoken by Paul, contradicting and blaspheming" (13:45). The Jewish majority had angrily rejected the gospel, and so Paul and Barnabas now turn to the Gentiles. Paul and Barnabas use Old Testament Scripture, quoting Isaiah 42, verses 6 and 7, as the basis for their action. Then in Acts 13:46, Paul says of the Jews, "but seeing that ye put it from you, and judge yourselves unworthy of everlasting life, lo, we turn to the Gentiles." Verse 48 stands as a contrast between the Jews who set themselves against the gospel and the Gentiles who disposed themselves to believe it. So we read, "as many as were disposed to eternal life believed" (Acts 13:48 Alford).

Much of the interpretation of this passage turns on the Greek verb tasso, translated in the KJV as "ordained," but generally agreed to have the broader meaning of "to decide" or "be disposed to," The Greek scholar Dean Alford translates it, "as many as were disposed to eternal life believed"[13] The Liddell and Scott Greek Dictionary suggests a number of alternative meanings for the verb "tasso," but the word "ordain" is not among them. Scholars are very much divided concerning the use of "ordain" as the meaning of the Greek verb "tasso," It has been suggested that it would be unwise to build a doctrine on a word meaning that is questionable. The Baptist Greek scholar Dr. A. T. Robertson writes:

> "The word 'ordain' is not the best translation here...The Jews had voluntarily rejected the word of God. On the other side were those Gentiles who gladly accepted what the Jews rejected...Why these Gentiles ranged themselves on God's side...Luke does not tell us. This verse does not solve the vexed problem of divine sovereignty and human free agency. There is no evidence that Luke had in mind an absolutum decretem (absolute decree) of personal salvation."[14]

On the other hand, we see that God was working in the hearts of the Gentiles. The Gentiles were ready to hear and believe the gospel. This verse does not teach that God, by eternal decree, had chosen these Gentiles to believe; rather, these Gentiles, after being drawn by the Spirit of God and hearing the gospel preached, were disposed to the truth and believed. The Gentiles were not chosen to believe while the Jews were passed over. No, both had made a choice; one for Christ, and one against Christ. The door of faith was now opened to the Gentiles and many believed. It was not that every Jew had rejected the gospel, nor that every Gentile had believed, but that God in His sovereignty was now turning to the Gentiles and the Gentiles were responding by faith. When Paul and Barnabas had returned to Antioch and were recounting the work of God among the Gentiles, they declared "all that they had done and how God had opened the door of faith to the Gentiles" (Acts 14:27).

JOHN 6:37 — "All that the Father giveth Me shall come to Me; and him that cometh to me I will in no wise cast out."

This verse in John six has been considered by Calvinists to be incontrovertible evidence for their position. The words, "All that the Father giveth to Me shall come to Me," have been taken to mean that God, in eternity past, has chosen a small group of persons, called the elect, for salvation. Now He is irresistibly drawing them to Himself so that they alone may be saved. However, at the outset we cannot help but notice the absence of words such as "elect," "irresistible," and "eternal decree." At times Calvinists, in their sincere desire to convince others of their position, over reach and assume that certain "suggestive" phrases set forth the Reformed view of election. John's gospel contains the phrase "All that the Father giveth..." or "which Thou has given..." on at least four different occasions (Jn. 6:37; 17:2, 6, 9). It is assumed by the majority of Calvinists that these "given ones" will all be saved. while the others are passed over by God. Others have suggested that God, by virtue of His foreknowledge, knew those who would trust Christ and these are given to Christ. Dr. Henry C. Theissen, a past chairman of the faculty of Wheaton Graduate School, in IL, writes:

> "There is a recurring declaration that certain men have been given to Christ, and it is assumed that this was an arbitrary act of God by which the rest were left to perish. But we reply that it is nowhere indicated what caused God to give certain men to Christ and not others. In light of God's revealed character, it is more probable that He did this because of what He foresaw they would do, than merely to exercise sovereign authority"[15]

Who are they which the Father has "given" to Christ in John 6:37? It seems from a study of relevant verses in John's gospel that the "given ones" are those who believe on Him and have personal knowledge of Him. The "given ones" are those: who kept God's Word (Jn. 17:6); who were with Christ in the world (Jn. 17:12); to whom Christ gave God's Word (Jn. 17:8); to whom Christ declared the Father's Name (17:26). In context, these "given ones" seem to be: (1) His own disciples, excepting, of course, Judas who was lost (Jn. 17:12); but also (2) all those who believe on Him (Jn. 17:20).

We might also ask, are the "given ones" persons who do not possess a free will, but who are irresistibly drawn by the Father to salvation in Christ? This is the suggested view of many Calvinist writers. But it does not seem to meet the demands of Scripture. If the "given ones" are drawn irresistibly, then John 6:37 is in conflict with John 6:40: "This is the will of Him that sent Me, that every one which sees the Son and believes on Him may have everlasting life..." (6:40). According to the Calvinist John 6:37 speaks of a select number who are chosen for salvation, regardless of free will but John 6:40 states that the gospel is open to "every one which sees the Son and believes on Him may have everlasting life." Free will and the exercise of faith seem to be the key factors in salvation. Theology seems to be in conflict with divine Scripture.

What is Jesus teaching in John six? Christ's main teaching should be the interpreter's main focus. When the focus is exclusively on Calvinist proof texts, the larger and more important meaning of the passage can be lost. Jesus is teaching that a vast group of people are on their way to a glorious destination: resurrection to life everlasting. Jesus assures us that He will not lose any believer...; "I will in no wise cast out." They will all attain to the resurrection. This is God's will. However, there is a divine side and a human side. The divine side is that God is drawing men to Himself, "No man can come to Me, except the Father which sent me draw him..." (6:44). No man can come to Christ unless the Father draw him. The conviction of sin by the Holy Spirit (Jn. 16:8), the drawing of the Father, and the Scripture's power to produce faith (Rom. 10:17) are all working in the hearts of the lost to bring men to Christ. Eternal salvation is of God. However, we must not make the mistake of thinking that God draws in some irresistible way the elect, while passing over others. For John 12:32, using the same Greek word for "draw"(helkuo), says, "And I, if I be lifted up from the earth, will draw all men unto me." This, on one hand, is the divine side of salvation.

Then there is the human side of salvation, which we call "free agency:" "him that cometh to Me I will in no wise cast out;" and "every one which sees the Son and believes on Him may have everlasting life" (Jn. 6:40). Everlasting life is not for those who just think about Christ, nor for those who simply know about Christ, nor for those who are merely willing; it is for those who come to Christ by faith. These are the ones whom the Father gives to Christ; these are the ones who have eternal life, and will attain unto the resurrection from out of the dead.

Endnotes

[1] John Parkinson, *The Faith of God's Elect*, (Glasgow, Scotland: Gospel Tract Publications, 1999), p. 18
[2] Dr. Willem J. Owneneel, *What is Election?*, (Sunbury, PA : Believer's Bookshelf, 1985), p.16

[3] G. C. Berkhouwer, *Divine Election*, (Grand Rapids, MI: Eerdmanns, 1960), 135, 149, 162

[4] Alan Richardson, *An Introduction to the Theology of the New Testament*, (London: SCM, 1958), p.279

[5] William Klein, *The New Chosen People- A Corporate View of Election*, (Grand Rapids, MI: Zondervan, 1990), p.180

[6] F. B. Hole, *Ephesians*, (Northumberland, GB: Central Bible Trust, ND), p. 34

[7] William Kelly, *Ephesians*, (Addision, IL: Bible Truth Publishers, 1970)

[8] H. A. Ironside, *What's the Answer*, (Grand Rapids, MI: Zondervan, MI, 1944), p.43

[9] William MacDonald, *Justification by Faith*, (Kansas City, KS: Walterick, 1981), p. 93

[10] W. E. Vine, *Expository Dictionary of New Testament Words*, (Old Tappan, NJ: Revell, 1981), p. 190

[11] Samuel Fisk, *Divine Sovereignty and Human Freedom*, (Neptune, NJ: Loizeaux, 1981), p. 37

[12] Sir Robert Anderson, *The Gospel and Its Ministry*, (Grand Rapids, MI: Kregel, 1980), p. 76

[13] Dean Alford, *The New Testament for English Readers vol. 1*, (Grand Rapids, MI: Baker Book House, 1983), p. 745

[14] A. T. Robertson, *Word Pictures in the New Testament, vol. 3*, (New York: Harper and Brothers, 1930), p. 200

[15] Henry C. Theissen, *Lectures in Systematic Theology*, (Grand Rapids, MI: Eerdmans, 1976), p. 348

- 6 -
Reformed Theology and Limited Atonement

Aurelius Augustine (354-430 AD), the learned university professor of rhetoric, knew of Christ's death, but never thought of it as extending to him. He saw himself as being too far from God and his sins as too loathsome to God for Christ to have died for him. If there was such a truth as unlimited atonement, his fertile mind never contemplated that it included him. He wrote in the book called Confessions, which describes his conversion to Christ, "Lord, how loathsome I was in Thy sight; lust stormed confusingly within me, whirling my thoughts over the precipices of desire, and the torrent of my immorality tossed, boiled, swelled and ran over…"

However, on a warm July day in the year 386 AD, Augustine was staying in the seacoast villa of a friend named Alypius in Milan, Italy. While settled in his quarters, busily composing a speech in praise of the emperor, there was a knock on the door. A decorated officer of the imperial guard, who was a serious Christian, had come for a visit. As they sat together, the visitor observed a book on a table. As he opened the book, he noticed it was a Greek version of the epistles of Paul. With this opening, the visitor began to tell of his conversion. He then told of person after person, whom he had met in different parts of the world, who were changed by faith in Christ. After the visitor left, Augustine, who was visibly moved, said to Alypius, "What is the matter with us? Didn't you hear? Simple men and women gain heaven by faith...but what of us?...We are noble and learned, but have not Christ. How long, how long? Tomorrow and tomorrow. Will there ever be an end to my uncleanness?"

At that moment, Augustine heard a child crying out on a nearby rooftop, "Take up and read, take up and read..." Augustine went back into the villa and took up the book of the writings of Paul. He went into the gardens, and sitting under a fig tree, he read, "...Let us live honorably, as in the day, not in reveling and drunkenness, not in debauchery and licentiousness, not in quarreling and jealousy. Instead, put on the Lord Jesus Christ, and make no provision for the flesh, to gratify its desires" (Rom. 13:13,14). At that moment, he realized that Christ's death truly extended to him. There in the garden he bowed before God, repented, and, through faith, trusted Christ as his Savior. From that point on, he would often say, "It was under the fig tree that God poured the light of salvation into my heart..." Augustine was 32 years old at his conversion. Nine days later Monica, his devoted mother, who had prayed for his salvation for 20 years, unexpectedly died.

Just as Augustine did not believe that the death of Christ extended to him personally, similarly many have taught that the death of Christ does not extend to all men, although not for the same reasons. Augustine thought the death of Christ did not extend to him because of the gravity of his sins. Others teach that the death of Christ does not extend to all men because many are not "elect." Since the time of the Reformation, Calvinist leaders have argued for the teaching called "limited atonement." This doctrine, simply put, teaches that the death of Christ did not atone for the sins of all men; but only atoned for the sins of the elect. This doctrine does not dispute that the power of the death of Christ is infinite and is sufficient to atone for the sins of the whole world, but contends that the extent of the atonement is applied to the elect alone. Limited atonement representing the "L" in the "TULIP" acrostic is probably the most debated point within all of Calvinism. Many who would count themselves as thorough Calvinists in other points, reject this point of doctrine, and they refer to their position as "moderate Calvinists" or "four-point Calvinists." This teaching is considered by leading proponents on both sides of the issue to be the weakest major tenet of Reformed theology.

LIMITED ATONEMENT AND CHURCH HISTORY

This point of theology, however, was never in question from the time of the early church until the days of the Reformation. The early church creeds, the early church fathers, the councils, and the overall consensus of the church agreed that the death of Christ atoned for the sins of all men. Athanasius (293-373 AD), a strong defender of orthodox belief, wrote in a work called The Incarnation of the Word of God:

> "Thus, taking a body like our own, because all our bodies were liable to the corruption of death, He surrendered His body to death instead of all, and offered it to the Father."

And again later in the same work, he writes:

> "...Death there had to be, and death for all so that the due of all might be paid."[1]

Many years later at the time of the Reformation, the Heidelberg Catechism (1563), the instructional standard for the German Reformed church, also espoused unlimited atonement. In its answer to the thirty-seventh question, we read:

"...What do you understand by the word 'suffered?' — That all the time Christ lived on earth, but especially at the end of His life, He bore, in body and soul, the wrath of God against the sin of the whole human race..."[2]

Martin Luther did not hold to the teaching of limited atonement, nor did other Lutheran Reformation stalwarts, such as Philip Melanchthon and Martin Bucer. Many contend, as well, that even John Calvin did not hold to this teaching, for he wrote, on more than one occasion, that Christ's death made provision for the salvation of all. In his comments on Galatians 5:12, John Calvin wrote: "...for God commends to us the salvation of all men without exception, even as Christ suffered for the sins of the whole world." The Church of England's official statement of faith, *The Thirty-Nine Articles* (1553), written about the time of John Calvin's death, is equally clear in its acceptance of unlimited atonement. Article thirty-one of *The Thirty -Nine Articles* reads:

"The offering of Christ once made is that perfect redemption, propitiation, and satisfaction, for all the sins of the whole world, both original and actual; and there is none other satisfaction for sin, but that alone."[3]

The doctrine of unlimited atonement is not a new doctrine; on the contrary. It has been the majority view and historic doctrine of the church from its earliest days. Presbyterian author Walter Elwell admits:

"Those who defend general redemption (unlimited atonement) begin by pointing out that it is the historic view of the church, being held by the vast majority of theologians, reformers, evangelists, and fathers from the beginning of the church until the present day, including virtually all the writers before the Reformation, with the possible exception of Augustine. Among the Reformers the doctrine is found in Luther, Melanchthon, Bullinger, Latimer, Cranmer, Coverdale, and even Calvin in some of his commentaries."[4]

In fact, numerous learned men held to unlimited atonement: Clement of Alexandria (150-220), Eusebius (260-342), Athanasius (293-373), Cyril of Jerusalem (315-386), Gregory Nazianzen (324-389), Ambrose (340-407), Martin Luther (1483-1546), Richard Hooker (1553-1600), James Ussher (1581-1656), Richard Baxter (1615-1691), John Bunyan (1628-1688), John Newton (1725-1807), Alfred Edersheim (1825-1889), B. F. Westcott (1825-1901), J. B. Lightfoot (1828-1889), Augustus Strong (1836-1921), A. T. Robertson (1863-1934), and Lewis Sperry Chafer (1871-1952). In addition, the numerous confessions from the Reformation period teach unlimited atonement: the Augsburg Confession (1530), the First Confession of Helvetia (1536), the Confession of Saxony (1551), the Thirty Nine Articles of the Church of England (1553), the Heidelberg Catechism (1563), and the Latter Confession of Helvetia (1566).

THE CALVINIST VIEW: FOR WHOM DID CHRIST DIE?

In the face of convincing evidence from the Bible and the testimony of many learned men, the Calvinist continues to argue the view that Christ died only for the elect. The Calvinist argues that restrictive words such as "sheep," "many," and the "Church" indicate a limited atonement. The other camp responds that those terms refer to the redeemed, those to whom the atonement has been applied. The two camps have continued to debate this doctrine for centuries. Unfortunately, this theological sparring has sadly produced more heat than light. In the process, scholars have not been persuaded and believers have not been edified. Yet, as in every biblical debate, the Scriptures must be our standard and divine compass. We must ask the questions: what does the Bible teach? For whom did Christ die? For the elect only or for all men? We read in the Scriptures that: He died for all (1 Tim 2:6); He died for every man (Heb. 2:9); He died for the whole world (Jn. 3:16); He died for the sins of the whole world (1 Jn. 2:2); He died for the ungodly (Rom. 5:8); He died for false teachers (2 Pt. 2:1); He died for many (Matt. 20:28); He died for Israel (Jn. 11:50-51); He died for the Church (Eph. 5:25); and He died for "me" (Gal. 2:20).

The general tenor of Scripture is that Christ's death is for all men, but there are three texts that warrant special attention. The first text is: "And He is the propitiation for our sins, and not for ours only, but also for the sins of the whole world" (1 Jn. 2:2). There are three reasons why the term "the whole world" must refer to the world of all mankind. First, because the word "world" refers to all men, unless the context indicates that it should be restricted. Second, because "our" and "world" are contrasted, the one referring to Christians and the other to all men. Third, because the expression "the whole world" is also used in 1 John 5:19, "the whole world lieth in the evil one," to denote unsaved persons. It is reasonable and certainly the normal sense that the expression "the whole world" should refer to Christ's death for all men.

The second verse is: "Behold the Lamb of God that takes away the sin of the world" (Jn. 1:29). In light of the context and the use of the word "world" by John, it is clear that the phrase "sin of the world" refers to all fallen human beings. The straightforward and normal use of the word "world" should and must be the meaning here. It cannot mean anything less, since there are no restrictive words linked to the phrase. Moreover, that which John intended is clarified only three verses later, when he writes, "And this is the condemnation, that light is come into the world, and men loved darkness rather than light because their deeds were evil" (Jn. 3:19). Clearly, the world of all fallen human beings is in view here, as it is also later in John, where we read, "And when He (Holy Spirit) is come He will reprove the world of sin, and of righteousness, and of judgment: of sin, because they believe not on Me." (Jn. 16:8).

Finally, the third verse is: "But we see Jesus, who was made a little lower than the angels for the suffering of death, crowned with glory and honor, that He, by the grace of God, should taste death for every man" (Heb. 2:9). This verse clearly suggests that the penal substitutionary death of Christ made provision for the sins of every man. The phrase "should taste death" must certainly refer to the awful experience of Christ bearing God's righteous wrath against sin on the cross. There our Savior profoundly experienced being stricken, smitten of God, and afflicted (Isa. 53:4) for every man. John Calvin's comments on this verse eloquently set forth the argument for an unlimited atonement. He writes:

> "When he says for every man, he does not mean that He should be merely an example to others. He means that Christ died for us, because He took on Himself our lot, and redeemed us from the curse of death."[5]

Many have objected, stating that if Hebrews 2:9 teaches atonement for all men, why does this verse say "every man" and not simply "all men?" Henry Alford, the eminent Greek scholar gives us a very satisfying answer. He writes:

> "If it be asked, why 'every man' rather than 'all men,' we may safely say, that the singular brings out, far more strongly than the plural word, the applicability of Christ's death to each individual man."[6]

THE CALVINIST VIEW OF "SECURED" ATONEMENT

Many misunderstand the doctrinal underpinning of the Calvinist view on the atonement. It is assumed that limited atonement is simply the view that only the elect will place faith in the death of the Lord Jesus Christ, and when each elect individual places faith in Christ, he is saved eternally. Most Calvinists will vigorously disagree with this view of limited atonement. The Reformed view of limited atonement sets forth the idea that the cross alone saves. The Calvinist does not believe that the cross of Christ provided the basis of eternal salvation. Nor does the Calvinist believe that personal faith is a decisive condition for salvation. But rather, the Calvinist believes that the death of Christ upon the cross of Calvary secured salvation for the elect alone. That is, at the death of Christ, all the elect of all ages were actually, completely, and entirely saved and nothing more was needed; every condition was fully met. This, according to Calvinism, is true of those elect who were not yet born, of those who have not knowledge of Christ, and of those who do not yet believe. Calvinist author David N. Steele, in this book *The Five Points of Calvinism* writes:

> "Christ's redeeming work was intended to save the elect only and actually secured salvation for them. His death was a substitutionary endurance of the penalty of sin in the place of certain specified sinners. In addition to putting away the sins of His people, Christ's redemption secured everything necessary for their salvation."[7]

The Calvinist view of the atonement fails to distinguish between the work of atonement and the application of the benefits of the atonement. To the Calvinist they are both one and the same, indivisible and indistinguishable. According to Calvinism, when Christ died on the cross, His penal sacrifice paid the price for our guilt and applied the benefits of salvation to the elect at the very same moment. However, this view does not seem to agree with the teaching of the Scriptures. The Scriptures state that all men are under the wrath of God until they place faith in the finished work of Christ. Scripture never gives us the idea that the elect have been saved since the death of Christ in 33AD. Are the elect "in Christ" from birth? Do they possess peace with God at birth? Do they experience the Spirit's witness with their spirits that they are sons of God when their lives begin? Do they possess from birth the many other marks that characterize all children of God? According to Calvinism, these things must be true from birth, for salvation was secured and made actual at the death of Christ. But Paul tells his readers at Ephesus that they were once "children of wrath" and they were "children of disobedience," This is very unusual language indeed, if they were saved already, and if the benefits of the cross were applied to the elect already at Calvary. We read of these believers, "in times past you walked according to the course of this world, according to the prince of the power of the air, the spirit that works in the children of disobedience; among whom also we all had our manner of life in times past in the lust of our flesh, fulfilling the desires of the flesh and of the mind, and were by nature the children of wrath, even as others" (Eph. 2:2-3). It is clear from Scripture that the benefits of the death of Christ are not applied to the believer until faith is exercised in the finished work of Christ. The provision of salvation was made through the death of Christ, but the application and enjoyment of the benefits come at the time personal faith is exercised (Eph. 2:8-9).

LIMITS THE NECESSITY OF FAITH

This leads us to consider the knotty problem of the role of faith in the Calvinist view of limited atonement. This may be the most serious problem with this doctrinal perspective. The Calvinist sees personal faith as an unbiblical condition for salvation; for if faith is a condition for salvation, then the result is a works-based salvation. To the Calvinist, faith cannot have a central or decisive role in our salvation, for this would result in man having a part in his salvation. Calvinist writer Keith Mathison explains:

"Unlimited atonement changes salvation into a cooperative effort between God and man. Jesus did His part on the cross by making us savable. Now we do our part by believing. What (according to non-Calvinists) makes salvation actual is our faith...but that is simply not biblical...it is a works salvation!"[8]

The Calvinist fully realizes the problem his theology poses. He knows that the Bible clearly teaches that faith is a necessity for salvation. The message of the gospel is everywhere evident, "Believe on the Lord Jesus Christ and you will be saved" (Acts 16:31, Rom. 10:9). Reformed writers realize that this glaring inconsistency must be addressed. The Calvinist suggests a solution; however it is a solution that strikes many as being so forced and unnatural that one wonders if he believes it himself. The solution is that God procured, in some way, personal faith for the elect at Calvary, thus doing away with the condition of personal faith for salvation. Although God has already procured faith in the death of Christ, the elect must still place personal faith in Christ at a later point. This second faith strikes many as unnecessary and redundant, and Calvinism has never adequately explained why two "faiths" are required. Calvinist R. C. Sproul explains this view by posing a series of rhetorical questions, all of which he supposes to be true. He writes:

"Let me consider the benefit of Christ's atonement for me. I am presently a believer in Christ. Today I enjoy the benefit of an atonement made for me centuries ago. Did that atonement satisfy the demands of God's justice on all my sins? If it did, then it satisfied the penalty for the sin of my previous unbelief. Was the sin paid for before

I believed? Or was Christ's atonement not complete until I came to faith? Did His death cover my unbelief or not? If it did, why then does His atonement not cover the unbelief of unbelievers?"[9]

Circular reasoning, such as is offered by R. C. Sproul, unfortunately falls short in helping us gain a greater understanding of Biblical truth. Such rationale may be compelling to the casual reader, but upon closer examination, one finds that it fails to satisfy the Biblical standard. One would like some Scriptural support for the idea that Christ purchased personal faith for the elect, therefore removing the need for individual faith. The truth of the matter is that there is simply no Biblical support for this idea. The benefits of the atonement and the work of the atonement must never be confused. God's justice was fully and righteously satisfied by the death of Christ alone. Before Pentecost, before the birth of the church, before one person ever enjoyed the benefits of the atonement, the Father raised Christ and seated Him on the throne of His right hand, demonstrating His satisfaction in the atoning death of Christ. The atonement made available salvation for all, even those who would never believe on Christ. However, personal faith in Christ's death would apply or appropriate the benefits of the atonement to the believer. These two aspects of the atonement are complementary yet clearly distinguishable in the Word of God. We read, "And by Him all that believe are justified from all things, from which you could not be justified by the Law of Moses" (Acts 13:39). In Romans, Paul writes, "The righteousness of God which is by faith of Jesus Christ unto all (provision) and upon all (application) them that believe" (Rom. 3:22). To Timothy, Paul writes, "…who is the Savior of all men, and especially those who believe" (1 Tim. 4:10).

LIMITS THE LOVE OF GOD

This leads us to another serious problem within Calvinist theology, that is, the love of God for the whole world. It may sound strange to hear that there are Christians who do not believe that God loves the whole world; nevertheless it is true of Calvinist theology. If Christ, as we have attempted to show, by His death made provision for the lost, it must also be true that Christ loves those who are lost. If God loves all people equally, then the atonement must extend to all people. The two go together: an infinite love and an infinite atonement, an all-inclusive love and an all-inclusive atonement, an unlimited love and an unlimited atonement. We may certainly be justified in such reasoning, but what does the Bible say? The Bible makes it clear that those whom God loves are also those for whom Christ died. Paul tells us in Romans, "But God commends His love for us in that, while we were yet sinners, Christ died for us (Rom. 5:8). In another place John the apostle writes, "Herein is love, not that we loved God, but that He loved us, and sent His Son to be the propitiation for our sins" (1 Jn. 4:10). The love of God to man is linked with the death of Christ for man. Of course, this is a dilemma for the Calvinist. For he well knows that, those whom God loves are also those for whom Christ died. If God's love for the world is unlimited, then Christ's atonement for the world is also unlimited. Since the Calvinist rejects the doctrine of unlimited atonement, it must follow that he also denies God's love for the whole world. Edwin Palmer, author of the book, *The Five Points of Calvinism*, explains:

"God does not love all people with the same love...since the objects of the Father's love are particular, definite, and limited, so are the objects of Christ's death. Because God has loved certain ones and not all, because He has sovereignly and immutably determined that these particular ones will be saved, He sent His Son to die for them, to save them, and not all the world."[10]

However, what does the Bible say? Whom does God love? God certainly has a special love for the Church (Eph. 5:25). No one would deny that wonderful truth. But does God just love the elect; or does God love those who are not elect, the lost and ungodly? The Bible teaches that:

1. God loves the world (Jn. 3:16)
2. God loves the selfish (Mark 10:21)
3. God loves the ungodly (Rom. 5:6)
4. God loves those who love not God (1 Jn. 4:10)
5. God loves the children of wrath (Eph. 2:3-4)

Is not the Word of God abundantly clear? God's love extends to the whole world, and therefore, the atonement provided by the death of Christ extends to the whole world. These two complementary truths are set forth so beautifully in John's gospel, "For God so loved the world that He sent his only begotten son that whosoever believes in Him should not perish but have everlasting life" (Jn. 3:16). However, this leads us into another issue in Calvinistic theology, and that is, the meaning of the word "world."

LIMITS THE MEANING OF THE "WORLD"

The theologically astute Calvinist realizes at times that his theology has forced him into a difficult corner. Limited atonement is indeed one of those issues in Reformed theology. If God purposes to provide atonement for all those whom He loves, and He loves the whole world and not merely the elect, then the very foundation of Calvinist theology is severely weakened. The appropriate solution to this dilemma, it seems to many Calvinists, is to give a new meaning to the word "world." Some Calvinist writers teach that the "world" in John 3:16 and 1 John 2:2 means some elect individuals from every nation in the world; others disagree saying, that interpretation is too forced and unnatural. The majority of Calvinists teach that the word "world" must mean the world of the people of God, that is the elect. Popular Calvinist author A. W. Pink explains this view:

> "The 'world' in John 3:16 must, in the final analysis, refer to the world of God's people (the elect). Must, we say, for there is no other alternative solution. It cannot mean the whole human race...We may admit that our interpretation of John 3:16 is no novel one invented by us, but one uniformly given by the Reformers and the Puritans, and many others since them."[11]

A. W. Pink tells us that this has been the view in the teaching of the Reformers and many Puritans and other respected Reformed leaders down through the centuries. Pink also states that there is no other alternative than the one he suggests. But we ask respectfully, does this view make theological sense? Allow us to pose a question. If the "world" in John 3:16 is the elect, can one of the elect ever perish eternally? Without a moment's hesitation, the Calvinist would answer that it is an utter impossibility. If it is an impossibility, then there is a problem for the Calvinist, found in John 3:16 itself. For this verse suggests the very real possibility that some of the "world"(elect) may not believe and will therefore perish. We read, "...that whosoever believes shall not perish..." This problem is posed not only by non-Calvinists, but is such a difficulty that some loyal and devout Calvinists suggest it should be eliminated from serious consideration. Calvinist theologian Dr. Robert Dabney writes in his respected work, Systematic Theology:

> "Make 'the world' which Christ loved, to mean the "elect world;" and we reach the absurdity, that some of the elect may not believe, and perish."[12]

Might it make more sense to accept the plain and straightforward view that the "world" in John 3:16 means just what it says: God loved the whole world? This world is one composed of all: elect and non-elect, believers and non-believers, godly and ungodly. God loves them all. This issue is not minor and insignificant. It touches on the very character and person of God. The Word of God declares that God is love. One of the attributes of God is that He is omni-benevolent, that is, He is all-loving. God cannot be all-loving if He does not love all. Might the Calvinist, and might all Christians, strive to be more like the godly C. H. Spurgeon who once said, "I would rather be inconsistent a thousand times with myself than to be inconsistent once with the Word of God."

LIMITS THE PREACHING OF THE GOSPEL

Our theological convictions will lead to practical, and ofttimes unfortunate, consequences. The Calvinistic view of limited atonement is a vivid example. In the area of evangelism, the Calvinist believes that it is improper and wrong to tell an unbeliever that Christ died for him. Why is this so? Because our theology has consequences. The Calvinist reasons that since Christ's atonement is limited to the elect alone, and that the riches of God's redemptive grace extend only to the elect, therefore we cannot tell the unbeliever that Christ died for him. In fact, the Calvinist believes that it is not even permissible to say to the unbeliever that God loves him, because God only loves the elect. Nor can we say that God's offer of salvation is extended to the unbeliever, because it is only extended to the elect, and no one knows absolutely who is one of the elect. Will this affect our gospel efforts? Undoubtedly. Will it make the presentation of the gospel more difficult? Of course. However, this is a difficulty that the Calvinist is more than willing to risk. Calvinist author Edwin Palmer explains:

> "Some reason that if an evangelist cannot say to his audience, 'Christ died for you,' his effectiveness in winning souls will be measurably hurt. The answer to such reasoning is that, if there has to be a choice, it is better to tell the truth and not to win so many converts than to win many by a falsehood. The end does not justify the means. If the Bible says that Christ died for the elect, then an evangelist may not play God by stating that he knows everyone in his audience is elect and, therefore, that Christ died for them. He does not know it and should not state it."[13]

We find this same reasoning even in the arena of Christian counseling. Calvinist leaders teach those who give spiritual care that they must not tell an unbeliever that Christ died for him. Christian counselor Dr. Jay Adams, in *Competent to Counsel*, explains:

> "As a Reformed Christian, the writer believes that counselors must not tell any unsaved counselee that Christ died for him, for they cannot say that. No man knows except Christ Himself who are His elect for whom He died."[14]

Explaining to the unbeliever that Christ died for him has never been a problem to the many evangelists who are non-Calvinist. In fact, this evangelistic practice is used effectively every day in leading many to Christ. One can hardly imagine how the gospel can even be presented at all, if Christians cannot tell unbelievers that the death of Christ and His full and glorious salvation is for them. The Calvinist undoubtedly will reply that he earnestly tells unbelievers that they are sinners, that they must repent of their sins, and that they must believe the gospel. But the Calvinist omits an all-important detail; that is, he cannot tell the unsaved the reason why they should believe: because Christ died for them.

The writers of Scripture also do not seem to be aware of this difficulty in the preaching of the gospel. The apostle Paul tells us that Christ did indeed die for the ungodly, "For when we were without strength, in due time Christ died for the ungodly" (Rom. 5:6). In writing to Timothy, Paul writes, "For there is one God, and one mediator between God and men, the man Christ Jesus, who gave Himself a ransom for all" (1 Tim. 2:5-6). Our Lord Jesus Christ died for all, the elect and the non-elect, the Jew and the Gentile, the slave and the free, for He stated clearly, "For the Son of Man is come to seek and to save that which was lost"(Lk. 19:10). Certainly, it is permissible to tell all people that Christ died for them and that the Lord "is not willing that any should perish, but that all should come to repentance" (2 Pet. 3:9).

The Scriptures clearly teach that Christ died for all men and that all men can and must respond to the gospel. This is the very heart and substance of the gospel and Christian doctrine. The truth of unlimited atonement is not new; it has been the historic doctrine of the church. It is supported by learned and godly men from the earliest days of the church, but more importantly, it is supported by the Scriptures. This has led more than a few Calvinists to concede that this doctrine of unlimited atonement is indeed the doctrine of the Scriptures. The moderate Calvinist theologian, Dr. Millard Erickson in *Christian Theology* writes:

> "We find that some of the verses, which teach a universal atonement, simply cannot be ignored. Among the most impressive is 1 Timothy 4:10, which affirms that the living God 'is the Savior of all men, especially of those who believe.' Among the other texts which argue for the universality of Christ's saving work which cannot be ignored are 1 John 2:2 and Isaiah 53:6. In addition, we must consider statements like 2 Peter 2:1, which affirms that some for who Christ died do perish."[15]

The Calvinist is hard pressed to deny this truth, and yet he must; otherwise, his theology is severely weakened. If Christ loves all men and died for all, but on the other hand, elects only some to salvation, then the logic of Calvinism is threatened. However, the teaching of Scripture could not be clearer: Christ died for all.

Endnotes

[1] Robert L. Ferm, Readings in the History of Christian Thought, (New York: Holt, Rinehart, and Winston, 1964), p. 194, 196
[2] Philip Schaff, The Creeds of Christendom, (New York: Harper, ND) p. 319
[3] Philip Schaff, The Creeds of Christendom, (New York: Harper, ND) p. 50
[4] Walter Elwell, Evangelical Dictionary of Theology: Atonement, (Grand Rapids, MI: Baker Books, 1984), p. 97
[5] John Calvin, Calvin's Commentaries: Hebrews, vol. 12, (Grand Rapids, MI: Eerdmans, 1994), p. 24
[6] Henry Alford, The New Testament for English Readers, vol. 4 (Grand Rapids, MI: Baker Books, 1983), p. 1459
[7] David N. Steele, Curtis C. Thomas, The Five Points of Calvinism, (Phillipsburg, NJ: P & R. Publishing, 1963), p. 17
[8] Keith Mathison, Dispensationalism: Rightly Dividing the People of God, (Phillipsburg, NJ: P & R Press, 1995), p. 61
[9] R. C. Sproul, Grace Unknown, (Grand Rapids, MI: Baker Books, 1997), p. 167
[10] Edwin Palmer, The Five Points of Calvinism, (Grand Rapids, MI: Baker Books, 1979), p. 44
[11] A. W. Pink, The Sovereignty of God, (Grand Rapids, MI: Baker Books, 1992), p. 205-206
[12] Robert Dabney, Systematic Theology, 2nd edition, (Carlisle, PA: Banner of Truth, 1985), p. 525
[13] Edwin Palmer, The Five Points of Calvinism, (Grand Rapids, MI: Baker Books, 1979), p. 53
[14] Jay Adams, Competent to Counsel, (Grand Rapids, MI: Zondervan, 1986), p. 70
[15] Millard Erickson, Christian Theology, vol. 2, (Grand Rapids, MI: Baker, 1984), p. 835

- 7 -
Reformed Theology and Regeneration

In 1883 on the island of Krakatao, in the Straits of Sunda, a volcano erupted, splitting mountains from top to bottom and scattering rock, landscape, and debris into the sea. Nothing was left of the island but a lifeless mass 100 feet deep of lava and volcanic ash. Observers estimated that 36,000 people lost their lives, thereby making this one of the deadliest eruptions in history. Scientists declared positively that no animal or vegetable life would be able to survive. Nevertheless, over the next three years, flowers and ferns began to sprout out of the dark soil. The wind and the sea had carried the seeds there. By 1897, many portions of the ground were covered with vegetation. Soon the entire island was covered with plant growth, and an array of birds, animals, and insects populated the island. This account vividly illustrates what takes place spiritually when the life of God completely transforms the sin-darkened souls of men through faith in Christ. The name the Bible gives for this experience is regeneration or "quickening"(KJV).

The term "new birth" never occurs in the Bible; the noun "regeneration" occurs only twice in the Bible (Tit. 3:5, Matt. 19:28). The Greek word translated "regeneration" is "palingenes," which, when broken down into its component parts, means "born-again" ("palin"= again; "genesia"= birth). While the term new birth never occurs, related words occur many

'What is regeneration? Regeneration is the one-time experience of receiving new life in Christ, when the work of a new creation is begun, and the process of sanctification is set in motion. The regenerate man is no longer the man he once was. By virtue of the work of the Holy Spirit, the new life (created after the image of God) has come into the souls of men. This new nature has its own desires, affections, and interests. They are all spiritual, rooted in Christ, and God-centered. "That which is born of the Spirit is spirit;" the new nature is spiritual, for it shares the nature of the One who imparts it. The believer is made "a partaker of the divine nature…" (2 Pt. 1:4). However, the old nature remains within the believer, struggling with the new

THE REFORMED VIEW OF REGENERATION

Students of Holy Scripture offer differing views on the divine order in regard to the new birth. This debate is not merely an academic exercise, but one that has far-reaching consequences. Clear biblical thinking in this area greatly helps the serious Christian. Current Reformed theology teaches that regeneration, or new birth, must precede faith. It maintains that since unregenerate man is dead and unable to respond to the gospel, he must first be "born again" so that he can receive the gift of faith. This regenerative work of God will only take place in the lives of the elect as God irresistibly draws them. This all must take place in this order; otherwise biblical salvation, it is maintained, is no longer of God in His grace, but rather of man through self-effort. Calvinist professor Dr. R. C. Sproul sets forth this position when he writes:

> "In regeneration, God changes our hearts. He gives us a new disposition, a new inclination. He plants a desire

for Christ in our hearts. We can never trust Christ for our salvation unless we first desire Him. This is why we said earlier that regeneration precedes faith."[1]

In a similar vein, concerning regeneration Reformed psychologist Jay Adams writes:

"Only God can bring life to dead souls to enable them to believe. He does this when and where and how He pleases by His Spirit, who regenerates, or gives life leading to faith...As a reformed Christian, the writer believes that counselors must not tell any unsaved counselee that Christ died for him, for they cannot say that. No man knows except Christ Himself who are His elect for whom He died."[2]

On the other hand, non-Calvinists teach that new birth occurs after an unregenerate man exercises faith in Christ. The unregenerate man, after he is drawn by the convicting work of the Holy Spirit, enlightened by the power of the Word of God, gripped by grace, and prodded through prayer, is then enabled by God to exercise faith in the finished work of Christ. Although unregenerate man is dead in trespasses and sin and at enmity with God, this does not mean that he is unable to express faith. For it is God's sovereign design and plan that men should come to faith in Christ by the infinite power of the convicting work of the Holy Spirit, the grace of God, the will of God, and the Word of God. Without this work of God, no man would ever be saved.

REGENERATION AND INFANT SALVATION

Calvinism also teaches that infants, when yet unborn, are regenerated, even though they have no knowledge of Christ; and that, upon birth, infant baptism is to be practiced as a sign that the child is regenerate. John Calvin believed that all the children of believers were spiritually regenerated in the womb. To complete the salvation process Calvin also suggested that God granted a unique, supernatural faith to these infants in the womb. This would certainly add a new twist to the term "childlike faith." But how is this all possible? John Calvin writes:

> "But how, they ask, are infants regenerated, when not possessing knowledge of either good or evil? We answer, that the work of God, though beyond the reach of our capacity, is not therefore null. Infants who are to be saved (and that some are saved at this age is certain) must, without question, be regenerated by the Lord...Many He certainly has called and endued with true knowledge of Himself, by internal means, by the illumination of the Spirit, without the intervention of preaching."[3]

The issue of the salvation of the children of the elect soon occupied the minds of many leading Calvinists. How could one know if the children of the elect would eventually come to Christ, or might some never come to trust Him as Savior? Calvinists reasoned: if only the elect are regenerated and only the regenerated can be saved, is there any way of knowing if children are elect? John Calvin comforted the hearts of many by stating that God had already made provision for that need. He suggested that all the children of the elect would be saved.

Calvin writes:

> "Our children, before they are born, God declares that He adopts for His own when He promises He will be a God to us, and to our seed after us. In this promise their salvation is included."[4]

What are the spiritual consequences of such speculation? First of all, if this is true, we need not concern ourselves with the spiritual condition of our children and our grandchildren. Why? Because if we are elect, our children are also elect, which means their children are also elect, and so on, until our family line comes to an end. While a Calvinist may find comfort in this view, he needs to flip the coin to see what lies on the other side. If it follows that a "Calvinist" child is elect and will be saved because of his parents' election, would it not also be true that if that child never believes in Jesus Christ, this proves that the parents were never elect? If a parent proves not to be elect, it would mean that his father could not be elect either. The Calvinist "election domino" must logically fall in both directions. Furthermore, Scripture stresses that children are not saved because the parents were elect but because children themselves possessed faith in Jesus Christ unto salvation (Acts 16:31-32, 2 Tim. 3:14-15).

THE REFORMED VIEW AND THE SCRIPTURES

Many have noted that the Reformed view of regeneration is in stark contrast to Scripture. The Bible clearly establishes that the blessings of salvation, the indwelling Holy Spirit in the life of a believer, eternal life, and regeneration never precede faith, but are always the result of faith.

- Ephesians 1:13 states, "In whom also after that you believed, you were sealed with that Holy Spirit of promise." At the time of belief, as a result of faith, the believer receives the sealing of the Holy Spirit.

- John 3:16 "...that whosoever believes on Him should not perish but have everlasting life," Again the same truth is emphasized-belief precedes salvation.

- Acts 16:31 "Believe in the Lord Jesus, and you will be saved, you and your house." The order of salvation is clear; belief is first and then salvation follows. Faith is a condition of salvation.

- Romans 5:1 "Therefore, since we have been justified through faith, we have peace with God through our Lord Jesus Christ," Regeneration is not a condition for receiving justification. But notice it is faith first, followed by justification. This is the pattern we have throughout the Bible in virtually every verse that is connected to this subject.

The godly Bible teacher Samuel Ridout, setting forth the great importance of faith prior to new life, writes:

> "Being born again, not of corruptible seed, but of incorruptible seed, by the Word of God, which liveth and abideth forever" (1 Pt. 1:23). New birth is by the word of God. That it is a sovereign act of God, by His Spirit, none can question. But this verse forbids us from separating, as has sometimes been done, new birth from

faith in the gospel. It has been taught that new birth precedes faith; here we are told that the Word of God is the instrument in new birth. 'Faith cometh by hearing and hearing by the word of God;' 'the word which by the gospel is preached.' Thus while we can distinguish between faith and new birth, we cannot separate them. John 3:3 and 3:16 must ever go together. There is no such anomaly possible as a man born again, but who has not yet believed the gospel."[5]

Similarly, Dr. John Walvoord, former president of Dallas Theological Seminary, sets forth the necessity of faith before eternal life or regeneration is received:

"Eternal life is not possessed until faith in Christ is exercised. Eternal life is not to be confused with efficacious grace, or that bestowal of grace that is antecedent to faith. Eternal life is to be identified with regeneration and is received in the new birth. It is resultant rather than causative of salvation, but is related to conversion or the manifestation of the new life in Christ."[6]

Very often, Reformed writers will use Ezekiel 36:26 to garner support for the view that regeneration precedes faith. This verse reads, "I will give you a new heart and put a new spirit in you; I will remove from you your heart of stone and give you a heart of flesh." However, it appears from a careful contextual study of this passage and related verses, that the Calvinist view is not supported. Firstly, we find that this passage is not addressing individual believers and the manner in which they are to be saved, but rather, the prophetic "house of Israel" (v.

17). The thrust of the prophet's argument is what God in His grace will do to restore Israel to her land in a future day. Regeneration of the individual unbeliever is not the context, but rather, the nation of Israel. Secondly, in an earlier passage Ezekiel writes, "Cast away all your transgressions...and make yourself a new heart and a new spirit" (18:31). Here, the responsibility is placed in the hands of man for a new heart and a new spirit. The gift of a new heart signifies the new birth of the nation of Israel through the new covenant, by the renewal of the Holy Spirit. However, Ezekiel also conditions the reception of the new heart upon repentance (18:31). Those who use this passage to support the view that regeneration of the unsaved precedes faith appear to be guilty of stretching Scripture to fit a particular theological view.

THE REFORMED VIEW AND LOGIC OF C. H. SPURGEON

Many have seen great difficulty with the Reformed view of regeneration. One of the most obvious shortcomings is that if a man has been regenerated, what need does he have then for faith? For he is saved already, albeit without the biblical prerequisite: faith. If regeneration precedes faith, then faith is unnecessary, for the one regenerated is saved already. Even some respected Calvinists have pointed out this apparent theological contradiction. Calvinist C. H. Spurgeon, in his famous sermon "The Warrant of Faith," argues this point with his characteristic style:

> "If I am to preach faith in Christ to a man who is regenerated, then the man, being regenerated, is saved already, and it is an unnecessary and ridiculous thing for me to preach Christ to him, and bid him to believe in

order to be saved when he is saved already, being regenerate. Am I only to preach faith to those who have it? Absurd, indeed! Is not this waiting till the man is cured and then bringing him the medicine? This is preaching Christ to the righteous and not to sinners."[7]

Spurgeon, with great insight, points to three weaknesses in this traditional Reformed position. Firstly, regeneration prior to faith will be a great barrier to preaching the true soul-saving gospel. He says, "…it is an unnecessary and ridiculous thing for me to preach Christ." For if someone is regenerated already, why must the gospel be preached? Hereby, the great themes of the gospel message such as sin, judgment, love, and grace are rendered unnecessary. Secondly, it eliminates the reality of the spiritual battle in winning souls for Christ. Spurgeon says, "…and bid him to believe in order to be saved when he is saved already…Am I only to preach faith to those who have it?" Where is the spiritual battle, the prevailing prayer, and the power of the Holy Spirit in evangelism? For they are saved already. There is no earnest wrestling with souls for the cause of the gospel. Thirdly, it makes the preacher wait at bay with the gospel Spurgeon writes, "Is not this waiting till the man is cured and then bringing him the medicine?" Are preachers to wait with the spiritual cure, the gospel, until a lost soul is regenerated and then, when he is saved, bring him the gospel? This view takes the urgency and the "Now" out of gospel preaching. Scriptures are clear, "Now is the accepted time; behold, now is the day of salvation."(2 Cor. 6:2). According to the "prince of preachers" this view of regeneration is a hindrance to one who brings good news and a contradiction of the general tenor of Scripture.

REGENERATION AND THE PREACHING OF THE GOSPEL

This leads us to consider the consequences of the Reformed view of regeneration upon gospel preaching. We must admit that some great Reformed gospel preachers were used of God to bring many to Christ, including Whitfield and Spurgeon. But this was in spite of the inconsistency between their theological position and the message they so effectively proclaimed. Anyone reading Spurgeon's sermons, for example, will discover that while he frequently uses the word "elect," he did not do so in such a way that sinners could not be included if they so desired. However Reformed theologians have produced a system that is as unorthodox as it is inconsistent. Unfortunately, this theology has been a great hindrance to the unfettered proclamation of the gospel. Eighteenth century Calvinistic theologian Dr. John Gill illustrates the withering effect of Calvinist theology on the preaching of the gospel. During the tenure of Dr. Gill at a Reformed church, this congregation, which at one time numbered 1,200 dwindled down to a mere shadow of its original size. C. H. Spurgeon, though a Calvinist himself, pointed to Calvinism as the reason for the marked decline:

> "During the pastorate of my venerated predecessor, Dr. Gill, this Church, instead of increasing, gradually decreased...the system of theology with which many identify his (Gill's) name has chilled many churches to their very soul, for it has led them to omit the free invitations of the gospel, and to deny that it is the duty of sinners to believe in Jesus."[8]

To the Calvinist, the preaching of the gospel is an exercise in futility if a person has not been regenerated. According to the

Calvinist, the first thing that the unbeliever must get is regeneration. But God alone gives regeneration sovereignly and irresistibly. There is nothing an unsaved man can do to produce regeneration; furthermore, there is nothing he would want to do since he is dead, without even the slightest desire for spiritual things. We now discover one of the great inconsistencies in Calvinism: the work of the unbeliever as a "living-dead man." Calvinism states that total depravity means the complete inability to desire, understand, think, or learn about God and His salvation. However, on the other hand, Calvinism insists on the depraved man seeking, learning about, and praying to God for his regeneration. Notice the explanation of Calvinist writer, W. G. T. Shedd, in *Dogmatic Theology*, as he writes:

> "The Calvinist maintains that faith is wholly from God, being one of the effects of regeneration."[9]

In another place Shedd explains that since an unbeliever is unregenerate, there are certain steps necessary before he can be saved:

> "One, read and hear the divine Word…Two, give serious application of the mind, and examination of truth in order to understand and feel its force…Three, pray for the gift of the Holy Spirit both as a convicting and regenerating Spirit…prayer for regenerating grace is a duty and a privilege for the unregenerate man."[9]

The popular Calvinist writer A. W. Pink also insists that the unbeliever must plead with God for his regeneration before he can be saved. He writes:

131

"...His first duty is to set his 'seal that God is true.' His second duty is to cry unto God for enabling power—to ask God in mercy to over come his enmity, and draw him to Christ, to bestow on him the gifts of faith and repentance."[10]

Is this the New Testament message of salvation? Is the evangelist to exhort the lost to pray for the gift of the Holy Spirit? Is there a New Testament example of anyone ever charging one who is lost to pray for regeneration? I suggest there is no such example. Is the unbeliever to pray for the gift of regeneration or to believe on Christ? Our Lord has paid the high price of salvation in full, and He invites the sinner to believe on Him and receive eternal life. Does a criminal need to plead and beg for his prison release, while the warden stands before him with the signed pardon in his outstretched hand? It is not a time for a prisoner to beg and to seek, but a time to receive. In like manner, the work of the cross is complete, Christ has paid the ultimate price for every man, and the gospel offer goes to all, now the sinner must receive it by faith. This strange new gospel turns the salvation of God into something to be sought, instead of something that is to be received. Is our gospel message "believe and thou shalt be saved" or pray and seek and ask for regeneration? The New Testament is clear: the work of salvation is finished by the once-for-all sacrifice of Christ; the unsaved need not pray for regeneration, but believe on the Lord Jesus Christ "and thou shalt be saved,"

REGENERATION AND RELATIONSHIP TO CHRIST

Calvinism teaches that God first regenerates the elect, and then at a later point in time, this leads to faith in the Lord Jesus

Christ. In the Reformed view of regeneration, our new life in Christ is separated from a new relationship with Christ. Calvinism teaches that a baby is regenerated in the womb, and a person can be regenerated for years before he is saved. However, when the Holy Spirit does His work of regeneration in our lives, at the same time He relates us to a Person, and the gift of eternal life unites us to the person of the Lord Jesus Christ. John writes, "This is life eternal, that they might know Thee, the only true God, and Jesus Christ whom Thou hast sent" (Jn. 17:3). It is certainly a strange "regeneration," to be alive by the Spirit of God, but not know Christ by faith. Lewis Sperry Chafer, founder of Dallas Theological Seminary, in his *Systematic Theology* explains the link between regeneration and relationship:

> "The important fact, never to be forgotten in the doctrine of regeneration, is that the believer in Christ has received eternal life. This fact must be kept free from all confusion of thought arising from the concept of regeneration which makes it merely an antecedent of salvation, or a preliminary quickening to enable the soul to believe. It is rather the very heart of salvation."[11]

The Word of God teaches that a man receives life by receiving Jesus Christ as Savior. That is why our Lord said, "I am the way, the truth, and the life…" (Jn. 14:6). He did not say, "I have the way, the truth, and the life," as though the indwelling Christ was simply a force or power or merely an agent who gives eternal life. Our Lord, before raising Lazarus from the dead, says, "I am the resurrection, and the life…"(Jn. 11:25); not "I have life to impart." This brings home to us the fact that if we are to have life, we must have Jesus Christ. Since Jesus Christ is the life, the Spirit must bring us into a living, vital union with Him. New birth or regeneration can never be divorced from a living relationship with Christ. John the apostle writes, "He that has the Son has life; and he that has not the Son of God has not life" (1 Jn. 5:12). In the epistles of the apostle Paul, we find that he uses the carefully chosen and deeply meaningful term "in Christ" to explain this truth. Paul states, "If any man be in Christ, he is a new creature (creation)..." (2 Cor. 5:17). Paul never imagined regeneration to precede faith in Christ, which in turn would precede the relationship of Christ in us, the "hope of glory," The New Testament doctrine is clear: the Holy Spirit of God produces new birth, which gives us new life, and that new life is the Lord Jesus Christ Himself.

The work of regeneration is conditioned upon faith. Faith must precede new birth. It is God alone who imparts this new life in Christ. This new life in Christ provides a new nature or disposition, by which we now have a relationship with God. Sir Robert Anderson may have best summarized the spiritual order of God's work of regeneration when he wrote:

> "It is by the Word that the sinner is born again to God. As Scripture declares, 'We are born again by the Word of God'—'living and eternally abiding word of God.' And to bar all error, it is added: 'And this is the word by which the gospel is preached unto you'—preached, as the Apostle has already said, 'with the Holy Ghost sent down from heaven.' Not the Spirit without the Word, nor the Word without the Spirit, but the Word preached in the power of the Spirit. God is never arbitrary; but He is always sovereign. Men preach; the Spirit breathes;

and dry bones live. Thus sinners are born again to God."[12]

Endnotes

[1] R. C. Sproul, *Chosen by God*, (Wheaton, IL: Tyndale Publishers, 1986), p. 118
[2] Jay Adams, *Competent To Counsel*, (Grand Rapids, MI: Zondervan, 1970), p. 70
[3] John Calvin, *Institutes of Christian Religion, Vol. II*, (Grand Rapids, MI: Eerdmanns, 1962), p. 541, 542
[4] John Calvin, *Institutes of Christian Religion, Vol. II*, (Grand Rapids, MI: Eerdmanns, 1962), p. 525
[5] Samuel Ridout, *Numerical Bible, Vol. 6*, (NY: Loizeaux Bro. 1903), p. 148-149
[6] Everett F. Harrison, editor, *Wycliffe Dictionary of Theology*, (Peabody, MA: Hendrickson Publishers, 1999), p. 195
[7] C. H. Spurgeon, Sermon: *Warrant of Faith*, (Pasadena, TX: Pilgrim Publications, 1978), p. 3
[8] Iain Murray, *Spurgeon vs. Hyper-Calvinism: The Battle for Gospel Preaching*, (Carlisle, PA: Banner of Truth, 1995), p. 120
[9] W. G. T. Shedd, *Dogmatic Theology, Vol. II*, (Grand Rapids, MI: Zondervan, n.d.), p. 472, 512-514
[10] A. W. Pink, *The Sovereignty of God*, (Grand Rapids, MI: Baker, 1992), p.160
[11] L. S. Chafer, *Systematic Theology, Vol. VI*, (Dallas, TX: Dallas Seminary Press, 1948), p. 117
[12] Sir Robert Anderson, *Redemption Truths*, (Kilmarnock, GB: Ritchie, 1940), p. 152

- 8 -
Reformed Theology and Eternal Security

Reformed theology, for many years, has been vigorously opposed to the evangelical doctrine of the believer's assurance of salvation. This teaching has been the focal point of bitter controversy and division between Dispensationalists and Calvinists. Dispensationalists regard the assurance of salvation to be essential for a balanced and healthy Christian life. Reformed leaders consider it to be among the most spiritually harmful doctrines to Christians. They believe that this doctrine promotes a dangerous antinomian attitude among Christians. Moreover, in recent years the attacks have grown even shriller. Reformed theologian and editor of the journal *Reformation and Revival,* Dr. John Armstrong, speaking at a conference of Reformed leaders, shared his candid opinion on the doctrine of eternal security:

> "I was asked the question about a year ago by a group of pastors in Pennsylvania '…what do you think is the one doctrine that is the most destructive in the life of the church practically in America today?' And I said, 'the doctrine of eternal security.'"[1]

Reformed writer and pastor of Westminster Chapel in London, R. T. Kendall, comments on Calvinism's general dislike for this important doctrine:

"Many Calvinists I meet are almost scared to death of the teaching "once saved, always saved." They believe it, but are afraid to rest in it; they believe it in theory, but they are afraid of it in practice. The fear of Antinomianism, I suspect, has unwittingly put them in a bondage they don't know how to throw off. They fear if people really believe they are saved utterly and entirely by what Jesus did on the cross, that they will live lawless lives."[2]

The doctrine of eternal security teaches that a believer has been saved utterly and completely by faith in the death of the Lord Jesus Christ upon the cross. Such a Christian can never lose his salvation, for he is kept by the power of God. A Christian, however, because of his love for Christ and the activity of the Holy Spirit in his heart, will display a godly and consistent life for Christ. Reformed leaders reject the idea of the eternal security of the believer, and in its place, teach the doctrine of the perseverance of the saints. At the root of this teaching is the proper idea that true believers in Christ should live consistent and holy lives as evidence of their new life in Christ. However, over time this doctrine has been transformed by many Calvinists into an unbiblical condition and requirement for salvation. Thereby, the gospel of the grace of God has become a thinly veiled salvation by works and self-effort. Calvinist teachers fully grant that salvation is by faith alone initially, but after trusting Christ, their "message of salvation" stresses words such as law, works, and duties. If there are not enough works, they conclude the person who once trusted Christ is not saved after all. The idea of "enough works" is never explicitly defined; but is described by terms such as "faithfulness to the ten commandments," "perseverance," and "forsaking all sin," However, the questions that ever plague the heart of the believer steeped in Reformed theology are: "Have I done enough?" or "Have I repented, submitted, and obeyed enough since I have been saved?" If the answer is "not enough," then Calvinist teaching cannot offer any assurance of salvation to the believer. The "assurance of salvation" in Reformed thinking is soon discovered to be no assurance at all. Even those who have displayed exemplary Christian character all their lives are not granted the comfort of the assurance of salvation. Reformed leader Dr. R. C. Sproul, during a conference just before the death of Dr. James Boice, displays this unfortunate tendency within Calvinism:

> "During the first message presented at Ligonier's Conference in Orlando last June (2000), Dr. R. C. Sproul indicated that Dr. James Boice, a scheduled speaker at the conference, was dying in faith that very night. Then, at the end of the message he asked all 5,000 of us present to pray that Jim dies in faith. This struck me as sad. Here was a great pastor, theologian, teacher, and author. Yet Sproul was not sure that he was regenerate. (In Reformed thought, if a person fails to die in faith, he proved he was never saved in the first place.) I was reminded of R. T. Kendall's remark that nearly to a man the Puritan divines died doubting whether they were saved and fearing they were going to hell. Dr. Boice died that very night, June 15th."[3]

Furthermore, Reformed theology lays great emphasis on the persevering work of the believer to keep himself saved.

Edwin Palmer, the author of *The Five Points of Calvinism*, explains his perspective when he writes:

> "Perseverance of the saints means that the saints will persevere in their faith. And that faith is composed of sorrow and repentance from sin. If anyone is not sorry for his sins and abandons himself to them, then he never had faith in the first place and he is not saved."[4]

The solemn and nagging question arises in our hearts: Who then can be saved? If we are honest with ourselves, who has not at times neglected to repent of his sins and sinned willfully, not "abandoning them," but for a time continuing in them? Who will tell us: How much sorrow and repentance is enough? Is not the God of infinite grace greater than all our sins? Is the finished work of Christ not finished after all? This Reformed perspective, though well intentioned, does not provide assurance, but rather engenders doubt and morbid introspection.

Contrariwise, many others have looked deeply into the Scriptures and have concluded that the believer in Christ is not only saved by grace through faith, but is also kept by God through faith. Their watchword is: the believer is made eternally safe through the blood of Christ and made eternally sure through the Word of God. It is true that works are an evidence of salvation; but they should not be viewed as the proof of salvation or the sole basis of assurance. However, this truth must never be used as an excuse for lax and carnal living. While Reformed theology lays great emphasis on the persevering work of the believer, the Scriptures place great emphasis upon the power of God to keep the believer. Our Lord unfolds this truth when He says, "My sheep hear My voice and I know them, and they follow Me. And I give them eternal life, and they shall never perish; neither shall any one snatch them out of My hand. My Father, who has given them to Me, is greater than all; and no one is able to snatch them out of My Father's hand" (Jn. 10:27-29). The apostle Peter set forth this same comforting truth when he wrote, "...who are kept by the power of God through faith for salvation ready to be revealed in the last time" (1 Pt. 1:5). The believer will, indeed, endure in holiness and devotion as evidence of his love for Christ; but his salvation is a gift from God alone, and its basis is found in the deep bedrock of the work of the cross of our Lord Jesus Christ. Our assurance of eternal salvation cannot depend upon us, for that is much too fragile a foundation; but rather, it depends on the finished work of Jesus Christ.

PERSEVERANCE AND MATTHEW 24:13

Many Calvinist theologians, in seeking biblical support for the doctrine of the "perseverance of the saints," have placed great emphasis upon the statement of our Lord Jesus Christ in the Olivet Discourse, "But he who endures to the end shall be saved" (Matt. 24:13). This statement of our Lord is also recorded in Matthew 10:22 in virtually identical phrasing; additionally, the Greek rendering of Luke 21:19 sets forth a similar meaning. In all three verses, the immediate context is a statement concerning the future tribulation period that shall come upon the whole earth (Matt. 24:5-12). In that day, believers will be physically persecuted for their faith and many will be martyred. However, those that endure or survive to the end of the tribulation period will be "saved" from further persecution from the armies of the Antichrist. These will be "saved," or delivered, at the second coming by the Lord Himself. Surely to interpret a statement of our Lord regarding physical salvation and apply it to eternal salvation will lead to serious doctrinal consequences. With the biblical context in mind, it is especially surprising that virtually every Calvinist writer applies this verse to eternal salvation, rather than to temporal deliverance. It is disconcerting to see the ease and comfort with which Reformed writers link the requirement of works to salvation. Notice this view in the comments of famed Calvinist author Matthew Henry (1662-1714), in his well-known *Commentary on the Whole Bible,* when he writes:

> "'He that endures to the end shall be saved' (Matthew 24:13). It is eternal salvation that is here intended. They that endure to the end of their days, shall then receive the end of their faith and hope, even the salvation of their souls."[5]

Many Calvinist writers insist that endurance in faith is nothing less than endurance in works. This endurance, in their view, is a "condition for salvation," This flawed view continues among many Calvinist theologians and authors today. In our present day, the noted and respected Calvinist writer and lecturer, Dr. R. C. Sproul, unfortunately perpetuates this view when he links endurance in the tribulation period with salvation. He writes:

> "The New Testament speaks of enduring to the end, promising that 'he who endures to the end shall be saved' (Matt. 24:13). This may be understood to be a condition or proviso for salvation. Endurance in faith is a condition for future salvation. Only those who endure in faith will be saved for eternity."[6]

Our interpretation of Matthew 24:13 will have far reaching consequences. Calvinism approaches Roman Catholic theology with its idea that salvation is a process. The Reformed salvation order is: first faith, followed by perseverance, works, and duty, and then eventually a future salvation. Matthew Henry says, "...shall receive at the end...the salvation of their souls." R. C. Sproul writes, "Endurance in faith is a condition for future salvation," Is salvation a life-long process of endurance, works, and self-effort and then finally future salvation? All evangelical Christians must vigorously maintain that salvation is obtained by faith alone, followed by works; not faith plus a lifetime of works, which eventually may lead to eternal salvation.

The views of most dispensational Bible teachers on this verse differ greatly from many of the Reformed writers. Dispensational writers have duly noted the tribulation context of this passage, and that is reflected in their interpretation. These authors clearly teach that the word "save" indicates a physical deliverance of believers at the end of the tribulation period and that the spiritual "salvation" view of Matthew 24:13 does violence to the tenure and teaching of Scripture. Dispensational Bible scholar and author Dr. Louis Barbieri, now at Moody Bible Institute, interprets Matthew 24:13 within its biblical context and concludes that spiritual endurance cannot result in eternal salvation. He writes:

> "Those who remain faithful to the Lord until the end of that period of time will be saved, that is delivered (Matt. 24:13). This does not refer to a personal self-effort at endurance that results in one's eternal salvation, but to physical deliverance of those who trust in the Saviour during the Tribulation period. They will enter the kingdom in physical bodies."[7]

John Walvoord, respected scholar and former President of Dallas Theological Seminary, concludes that "endurance to the end" cannot refer to salvation from sin. He writes:

> "The age in general, climaxing with the second coming of Christ, has the promise that those that endure to the end (Matt. 24:13), that is, survive the tribulation and are still alive, will be saved, or delivered, by Christ at His second coming. This is not a reference to salvation from sin, but rather deliverance of survivors at the end of the age. Many, of course, will not endure to the end, in the sense that they will be martyred, even though they are saved by faith in Christ, and the multitude of martyrs is mentioned in Revelation 7:9-17."[8]

William MacDonald warns of the doctrinal pitfalls in this verse. Our failure to do the work of a careful interpreter may result in doing damage to the gospel of God's grace. He writes:

> "'But he who endures to the end will be saved' (Matt. 24:13). This obviously does not mean that men's souls will be saved at that time by their enduring; salvation is always presented in the Bible as being a gift of God's grace, received by faith in Christ, and based upon His substitutionary death and resurrection. Neither can it mean that all who endure will be saved from physical harm, because we have already learned that many true believers will be martyred (Matt. 24:9). It is a general statement that those who stand fast in their confession of Christ, enduring persecution without apostatizing, will be delivered at Christ's Second Advent."[9]

PERSEVERANCE AND WORKS-SALVATION

Reformed theologians are among the most gifted and learned as to the teaching of Scripture and theology generally. Among their numbers are giants of the Word, such as John Calvin, C. H. Spurgeon, B. B. Warfield, and in our own day, J. I. Packer, R. C. Sproul, and D. Martyn Lloyd-Jones. Their understanding concerning the gospel should be beyond reproach. It is, therefore, troubling to find leaders in Reformed circles linking human effort with salvation. The question must be raised as to why such men would be so comfortable themselves and be so supportive of others who connect the principle of works with salvation? I would suggest that, although these men are extremely able and gifted teachers of the Word, they are also devoted and beholden to a school of theology that shadows their doctrinal perspective. One must be ever watchful to insure that theology does not determine one's view of Scripture, but rather that Scripture determines one's view of theology. A few years ago the Calvinist radio pastor John MacArthur, in a radio address on the subject of "Lordship," stated:

> "Listen! No one who is saved will fail to repent, will fail to submit, or fail to obey...True faith results in an absolutely and totally transformed life."[10]

A number of years ago, noted Calvinist A. W. Pink, in the book *Practical Christianity*, staked out his position that obedience is a condition for salvation after we have trusted Christ, writing:

> "Reader, if there is a reserve in your obedience, you're on the way to hell."[11]

The extreme words of these two Calvinists must not go unnoticed. "No one who is saved will fail to repent, obey, or submit"…"If there is a reserve in your obedience then you are on your way to hell." The implication of these words is clear. If you fail to do these things, you are not saved. Personal spiritual experience and the sound interpretation of Scripture prove this Reformed perspective to be utterly false. Doubtless, everyone who reads those words realizes, if this is true, none will be saved. What true child of God has never known reserve in his obedience? Who has never failed to repent, or obey, or submit in one area or another? This is true of each one of us and of every man of God found in Scripture. The sincere and godly Christian becomes not only startled by these statements, but also wonders at the spiritual reasoning behind them. Doubtless, these Reformed teachers have upright motivations and well-intentioned convictions. These statements may be sincere attempts to effect greater zeal and greater perseverance in Christians through fear. Many are convinced that well-placed guilt and fear concerning one's eternal salvation will result in more fervent and more devoted followers of Christ. John Calvin, in commenting on 1 Timothy 4:16, sets forth this perspective:

> "The zeal of pastors is greatly increased when they are told that both their own salvation and that of their people depends upon their serious and earnest devotion to their office."[12]

This approach may result in greater zeal, but not greater love for Christ. Many soon discover that attempts to force zeal and coerce devotion are usually very short lived. This method is not only ineffective but furthers a misguided works-based salvation. This approach is very subtle and unassuming, and yet very troubling. For its message is couched in Christian terms of sacrifice and discipleship. These terms are biblical and important when understood in their proper place and proper context. However, when sacrifice, zeal, and self-effort are set forth as conditions for salvation, the writers of Scripture roundly condemn it. The New Testament is uncompromising in its condemnation of any works-based salvation. It does not matter if the message of works in salvation is placed before faith in Christ or after faith in Christ. The Word of God equally condemns both approaches. In Acts 15, the elders of the Jerusalem assembly, the believers, and the apostles gathered to consider the issue of salvation by faith alone, plus nothing. A Jewish sect within the church insisted that only those who trusted in Christ and then afterwards submitted to the Law of Moses and circumcision were saved. This issue would define the Christian character of the church. Alexander Maclaren, the Scottish Baptist expositor, charges that the issues discussed at the Jerusalem council in Acts 15 strike at the very heart of the salvation charter. He sets forth with clarity the incompatibility of works and the gospel:

> "Paul saw that if anything else than faith was brought in as necessary to knit men to Christ, and to make them partakers of salvation, faith was deposed from its place and Christianity sank back to a religion of 'works.' Experience has proved that anything whatever introduced as associated with faith ejects faith from it place, and comes to be recognized as the means of salvation. The controversy started then is a perennial one, and the

church of the present needs Paul's exhortation, 'Stand fast therefore in the liberty wherewith Christ hath made us free, and be not entangled again with the yoke of bondage.'"[13]

The apostle Paul is the most uncompromising of all the New Testament writers in teaching that works must have no part of salvation. Paul charges the Christian and non-Christian, "For by the works of the law shall no flesh be justified" (Gal. 2:18). Earlier in Galatians, Paul reserves his strongest rebuke for these "works" teachers. "I marvel that ye are so soon removed from Him that called you into the grace of Christ unto another gospel ...But, though we, or an angel from heaven preach any other gospel unto you than that which we have preached unto you, let him be accursed" (Gal. 1:6, 8). The gospel of the grace of God must be left free and unencumbered by our theology. Calvinist author A. W. Pink, in his book *Eternal Security*, shows the extreme lengths to which some Reformed leaders will go in detail and minutia to press their works-based salvation. In listing the works necessary for salvation after faith in Christ, he practically eliminates everyone from being saved, including himself. He writes:

> "One who regards sin lightly, who thinks nothing of breaking a promise, who is careless in the performance of temporal duties, who gives no sign of a tender conscience...who is vain and self-important, who pushes to the fore seeking the notice of others...who is hyper-sensitive, who is hurt deeply when someone slights them, who betrays a humble and teachable spirit...who frets over disappointments, who is thoughtless of others...

(such a one) has no title to be regarded as a new creature in Christ."[14]

Many modern Calvinist teachers, in their zeal to stir believers to greater faithfulness to Christ, have sadly turned devotion to Christ into a condition for salvation. The finished work of Christ, it seems, is not finished after all. Works that should follow salvation have been turned into requirements for salvation. No matter how sincere or winsome a teacher may be and regardless of his soundness in the faith in other areas, when he teaches something that adds to or diminishes the simplicity of the glorious gospel message we must not give him our ear.

PERSEVERANCE AND ETERNAL SECURITY

While Reformed theology, with the most honorable of intentions, seeks to provide the sincere believer with the assurance of eternal salvation, it fails to do so. Instead of instilling assurance, it instills doubt. Instead of engendering trust in the finished work of Christ, it encourages trust in self-effort, leading to introspection. Calvinism stresses a confusing and contradictory array of doctrines, which do more to hinder than to help. There is no longer a sin nature, but the "sinful remnants of the flesh;" there is a "functioning faith" that may not be "saving faith;" and there is a deep heart-felt sorrow for sin that is not true repentance. The sad result of all of this is more doubt, uncertainty, and confusion. Author Michael Eaton was once an enthusiastic supporter of Calvinism until he looked more carefully at the doctrine of the perseverance of the saints. While looking for assurance, he unfortunately found doubt and uncertainty. He writes:

"I have already urged that introspection is implicit in many aspects of the Reformed doctrine of grace in late Calvinism. Now, I wish to underline the fact that the most intense introspection follows if many or all of these emphases are combined. If Christ did not die for all, and if it is possible to have sorrow for sin that is not true repentance, a faith which is not true faith, a possessing of the Spirit which falls short of true regeneration, if despite any and every 'experience' of the gospel there is a way to Hell even from the Gates of Heaven, if Paul himself feared loss of salvation, then what remains of the Calvinist's assurance? It has died the death of a thousand qualifications."[15]

This lack of assurance is intrinsic in Calvinism. This was a mark of Calvinism during the colonial period in America. Calvinist John Gerstner, the late professor at Pittsburgh Theological Seminary, comments on Calvinist theologian Jonathan Edwards (1703-1758) and his followers:

"Jonathan Edwards, being a Calvinist, taught perseverance of the saints. However, the marks of grace and the signs of salvation were so meticulous, exacting, and searching on one hand; and the deceitfulness of sin, the counterfeits of Christian experience, and the difficulty of being truly objective about the state of one's soul were so great, on the other, that assurance became a relatively rare thing... It has been said that none of Edward's followers claimed to have assurance of salvation, but remained dubious to the end of their lives."[16]

These comments are not made in isolation, but are comments commonly found among those influenced by Reformed theology. David Brainerd, the Calvinistic missionary to Indians in New Jersey, is an example of the effect the Reformed doctrine of perseverance can have upon the Christian life. Brainerd, in his journals, shows his profound doubt and uncertainty concerning his assurance of salvation. These journal writings, edited and published by Jonathan Edwards, are filled with introspection, sorrow for sin, a heavy burden of sin, and guilt. Although David Brainerd was obviously saved by the blood of Christ, he seemed to know so little of being safe through the work of Christ. His sin nature and past sins plagued him so deeply that he longed for deliverance and assurance, which unfortunately seemed to elude him. Although he studied Reformed theology at Yale College, later called Yale University, his writing evidenced a deep lack of security in Christ:

> "I have been for some time extremely oppressed with a sense of guilt, pollution, and blindness, 'the iniquity of my heels hath compassed me about: the sins of my youth have been set in order before me; they have gone over my head, as an heavy burden, too heavy for me to bear.' Almost all the actions of my life past seem to be covered over with sin and guilt; and those of them that I performed in the most conscientious manner, now fill me with shame and confusion that I cannot hold up my face. O, the pride, selfishness, hypocrisy, ignorance, bitterness, party zeal..."[17]

Reformed theology's attempt to provide the Christian with assurance of salvation has fallen far short of the scriptural standard. Calvinism's influence in the lives of believers has not increased the assurance of salvation, but has decreased it. A dear Reformed believer in Michigan was once asked if she knew she was saved and on her way to heaven. She replied, "Oh, no one can know that until they die." Sadly, Calvinism provided her with little assurance and certainty in the power of the finished work of Christ. John, the apostle, frames the doctrine of eternal security well when he writes, "These things have I written unto you that believe on the name of the Son of God; that you may know that you have eternal life" (1 Jn. 5:13).

PERSEVERANCE AND ARMINIANISM

Although Reformed theology vehemently denies that a true believer can ever lose his salvation, its interpretation of the key assurance texts in Scripture is strikingly similar to modern Arminianism. The modern Arminian teaches that, although a believer is saved by faith in the finished work of Christ, he can, by sinning, lose his salvation. The modern Calvinist teaches that, although a believer is saved through the finished work of Christ, he must without reservation, in submission to the law and by self-effort, persevere in works, because he can through sin show he was never saved. Calvinism denies the believer the assurance of salvation, whereas Arminianism denies the believer the security of salvation. There is a difference in the Reformed and Arminian views of assurance of salvation; however when one takes a closer look, these two views seem to be virtually identical. Consider for a moment the classic so-called "falling away" text of 1 Cor. 9:26-27, "I therefore run, not as uncertainly; so fight I, not as one that beateth the air: But I keep under my body, and bring it into subjection: lest that by any means, when I have preached unto others, I myself should be a castaway." Commenting on this verse, the respected Calvinistic Professor of Systematic Theology, Charles Hodge writes:

> "What an argument and what a reproof is this! The reckless and listless Corinthians thought they could safely indulge themselves to the very verge of sin, while this devoted apostle considered himself as engaged in a life struggle of his salvation."[18]

The Reformer John Calvin expresses similar views when he writes:

> "Now, in order to impress it on the minds of the Corinthians, he adds an exhortation. In short, he says that what they had attained so far is nothing, unless they keep steadily on; because it is not enough that they once started off on the way of the Lord, if they do not make an effort to reach the goal. This corresponds to the word of Christ in Matthew 10:22: 'He that endureth to the end, the same shall be saved.'"[19]

Both Charles Hodge and John Calvin stress that the Corinthian believers must continue to struggle and endure in works to ensure their salvation. In fact, Hodge states that Paul was "engaged in a life struggle of his salvation." Is this position different from the views of the modern Arminian commentators? Not at all. Notice the similar comments by a leading Arminian commentator Richard Lenski:

> "What a calamity when a professing Christian finds himself 'rejected' in the end! How much worse is it then

when one of the Lord's own heralds have this experience! Paul regards his work with extreme seriousness. The fact that he is an apostle is not yet proof to him that he will be saved. He knows the test that he must face."[20]

The Calvinist interpretation on the so-called "falling away" texts is so similar to that of Arminian commentators that one fails to see any real difference. The same doubt and confusion over assurance of salvation that plagues the Arminian also plagues the Calvinist believer as well.

ETERNAL SECURITY ACCORDING TO THE SCRIPTURES

The Scriptures, however, provide a very different picture of eternal security. The apostle Paul did not doubt his eternal salvation, as both the Calvinist and Arminian suggest. Much to the contrary, he was confident in the knowledge of his eternal salvation. In Romans 8 he writes, "For I am persuaded, that neither death, nor life, nor angels, nor principalities, nor powers, nor things present, nor things to come, nor height, nor depth, nor any other creature, shall be able to separate us from the love of God, which is in Christ Jesus, our Lord" (Rom. 8:38-39). Again in a letter to Timothy, Paul writes, "I know whom I have believed, and am persuaded that He is able to keep that which I have committed unto Him against that day" (2 Tim. 1:12).

It is true that the Christian is to persevere in his faith in Christ. The Scriptures tell the Christian repeatedly to live for the Lord, but never as a way to prove or maintain his salvation. The Christian is exhorted to live a life that produces good works. These good works are those that will be judged at the Judgment Seat of Christ, but again they do not concern his salvation. The motivation for devotion, zeal and good works is the believer's love for Christ and not fear of failing to persevere. The Lord Jesus Christ illustrated this when He said, "If a man love Me, he will keep My words" (Jn. 14:23), and in another place He said, "He that hath My commandments and keepeth them, he it is that loveth Me" (Jn. 14:21). The Christian, because of his love for Christ, will continue on in obedience, works of service, and devotion for Christ. However, this does not determine his salvation. The Christian is assured of his salvation by faith alone in the Lord Jesus Christ and because of the finished cross work. "Not by works of righteousness which we have done, but according to His mercy He saved us, by the renewing of the Holy Spirit, which He shed on us abundantly through Jesus Christ, our Savior" (Tit. 3:5-6).

Endnotes

[1] Transcript of a message by Dr. John Armstrong, *Reflections from Jonathan Edwards on the Current Debate Over Justification By Faith Alone,* given at Annapolis, MD 2000
[2] R. T. Kendall, *Once Saved, Always Saved,* (Chicago, IL: Moody Press, 1983), p. 211
[3] Michael Makidon, Book Review: Whatever Happened to the Gospel of Grace: Recovering the Doctrines That Shook the World by James Boice, Journal of the Grace Evangelical Society, Fall 2001
[4] Edwin H. Palmer, *The Five Points of Calvinism,* (Grand Rapids, MI: Baker Book House, 1979) p. 79
[5] Matthew Henry, *Commentary on the Whole Bible, vol. 5,* (Peabody, MA: Hendrickson, 1991), p. 284
[6] R. C. Sproul, *Grace Unknown,* (Grand Rapids, MI: Baker Books, 1997) p. 198
[7] Louis Barbieri, Jr., *Bible Knowledge Commentary: Matthew,* (Wheaton, IL: Victor Books, 1983) p.77
[8] John Walvoord, *Matthew,* (Chicago, IL: Moody Press, 1974) p. 184
[9] William MacDonald, *Matthew,* (Kansas City, KS: Walterick Publishers, 1974) p. 269

[10] John MacArthur, Tape GC 90-21 Lordship, quoted in George Zeller, Teachings of John MacArthur, Middletown Bible Church, Middletown, CT)
[11] A. W. Pink, *Practical Christianity*, (Grand Rapids, MI: Guardian Press, 1974), p. 16
[12] John Calvin, *Calvin's Commentaries, vol. 10*, (Grand Rapids, MI: Eerdmans, 1994) p. 248
[13] Alexander Maclaren, *Expositions of Holy Scripture, Acts, vol. 12*, (Grand Rapids, MI: Baker Book House, 1992) p. 80-81
[14] A. W. Pink, *Eternal Security*, (Grand Rapid, MI: Baker Book House, 1979) p. 67-68
[15] Michael Eaton, *A Theology of Encouragement*, (London: Paternoster Press, 1995), p. 23
[16] John Gerstner, *Jonathan Edwards, Evangelist* (Morgan, PA: Soli Deo Gloria Publications, 1995), p. 192
[17] Jonathan Edwards, *Life of David Brainerd*, (Grand Rapids, MI: Baker Book House, 1980) p. 64
[18] Charles Hodge, *1 & 2 Corinthians*, (Carlisle, PA: Banner of Truth, 1974) p. 169
[19] John Calvin, *Calvin's Commentaries, vol. 9*, (Grand Rapids, MI: Eerdmans, 1994), p. 197
[20] R. C. H. Lenski, *The Interpretation of St. Paul's 1st & 2nd Epistles to the Corinthians* (Minneapolis: Augsburg Publishing House, 1963) p. 388

- 9 -
The Sovereignty of God

The blazing African sun beat down upon the crowded Arab marketplace as women busily bartered with the merchants. The bustling walkways were lined with storekeepers selling their wares, as children played nearby. The air was filled with the pungent smell of spices, and the confusing din of a thousand voices. Amid these dusty streets teeming with people, a pregnant woman began to slowly make her way across a wide thoroughfare. Suddenly, there was a great noise and commotion in the marketplace, and in an instant, an out-of-control wagon, being pulled by a team of horses in full gallop, raced through the marketplace. Without warning, the team of horses trampled down the helpless woman with tremendous force. Immediately, a crowd began to gather to see what had happened. The driver, now realizing what he had done, brought the horses to an abrupt stop, and while looking at the woman lying dead on the ground, said with callous indifference, "It was the will of Allah," and continued on his way.

To many, this account describes their view of the sovereignty of God. To them, God's actions are arbitrary, capricious, and often unjust. Their attitude is "whatever will be will be." No matter what happens, it is God's will. This is the fatalistic view of God. Such a God will be feared, but how can He be loved? If he cannot be loved, how can He be trusted?

DIVINE SOVEREIGNTY AND THE ATTRIBUTES OF GOD

Thankfully, the Bible does not present such a view of God's sovereignty. The Bible presents God as both infinitely all-powerful and infinitely good. In the early chapters of Genesis we read, "...God created the heavens and the earth" (Gen. 1:1). Here we see God's great power and might displayed. But we also see God's goodness in creation, as later we read, "God saw it was not good that a man should be alone...." God's goodness, justice, mercy, grace, and His numerous other attributes meet together to form the righteous and holy sovereign actions of God. God's sovereignty may sometimes involve testing in the form of calamity and trials, but never without love, faithfulness, and compassion. His sovereign will may appear for the moment to be without purpose or sense, yet the ways of God are always perfect. He is a God whom we can trust, love, and worship for His sovereign will. While sovereignty is surely to be believed by all who love sound doctrine, it must not be understood to be exercised in conflict with God's attributes, such as love, justice, truth, and immutability. Some have erred in this respect and have raised sovereignty to such a level that all the attributes of God become secondary, thereby causing discord in the nature of God. The sovereignty of God can never be exercised at the expense to His divine nature, which is love (1 Jn. 4:8). Concerning this conflict, Dr. James Orr, general editor of the International Standard Bible Encyclopedia, writes:

> "Calvin exalts the sovereignty of God, and this is right, but errs in placing his root-ideas of God in the sovereign will rather than in love. Love is subordinated to sovereignty, instead of sovereignty to love."[1]

DIVINE SOVEREIGNTY AND THE GOODNESS OF GOD

The biblical principle that God is good and does good applies to His sovereign actions. God's nature and God's holy purposes cannot be divorced, for God will not act contrary to His holy nature. Throughout the canon of Scripture, the sovereign actions of God are guided by His holy character. Abraham echoed this very principle, when he said, "Shall not the judge of all the earth do right?" (Gen. 18:25). Scripture reveals that God's mercy, goodness, grace, and compassion all undergird His sovereign purposes and will. "God's tender mercies are over all his works," and even when affliction and suffering are God's divine will, these too are ruled by "compassion and unfailing love." Jeremiah the prophet explains, "Though He brings grief, He will show compassion, so great is His unfailing love. For He does not willingly bring affliction or grief to the children of men" (Lam. 3:32-33). Isaiah, the prophet, penned a striking portrait of the majestic God, who is also the wise and gentle Shepherd, when he wrote, "Behold, the Lord God shall come with a strong hand and His arm shall rule for Him...He will feed His flock like a shepherd; He will gather the lambs with His arm and carry them in His bosom and gently lead those who are with young" (Isa. 40:10-11). The Psalmist lays bare the very essence of God's sovereign nature, when he writes, "Thou art good and doest good..." (Ps. 119:68). In another place he writes, "The Lord is gracious and full of compassion...the Lord is good to all, and His tender mercies are over all His works" (Ps. 145:8-9). Five times the Scriptures link God's holy nature and sovereign acts by proclaiming, "The Lord is good, His mercy endures forever..." (Jer. 33:11; Ps. 100:5; 2 Chr. 5:13; 2 Chr. 7:3; 1 Chr. 16:34).

Theologians have called this biblical linking of God's sovereign rule with God's infinite goodness the doctrine of "providence." Providence is divine care, sustenance, and love, and His sovereign rule over creation for His glory and the good of man. The two-fold goal of providence is the glory of God and the good of His people. These two goals are never in conflict with each other, but are always in harmony with each other. God never pursues His glory at the expense of the good of His people, nor does He ever seek our good at the expense of His glory. He has designed His eternal purpose so that His glory and our good are inseparably yoked together. Alexander Carson writes:

> "God's sovereignty is always to His people in wisdom and in love. This is the difference between sovereignty in God and sovereignty in man. We dread the sovereignty in man, because we have no security of its being exercised in mercy, or even justice; we rejoice in the sovereignty of God, because we are sure it is always exercised for the good of His people."[2]

DIVINE SOVEREIGNTY AND THE WISDOM OF GOD

All God's sovereign actions are rooted in His infinite wisdom. God's wisdom enables Him to direct every act that occurs upon the world stage into a perfect plan that accomplishes His divine purpose. God is the master of every situation. Man can be frustrated by circumstances outside of his control, but this is never true of God. There is never a situation, problem, or difficulty which can ever frustrate the wisdom of God. For His sovereign actions are advanced by His unbounded omnipotence and ruled by His infinite wisdom. He will cause even the wrath of man to bring praise to Himself (Ps. 76:10). The Psalmist has said, "Great is our God, and of great power: His understanding is infinite" (Ps. 147:5). The Scriptures manifestly declare that all God's sovereign actions are in wisdom. Whether it is His acts of creation, redemption, or His many works within the world, they are all accomplished in wisdom. His ways are infinitely perfect. No act of God is flawed, marred, or suspect. No decision of God can ever be improved upon. We may not understand the ways of God, yet they remain rooted in perfect wisdom. It is not our place to raise doubts about our "God only wise," but rather to bow in worshipful submission. The psalmist writes of all the works of God, "O Lord, how manifold are Thy works! In wisdom hast Thou made them all: the earth is full of Thy riches" (Ps. 104:24). Solomon writes concerning the sovereign act of creation, "The Lord by wisdom hath founded the earth; by understanding hath He established the heavens" (Prov. 3:19). Likewise, the prophet Jeremiah writes, "He hath made the earth by His power, He hath established the world by His wisdom, and hath stretched out the heavens by His discretion" (Jer. 10:12; 51:15). The apostle Paul, after surveying the dizzying heights of God's sovereign plan of redemption exults, "Oh, the depths of the riches both of the wisdom and knowledge of God! How unsearchable are His judgments and His ways past finding out!" (Rom. 11:33). God desires that we completely trust His sovereign acts of infinite wisdom. He encourages us to know and believe that the "only wise" God is in control of the affairs of this world and of our individual lives. The high and lofty One, who inhabits eternity, permits and purposes every event in this world and, yes, all in wisdom. When God created the heavens and the earth; when the Eternal Son of God became flesh and dwelt among us; when He died upon the cross in complete darkness, and cried out, "Eloi, Eloi, lama sabachthani;" when He rose from the dead after three days—It was all in wisdom. It was God acting in goodness to bring to pass our highest good, and acting in wisdom to bring to pass His perfect and sovereign will. We will never know the answer to the question, "Why?" Yet submission to the ways of God is a lesson that must be learned repeatedly. Some visitors to a deaf and dumb school were invited to write on the blackboard any question they desired the children to answer. One person callously wrote, "Why did God make you deaf and dumb, while He gave other children speech and hearing?" There was tense silence for a few moments and tears moistened the eyes of some of the children. Then one boy took the chalk and wrote this sublime answer. "Even so, Father, for so it seemed good in Thy sight."

IS DIVINE SOVEREIGNTY AN ESSENTIAL ATTRIBUTE OF GOD?

While all Christians believe that God is sovereign, this does not mean that sovereignty is to be considered an attribute of God, nor the most dominant aspect of His person. Sound Bible teachers have defined the attributes of God to be characteristics that together describe, as much as is humanly possible, the nature and essence of God. There are the divine "non-moral" attributes, and among these would be His omnipresence, His omniscience, His omnipotence, and His immutability (unchangeableness). Secondly, there are the "moral" attributes of God, among which would be holiness, righteousness, love, and truth. Sovereignty is not rightly numbered among the attributes of God, but is better understood to be the authority of God over His work. It is something that God does, rather than what God is. Before the creation of the world and all that is in it, God was love, holy, and righteous but not sovereign, for this attribute expresses His rule. It was not until creation that God could properly be thought of as sovereign. 1 Samuel 2:8 reads, "He raiseth the poor out of the dust, and lifteth up the beggar from the refuse, to set them among princes, and to make them inherit the throne of glory; for the pillars of the earth are the Lord's, and He hath set the world upon them." It is noteworthy that so much of the Lord's sovereign work seems to be exercised in the earthy realm. He begins with the dust of the earth and ends with the pillars of the earth and the world. His authority on earth extends to all, from a poor beggar to the regal princes and on to the throne of glory. Lewis Sperry Chafer, co-founder of Dallas Theological Seminary, Texas, writes:

> "By many writers, sovereignty is not included among the attributes of God. It is more properly a prerogative of God than an attribute and owes all its reality to the divine perfections of God."[3]

This does not diminish God's sovereignty, but assigns it to its rightful place. It charges all Christians to view His sovereignty as deeply rooted in the holy attributes of God. God's sovereignty is exercised in love, holiness, truth, and righteousness, as well as in His attributes of immutability, omnipotence, and omniscience. To view God's sovereignty as superior to His attributes, as some have, is to do violence to God's holy character. Indeed, God is in control; He is sovereign in all the affairs of men. He does whatever pleases Him in the universe, determining and controlling all that occurs. Therefore, there is no creature, person, or empire that lies outside of His sovereign control.

THE BIBLICAL SCOPE OF DIVINE SOVEREIGNTY

The doctrine that God is sovereign in His created universe is a truth that must be believed by all Christians. It must be the very foundation of all biblical doctrine. That God is sovereign means that He is the highest and greatest, exalted above all. He is omnipotent and controls everything, working everything according to His eternal plan and purpose. "According to the purpose of Him who worketh all things after the counsel of His own will"(Eph. 1:11). The Bible states that God is eternal, self-existent, self-sufficient, unchanging, all-powerful, all-knowing and He alone stands unequaled, above all. "For Thou, Lord, are high above all the earth: Thou art exalted far above all gods" (Ps. 97:9). No less than nine times in the Book of Revelation, God is called the "The Almighty," or the "Omnipotent Lord." Since God is infinite, His rule must be absolute. His rule must involve total control of everything in His creation: every circumstance, every situation, every event. God's sovereignty means that He either directly causes or consciously permits all that happens in human history. God claims full responsibility for establishing and removing human rulers. The Psalmist tells us that the sovereign God controls the weather (Ps. 147:16-18, 148:8). God gives life and sustains the life of all His creatures in His strong hand (Job. 12:10). Paul said to the Romans, "For from Him and through Him and to Him are all things" (Rom. 11:36). God, according to His holy character, has the right to do those things that please Him. Yet we must never forget that those things that please Him most are marked by love, mercy, and justice. The Psalmist states, "But our God is in the heavens; He does whatever He pleases" (Ps. 115:3). The prophet Isaiah states, "I am God and there is none other…My purpose will be established, and I will accomplish all My good pleasure" (Isa. 46:9-10).

God is in complete control, and yet He does not manipulate people like mere puppets. He gives them the dignity and freedom to make decisions and holds them responsible for their choices. Those decisions may bring to pass untold misery and suffering, and yet God allows it. The majority of human suffering is ultimately linked in some way to man's sinful choices. In his book *Problem With Pain,* theologian and author C. S. Lewis has pointed out:

> "The possibility of pain is inherent in the very existence of a world where souls can meet. When souls become wicked they will certainly use this possibility to hurt one another; and this, perhaps, accounts for four-fifths of the sufferings of men. It is men, not God, who have produced racks, whips, prisons, slavery, guns, bayonets, and bombs."[4]

However, through divine omniscience God knows every choice that man would make, and through divine sovereignty He takes those choices and uses them to serve His purposes (Ps. 139:1-4). In this way God has complete control over every decision and action, and man has the freedom to make decisions. However, where divine wisdom deems it best, He will overrule man's decisions in order to accomplish His own matchless purposes. Only an omnipotent God can take man's choices and the suffering that follows and cause it to ultimately serve His sovereign and perfect will. God does not always allow man's sinful actions to run their full and natural evil course, but He intervenes and overrules. The story of Joseph serves as a wonderful illustration of God's sovereign plan being worked out. When Joseph was reunited with his brothers many years later, he said,

"As for you, you meant evil against me, but God meant it for good…" (Gen. 50:20). God overruled the sinful actions of Joseph's brothers to bring about blessing. God used Joseph's brothers' sinful actions to bring to pass God's ultimate purposes. God's ways are always perfect and "past finding out." Jeremiah, writing to the Jewish captives suffering in Babylon, assures them that the sovereign God has their welfare at heart in His divine purposes: "For I know the plans that I have for you, declares the Lord, plans for welfare and not for calamity, to give you a future and a hope" (Jer. 29:11). We do not question God's sovereignty, but rather yield to the good and perfect will of God. In all human history the sovereignty of God exercises overruling control. God, through the use of living and non-living things, through the use of voluntary and involuntary actions of man, through the use of evil and good in the world, causes all things to interact so that His will is perfectly accomplished for His glory and the good of mankind.

DIVINE SOVEREIGNTY AND THE SCOPE OF MAN'S FREE WILL

Some have wrongly concluded that if God is absolutely sovereign, then man does not have a free will. It is thought that man can only act insomuch as God will determine him to act and that man must act, as God desires. Therefore, according to this view, man cannot resist the sovereign will and desires of God. John Calvin wrote in his most important theological work, *Institutes of Christian Religion:*

> "We mean the eternal decree of God by which He determined with Himself whatever He wished to happen with regard to every man."[5]

John Calvin sets forth the view that man must act exactly as God desires; man cannot do otherwise. He concludes that man does not possess a free will. This appears logical and verses here and there in Scripture may seem to support Calvin's position, but it is not really biblical because the Bible balances God's sovereignty with His goodness and love, as we have already shown. Moreover, Scripture emphasizes that God has sovereignly granted to man the ability to make free choices. This is not man usurping God's role in the world, but this is God's sovereign design and purpose for man in the world. Man could not make free choices except that it was given by God. Our Lord Himself in His interview with Pilate states this principle before the crucifixion. Pilate charges the Lord, "Do You not know that I have power to crucify You, and have power to release You?" Jesus answers, "You could have no power at all against Me, except it were given to you from above..." (Jn.19:10-11). Pilate thought that his ability to make free decisions was a personal right. Our Lord rightly corrects Pilate and states that the ability to make free choices is from God;" it is given from above." Frequently throughout Scripture we see man acting in defiance to God's desires. This ability is granted to man from God. King Solomon in the book of Proverbs declares, "For that they hated knowledge, and did not choose the fear of the Lord: They would have none of my counsel: they despised all my reproof" (Prov. 1:29-30). The gospel writer, Luke, states "The Pharisees and the lawyers rejected the counsel of God against themselves" (Lk. 7:30). In John's gospel the Lord rebukes the Pharisees, saying, "You will not come to me that you might have life" (Jn. 5:40). Further, Matthew tells us that when the Lord Jesus Christ strongly desired that the Jewish people come to Him, they rejected the desire of the Son of God "O,

Jerusalem, Jerusalem, ...how often would I have gathered your children together, even as a hen gathers her chickens under her wings, and you would not" (Matt. 23:39). God has not determined and caused all things to come to pass as they do. God exercises sovereign control in the world; but within this control He permits certain events and purposes others. It is of great importance to carefully distinguish between these two aspects of God's sovereignty. For this reason, the sinful consequences of man must never be attributed to God. The Word of God clearly states that all sinful temptations, the acts of the flesh, wars, lust, killings, and the misery that results because of sin are not caused by God, but by the free choices of man. James writes, "Let no man say when he is tempted, I am tempted of God: for God cannot be tempted with evil, neither tempts He any man...." (Jas. 1:13) Further in the book of James, he writes, "Where do wars and fights come from among you? Do not they come from your desires for pleasure that war in your members?" (Jas. 4:1). The apostle John wrote, "For all that is in the world: the lust of the flesh, the lust of the eyes, and the pride of life-is not of the Father..." (1 Jn. 2:18)

The Word of God carefully sets forth both the infinite sovereignty of God and human responsibility. God is sovereign, and yet in this infinite sovereignty, God has granted to man a free will. To detract from either of these truths is to detract from the fullness of the Word of God. A proper biblical balance between the two must be rigorously sought and maintained. Respected author A. W. Tozer strikes this proper biblical balance between the sovereignty of God and man's free will when he writes:

> "God sovereignly decreed that man should be free to exercise moral choice, and man from the beginning has

fulfilled that decree by making his choice between good and evil. When he chooses to do evil, he does not thereby countervail the sovereign will of God but fulfills it, inasmuch as the eternal decree decided not which choice the man should make but that he should be free to make it. If in His absolute freedom God has willed to give limited freedom, who is there to stay His hand or say, 'What doest Thou?' Man's will is free because God is sovereign. A God less than sovereign could not bestow moral freedom upon His creatures. He would be afraid to do so."[6]

Respected theologian Dr. Norman Geisler adds further clarity writing:

"Human freedom is not contrary to God's sovereignty. God sovereignly gave man his freedom by creating him a free creature, and God sovereignly continues to allow man to exercise his freedom moment by moment in existence (Col. 1:17). Thus the sovereignty of God is not thwarted by human freedom but glorified by human freedom. For God gave man free will, He sustains man so he can act freely, and He brings about all His purposes without violating man's free will."[7]

The faithful scholar and gifted preacher C. H. Spurgeon draws together in a sermon the importance of these two lines of biblical truth:

"Man is a free agent, a responsible agent, so that his sin is his own willful sin and it lies fully with him and never with God, and yet at the same time God's purposes are fulfilled, and even demons and corrupt men do His will? I cannot comprehend it: without hesitation I believe it, and rejoice so to do, I never hope to comprehend it....I worship a God I never expect to comprehend."[8]

THE SOVEREIGNTY OF GOD AND PRAYER

Many Calvinists believe that prayer can have no effect upon God since He has already decreed what He will do. This is, indeed, an extreme position concerning prayer. For James 4:2 clearly states, "Ye have not because ye ask not." The fact that some Christians do not possess certain things because they have not prayed is the clear teaching of this verse. Therefore, the Bible teaches that God does act in response to believing prayer. He also acts in many instances without anyone praying about a particular need; and then He acts in other cases contrary to the prayers of Christians because they have not prayed according to His will. "And this is the confidence that we have in Him, that, if we ask any thing according to His will, He heareth us" (1 Jn. 5:14). In His foreknowledge He has taken all of these things into account, and in His power He brings them to pass according to His own eternal purpose. Thus there is harmony concerning God's sovereignty, foreknowledge, and earnest prayer. It seems in Scripture that God has voluntarily bound Himself to the prayers of His people for the accomplishment of some of His purposes. From the very beginning God has used men and women who have yielded themselves to the service of God. It may be said that prayer is a leading characteristic of a yielded Christian life. For reasons known to God alone, God has decided to use the prayers of His people to bring to pass His divine purposes. The words of the Lord Jesus Christ in Matthew 9 are but a flash of light, which reveal God's ways of accomplishing His purposes. The Lord says, "The harvest truly is plenteous, but the laborers are few. Pray ye therefore the Lord of the harvest that He may send laborers into His harvest" (Matt. 9:37-38). Jesus is teaching that God sends forth laborers into the harvest; but also that He does it in connection with the prayers of His people. Why would a sovereign God accomplish His purposes in this way? We do not know. "The secret things belong unto the Lord, our God: but those things which are revealed belong to us" (Deut. 29:29). But we can say with certainty that prayer changes things.

To some extreme Calvinists, this statement is the highest form of arrogance. To say that the prayers of a mere sin-marred creature could ever influence the divine purposes of an eternal, omnipotent God is unthinkable. But we must remember that God's thoughts are higher than our thoughts, and man, in his brightest hour, will only know but the "edges of His ways." Does this not clearly show the unequaled privilege to which a Christian has now been brought before God, through grace, because of the death of the Lord Jesus Christ? Truly, the poor vile sinner has now been brought into the house of wine. Clearly, the assertion that prayer changes things is not an assault upon God's sovereignty, but rather a tacit acknowledgement of it. Who, indeed, would pray unless he believed that God was over all and the controller of all things? It is because the one who prays believes that God has the right and the power to alter the course of events that he prays. The view that prayer changes things, therefore, is consistent with and faithful to the biblical view of divine sovereignty. May we be ever watchful so that a system of theology does not rob us of rich and important spiritual blessings? Respected author C. H. Macintosh has wisely counseled in regard to this danger in extreme Calvinism:

> "...Difficulty is occasioned by the influence of a one-sided theology, a system that we can only compare to a bird with one wing or a boat with one oar. When we turn to the sacred page of God's Word, we find truth, not one side of truth, but the whole of truth in all its bearings. We find, laying side by side, the truth of divine sovereignty and human responsibility. Are we called to reconcile them? No, they are reconciled already because they are both set forth in the Word of God. We are to believe and obey. It is a fatal mistake for men to frame systems of divinity. You can no more systematize the truth of God than you can systematize God Himself. Let us abandon, therefore, all systems of theology and schools of divinity, and take the truth. All may contain some truth, not one contains all. And very often you find that whatever little truth the system contains is misplaced and turned the wrong way, to the serious damage of truth as a whole, and the stumbling and injury of souls. Every day we live we are more and more struck with the vast difference between the dogmas of divinity and the heart, the world, the Christ of God."[9]

Finally, the doctrine of the sovereignty of God must never provide man with excuses. Systems of theology may give reasons to do so, but not the Word of God. For no man can deny full responsibility for his actions, claiming that he was irresistibly led by God; for God never does violence to the free will which He has graciously given to man. God's sovereignty and man's freedom dwell side by side in such a way that the former does not force itself upon the latter; but in some cases He does overrule for His highest eternal purpose. In a future day we will see that mankind, in complete freedom, in uncoerced decisions, has been working out God's eternal divine plan. How can this be brought to pass? It is only by and through a sovereign God who is characterized by infinite power, wisdom, love, and goodness that such a plan can ever be realized. "O the depth of the riches both of the wisdom and knowledge of God! How unsearchable are His judgments, and His ways past finding out! For who hath known the mind of the Lord? Or who hath been His counselor? For of Him, and through Him, and to Him are all things: to whom be glory forever. Amen" (Rom. 11:33-36).

Endnotes

[1] James Orr, *The Progress of Dogma,* (Grand Rapids: Eerdmans, 1952), p. 292
[2] Alexander Carson, *Confidence in God in Times of Danger,* (Swengel, PA: Reiner Publications, 1975), p. 25
[3] Lewis Sperry Chafer, *Systematic Theology,* (Dallas, DTS Press, 1947), p. 222
[4] C. S. Lewis, *The Problem of Pain,* (New York, NY: Macmillan Co. 1963), p. 56
[5] John Calvin, *Institutes Vol. 2,* (Grand Rapids, MI, Eerdmans, 1952), p. 206
[6] A. W. Tozer, *The Knowledge of the Holy,* (New York, NY: Harpers and Row Publishers, 1961), p. 118
[7] Norman Geisler, *Evangelical Dictionary of Theology:* Ed. Walter Elwell, (Grand Rapids, MI: Baker Books, 1986), p. 429
[8] C. H. Spurgeon, *Metropolitan Tabernacle Pulpit, vol. 16,* (London: Passmore & Alabaster, 1907), p. 501
[9] C. H. Mackintosh, *Short Papers, Vol. 2,* (Sunbury, PA: Believer's Bookshelf, 1975), p. 267

- 10 -
Reformed Theology and Romans 9

Frederick the Great of Prussia once challenged Count Nicholas von Zinzendorf, the Moravian Christian leader, at his royal court to defend the truthfulness of the Bible. The count gave his theologically astute reply with two words: "The Jew." The history of the Jewish nation is the history of the sovereign workings of the eternal purposes of God. God had chosen the Jewish nation to be His people and to be His Servant attending to His affairs in the world. The preservation of the nation is a weighty testament to her divine election. Yet this election of Israel down through the centuries would be gravely misunderstood by the Jewish people as well as by Christians. Both groups, though devout and zealous, tended to drift in their convictions to the theological extreme, when the truth lay somewhere between. The Jewish rabbis looked deeply into this divine truth and coveted and gloried in the position they discovered in the Scriptures.

THE JEWISH VIEW OF ELECTION

The idea of the divine election of Israel was one of the most dominant and most important themes in the Old Testament. We find in the Pentateuch, "For thou art an holy people unto the Lord thy God: the Lord thy God hath chosen thee to be a peculiar people unto Himself above all peoples that are on the face of the earth" (Deut. 7:6). Later in the Psalms, "For the Lord hath chosen Jacob unto Himself, and Israel for His peculiar treasure" (Ps. 135:4). In the Prophets, "But thou Israel, My servant, Jacob whom I have chosen, the seed of Abraham My friend; whom I have taken hold of from the ends of the earth and called thee from the corners thereof, and said unto thee, 'Thou art My servant, I have chosen thee and not cast thee away' " (Isa. 41:8-9). The idea of Israel being the elect people of God was one of the most treasured and tenaciously held teachings among the Rabbis and Jewish people. Yet there were striking differences between the views held by first century Jewish leaders and the teaching of the Old Testament. In the Old Testament, election is always seen as an act of mercy and an expression of the love of God for Israel. It is for this reason that He redeemed them from bondage and made provision for the forgiveness of sin. In the Old Testament Israel has been chosen not merely for her own sake, but as an instrument of blessing in the hand of God; not merely to display His Divine power, but also for the benefit of other nations (Gen 12:3, Isa. 65:18-20).

> "But among the rabbis, the idea of election was looked upon as a covenant by which God is bound and over which He seems to have no control. 'Israel and God are bound in an indissoluble marriage' (Shemoth Rabba 1. 51); 'the holiness of Israel can never be done away with, even although Israel sins, it still remains Israel' (Sanhedrin 55); 'the worst Israelite is not profane like the heathen' (Bammidbar rabba 17); 'no Israelite can go into Gehenna' (Pesikta 38 a); 'all Israelites have their portion in the world to come' (Sanhedrin I).

Other Jewish leaders of the time of the epistle to the Romans had similar views: 'The planting of them is rooted for ever: they shall not be plucked out all the days of the heaven: for the portion of the Lord and the inheritance of God is Israel' (Ps. Sol. 14:3); 'Thou did choose the seed of Abraham before all the nations, and did set Thy name before us, O Lord: and Thou wilt abide among us forever' (ib. 9: 17). 'While Israel is always to enjoy the Divine mercy, sinners, that is Gentiles, are to be destroyed before the face of the Lord' (ib. 12:8). 'Israel is the end of the Divine action; for Israel the world was created' (4 Ezra 6:55); 'it does not in any way exist for the benefit of other nations, who are of no account; they are spittle, as the dropping into a vessel' (4 Ezra 6:55, 56). The Jew believed that his race was joined to God by covenant which nothing could dissolve, and that he and his people alone were the center of all God's action in the creation and government of the world."[1]

Paul opposes these current views among the rabbis, but shows, nevertheless, that Israel is elect and that God's promises to them have not failed. Romans chapter nine presents a theological argument proving the election of the nation, despite their widespread unbelief. Paul concerns himself with the solemn fact that most of the Jewish nation were in a hardened state and were refusing the offer of salvation in Christ. Yet how can this truth be reconciled with the truth of election? Throughout Romans nine Paul traces the future of two groups within the nation of Israel: a remnant, a small number of believing Jews who have come to Christ, and the larger number, who rejected Christ. He argues that the spiritual condition of the nation of Israel does not prove God's unfaithfulness or unrighteousness. Paul proves that it is in accordance with the Old

Testament Scriptures for God to reject those Jews who were seeking a righteousness of works and to accept those Gentiles who were willing to come to Christ by faith. Paul sets forth God's free and sovereign election of a nation. This election does not extend to the salvation of men, but is solely concerned with the privileges and eternal purpose of God for the nation of Israel. German theologian Erich Sauer explains,

> "On the theater of world history He moves His figures, as He will. He certainly does not compel the believer to believe or the unbeliever to disbelief; but out of the number of unbelieving He chooses certain individuals to be special examples of His power to judge (Pharaoh), and out of the number of believing He chooses others to be special agents for mediating His salvation (Patriarchs). Thus Romans 9 does not deal with the call unto salvation but to certain purposes connected with the history of salvation. It speaks less of God as a Redeemer of the individual than of Him as the One who directs general history."[2]

NATIONAL PRIVILEGES

Paul begins this chapter by revealing his great love and sorrow for his people: the nation of Israel. His great sorrow is because of the refusal of Israel to accept Christ as her chosen Messiah. He proceeds and explains how great are the privileges and promises that Israel possesses. He lists the privileges of Israel: adoption of sons, divine glory, promises, covenants, giving of the law, sacred worship (latreia), and the fathers. Saving the choicest provision for last, he says, "from whom, according to the flesh, came Christ." He stresses that the Christ was as much a man as we, but not such a man as we, touched with infirmities but untouched with sin. The point of the apostle would not be missed by a believing Jew: although the greater portion of those called Israelites have rejected the Messiah, the promises of God are nevertheless still in force.

THE CHOICE OF ISRAEL

Paul anticipates the Jewish objection: if God's promises to His people are still in effect, why then has the majority of the nation rejected Christ? Has God's Word failed? Paul replies that the promises are still in effect and God's Word has not failed, "Not as though the Word of God hath taken none effect"(v. 6). God's promises to Israel have not been forgotten. God in His sovereignty has determined that they should be fulfilled, not in the entire nation, but in a smaller group within the nation. God has chosen a remnant, spiritual Israel, Isaac's seed, on which to bestow His favor. God sovereignly chose, from among Abraham's sons, Isaac over Ishmael to be the seed of the nation of Israel. Election to salvation is not the issue. If election was to salvation, then only the nation of Israel would be saved, since only the nation of Israel was elect. This cannot be the case, for many Gentiles, who were not elect, have come to repentance. One thinks of Melchizedek and the city of Nineveh, as well as others. Election here is to a specific role, function, and purpose, as expounded or explained in Romans nine.

THE CHOICE OF ISRAEL IS EXPLAINED

God sovereignly chose Jacob's descendants to be a nation that He would use for His eternal purposes. Not all the children of Isaac and Rebecca are God's chosen people, those in whom the promises would be realized; but only those who descend from Jacob, and not those of Esau, "the children of the flesh" (v. 8). The children of Jacob are "the children of promise...counted for the seed." The basis of the election of Israel through the line of Jacob and not Esau was not upon works, but founded solely upon God's divine prerogative. Paul's states, "For the children being not yet born, neither having done good or evil" (v. 11). This divine prerogative is confirmed in Romans 9:13 where Paul states, "As it is written, Jacob have I loved, but Esau have I hated." This quotation is drawn from Malachi 1:2-3, " 'I have loved you', saith the Lord. 'Yet you say, "Wherein hast thou loved us?" Was not Esau Jacob's brother?' saith the Lord.' Yet I loved Jacob, and hated Esau, and laid his mountains and his heritage waste for the jackals of the wilderness.' "The hatred and love spoken of here is directed to the descendants of the nations represented in Jacob and Esau. It is privilege on earth, not election to salvation in heaven, and reprobation that is considered here. William MacDonald's comments are of interest here:

> "'I loved Jacob, and I hated Esau.' Here God is speaking of two nations, Israel and Edom, of which Jacob and Esau were heads. God marked out Israel as the nation to whom He promised the Messiah and the messianic kingdom. Edom received no such promise...This passage refers only to earthly blessings, and not to eternal life. God's hatred of Edom doesn't mean that individual Edomites can't be saved, any more than His love of Israel means that individual Jews don't need to be saved."[3]

God blessed the house of Jacob with the law, prophets, God's presence in their midst, shepherd-leaders, and revelation. All of this was withheld from Esau's descendants. We see in verse 11, "Not being yet born," and in...v. 12, "The elder shall serve the younger." This prophecy does not refer to Jacob and Esau individually but to their descendants. History will show that Esau, the older brother, in his life never served Jacob, the younger; but his descendants, the Edomites did serve the Jewish nation (2 Sam. 8:14). Genesis 25:23 adds light to this truth, "And the Lord said unto her; Two nations are in thy womb, and two manner of people shall be separated from thy bowels; and the one people shall be stronger than the other people; and the elder shall serve the younger." God chose the descendants of Jacob to be that nation through whom He would fulfill His purpose on earth. God righteously chose Jacob, and not Esau, from before they were born, but His judgment upon them, His holy assize, was not declared until they had lived out their lives, and their descendants had displayed their spiritual character.

THE CHOICE OF DIVINE MERCY

Is God unrighteous to show mercy to Jacob and not to Esau? To Moses and not to Pharaoh? No. "I will have mercy...I will have compassion...not of him that willeth or runneth, but of God...I raised thee up...that I might show My power...that My Name might be declared throughout all the earth " (Rom. 9:15-17). Calvinists, will often point to Romans 9:16 as a proof for the Reformed view of divine election. They argue that election is not based upon he who runs or wills but upon the mercy and election of God alone. None will argue that salvation is of God alone, or that mercy is unmerited; these both are true and biblical. However, we must resist using Romans nine to prove election to salvation, for the election here is not to salvation but, is referring to God's sovereign will concerning Israel. God is sovereign, and has the right to do as He pleases with individuals and nations. Paul holds up two great individuals at the time of Israel's birth as a nation, Moses and Pharaoh. God's purposes will be established regardless of that which Moses wills or that which Pharaoh opposes. This sovereignty extends to Isaac and Ishmael, to Jacob and Esau, to Moses and Pharaoh, and to the nation of Israel and the Gentile nations (Rom. 9:24, 30). The purpose of this section is to prove that God is just and righteous to show His abundant mercy to Israel on the one hand, and is righteous to harden Pharaoh and demonstrate His power on the other hand. Scripture is clear that God is full of mercy and loves to bestow it, and yet His mercy is never merited or deserved. God's merciful acts are never arbitrary or capricious, but they are based upon the just will and purposes of God. Human effort and resolve avail nothing. He alone reserves the right to bestow mercy, when and upon whom He sovereignly chooses. The reason He bestows mercy on one and hardens another is a mystery hidden in God alone. Concerning God's mercy, Dr. W. H. Griffith Thomas writes:

> "God's mercy is not merely a response to human resolve ('him that willeth'), or to human effort ('him that runneth'). His Divine will is the one and only source of His mercy. All men are sinners, and as God pardoned Israel when they were rebels, why may He not pardon the Gentiles also?"[4]

Romans 9:15, "I will have mercy upon whom I will have mercy," is a quotation taken from Exodus 33:19. The reference to Exodus sheds light upon the eternal purpose of God alluded to in Romans nine. Israel had sinned greatly in setting up an idol of a golden calf. God's anger burned hot against Israel, and He disclosed to Moses that He would destroy all Israel and start anew with Moses' seed. God would have been fully righteous and just to judge Israel. Moses, however, interceded for Israel saying, "Lord, why does Thy wrath wax hot against Thy people, which Thou has brought out of Egypt with great power, and with a mighty hand?" (Ex. 32:11). God relented and showed full and unmerited mercy to Israel. Just as God was righteous in showing mercy to Moses and the children of Israel, in like manner, He would be righteous in withholding mercy from Pharaoh. In both cases God's glory would be displayed, however, the outcome would be markedly different. Moses and Israel submitted to the will of God and received mercy; Pharaoh hardened his heart and came under the Lord's sovereign hand of judgment.

God sent His servant Moses to Pharaoh demanding submission. Pharaoh, in his pride and arrogance, refuses obedience saying, "Who is the Lord, that I should obey Him?" He challenges the Almighty's divine will and purpose. However, the purpose of God in Pharaoh would not be hindered. "Even for this same purpose have I raised thee up, that I might show My power in thee, and that My name might be declared throughout all the earth"(v. 17). The phrase "...have I raised thee up" does not have reference to the birth of Pharaoh. New Testament Greek authorities suggest that the expression "raised up" means, "carefully kept." This statement speaks to the fact that God brought Pharaoh to such a position upon the world stage in order to teach generations to come the uselessness of fighting against God. God demonstrates His righteousness in having mercy on whom He will have mercy, and in hardening whomsoever He will. He is the moral ruler of the universe, and He works all things according to the counsel of His will. God is righteous in His bestowal of mercy, and He is righteous and just in His dealing with Pharaoh. We may not understand the purposes or mercy and justice of God, nevertheless we must always acknowledge that "God's ways are higher than our ways, and His thoughts are higher than our thoughts"(Isa. 55:8-9).

Did not God, one will ask, harden Pharaoh's heart so that he could not receive God's mercy? Eighteen times we are told that Pharaoh's heart was hardened in refusal. Half of those times the hardening is attributed to Pharaoh himself and the rest to God. But the very source of the hardening must be interpreted in light of Exodus 3:19, "The king of Egypt will not..." Before this contest between God and Pharaoh began, the will and heart of Pharaoh was already set. The heart of this Egyptian king was already hardened by his own doing. The plagues sent by God revealed clearly, and crystallized further, the hardness of his heart. The eloquent Scottish Bible expositor, Alexander Maclaren, explains:

> "God hardens no man's heart who has not first hardened it himself. We do not need to conclude that any inward action on the will is meant. Was not the accumulation of plagues, intended, as they were, to soften a cause of hardening? The same fire softens wax and hardens clay...Pharaoh's obstinacy had not thwarted the divine purpose but had been the dark background against which the blaze of God's irresistible might

shone brighter. He turns opposition into the occasion of more conspicuously putting forth His omnipotence."[5]

Furthermore, the grammatical construction of the Hebrew text suggests that God was strengthening that which was already present in Pharaoh's heart. God did not arbitrarily harden Pharaoh's heart, but rather hardened a will already angered against the Israelites. Author and biblical scholar Dr. Norman Geisler, writes:

> "The Hebrew word 'hardened' (chazaq) can and often does mean to 'strengthen' (Judg. 3:12, 16:28) or even to 'encourage' (Deut. 1:38, 3:28). Taken in this sense, it would not carry any sinister connotations but would simply state that God made Pharaoh strong to carry through with his (Pharaoh's) will against Israel."[6]

In the process of God displaying His power in the judgment of Pharaoh, the mercy of God was also in view. The Lord, as Sovereign of the universe, can do as He desires, and what He desires most is to show mercy. Did not God show a measure of mercy to Pharaoh, even as He was merciful to Moses and Israel? Was not God longsuffering with Pharaoh from the very outset when he hardened his heart and would not let Israel go (Ex. 3:19)? Was not God's mercy to Pharaoh seen when Pharaoh asked Moses to pray to the Lord so that the plague of frogs would end? Moses prayed and God responded by ending the plague of frogs as Pharaoh requested (Ex. 8:9-11). Yet Pharaoh hardened his heart even more. Therefore, Pharaoh came under the judicial hardening and fearful judgment of a gracious, merciful, and just God. Pharaoh was allowed by God to raise himself to the very pinnacle of political power and human ambition, only to see it come crashing down, so that God could declare His unmatched glory and display His divine power to all the world. This would be a lesson to the generations that would follow of the utter folly of fighting against God.

THE CHOICE OF ISRAELITE VESSELS

Paul anticipates another question by a Jewish objector: If Pharaoh did what God willed, why then does God find fault? (v. 19). Paul counters that the reply is wrong on two counts: in using Isaiah 29:16, he firmly states that finite man is in no position to question a sovereign God (v. 20, 21), and that God's sovereignty is always expressed righteously, ever tempered with mercy (v. 22, 23).

Paul sets forth the divine right of a sovereign God over the Israelite nation. God has the absolute right to shape and to mold Israel, to execute judgment, and to withhold or to mete out blessing according to His will. Paul draws upon the potter and clay analogy, alluding to the Old Testament passages Isaiah 29:16 and Jeremiah 18:6. In this analogy of the potter and the clay, Paul's use of the word "forms" instead of "creates" is important. The apostle is not referring to original creation, but to spiritual destination. From one lump of clay, the nation of Israel, God is seen as taking two separate groups of Israelites as He finds them, and then molding them into a vessel of His design. Scripture calls the one a vessel of honor, and the other vessels of dishonor or "no honor." The vessel of honor is made up of vessels of mercy, and the vessel of dishonor is made up of vessels of wrath. The vessel of honor seems to refer to the small believing Jewish remnant and believing Gentiles, and the vessel of dishonor refers to the unbelieving Israelites. This seems to be evident from Paul's words in verse 24: "...even of us whom He called, not of the Jews only but also of the Gentiles." W. H. Griffith Thomas' comment on this verse underlines this point,

> "At the close of verse 24 the calling of the Gentiles is introduced for the first time. Hitherto the argument has only been concerned with two distinct portions of the Jews."[7]

In his allusion to the potter and the clay, Paul points to God's right to do with Israel what He desires. The Potter made a vessel of clay; when it became marred by unbelief He made another vessel. "'...House of Israel, cannot I do with you as this potter?' saith Jehovah. Behold, as the clay is in the potter's hand, so are you in My hand, house of Israel'" (Jer. 18:5-6). The reference is to two groups within Israel, a faithful remnant and those who do not believe and are evil. Whom will God use to make a new vessel? Upon what basis does He reject the old vessel and select a new vessel? God tells us by applying the potter and clay illustration, "At the moment that I speak concerning a nation and concerning a kingdom, to pluck up and to break down, and to destroy, if that nation, concerning which I have spoken, turn from its evil, then I will repent of the disaster which I thought to bring upon it" (Jer. 18:7-8 NKJV). If unbelieving Israelites would turn from their unbelief, they would, in God's sovereign plan, become vessels of mercy. If they remain steadfast in their unbelief then they will become a vessel of dishonor. If Israel turns from her unbelief, God will turn from His judgment that He planned to execute. Israel did not turn from her evil, and God, faithful to His word, displayed His power and wrath upon the unbelieving Jews, who are called vessels of wrath. God has shown Himself to be long-suffering and patient, desiring them to come to repentance and faith and holding back sure and certain destruction. "...Endured with much long-suffering the vessels fitted to destruction" (v. 22). However, they did not believe, and the destruction of a sovereign God came upon the nation of Israel. God reserved His divine right to execute judgment upon them by using political movements and the military might of that day. At the time of the writing of the epistle to the Romans, the Temple in Jerusalem was yet standing. But in 70 A.D., the Temple in Jerusalem was destroyed and the nation was scattered by the Roman commander-in-chief Titus Flavius Vespasianus and his 60,000 legionary soldiers. The Jewish historian Josephus recorded in his annals, *The Jewish War*, the severity and scope of this judgment. He writes that 97,000 men above the age of seventeen were taken prisoner, 11,000 died of starvation, 1,100,000 were killed during the siege and the entire city was burned and destroyed. After chronicling the razing of the city, he states:

> "All the fortifications encircling the city were so completely leveled with the ground that no one visiting the spot would believe that it had once been inhabited."[8]

The destruction and judgment upon the "City Of David" was a landmark event, yet the theological implications of this Roman conquest are of equally great importance. The Swiss biblical scholar and commentator Dr. Frederick L. Godet writes, noting the theological purpose of this judgment of God:

> "The manifestation of wrath (Rom. 9:22) refers at once to the doom of destruction that was already suspended

over the nation in general, and to the unbelieving Israelites in particular...The near destruction of Jerusalem and of the Jewish people by the arm of the Romans, which was to be in this unexampled catastrophe the instrument of God's wrath and power. The execution of this destruction, long ago determined and clearly announced by Jesus Himself, God delayed for forty years; that is the long-suffering of which the apostle here speaks."[9]

The devastation pronounced by Jeremiah had come, "...the disaster which I thought to bring upon it" (Jer. 18:7-8 NKJV). God's judgment had fallen and His wrath was displayed. This judgment, as Scripture states, was not arbitrary, but fitting. God's wrath was displayed in allowing destruction to come upon the unbelieving Jewish nation. This is not the first time Jerusalem would be devastated by her enemies. In 586 BC, the Babylonians destroyed Jerusalem, because of Jewish unbelief, as recorded for us by Jeremiah in chapters 37-39. This siege of Jerusalem lasted just over 30 months before the city was taken and burned; Zedekiah, the king, was captured and his two sons were put to death. Paul now explains that another destruction will take place again because of unbelief of the Jewish nation. The destruction of Jerusalem in 586 BC by the Babylonians and the destruction of Jerusalem in 70 AD by the Romans both appear to be biblical fulfillments of the prophecy of Jeremiah 18:5-8.

The unbelieving Jews, by their rebellion, had fitted themselves to a judgment of destruction. This point deserves strong emphasis. The unbelieving Jews had prepared themselves for judgment by their rebellion and disobedience; whereas, these of the believing remnant, through faith and obedience, became vessels of mercy prepared beforehand for glory. It is noteworthy that the Greek construction of this verse (v. 22) does not ascribe the fitting of the vessels of wrath directly to God, but rather to the unbelieving Jews. New Testament Greek authority W. E. Vine's comment here is important:

> "The 'fitting' (v. 22) is not imputed to God as if God had prepared these vessels for wrath...God has not created men with a view to their destruction. The form of the word rendered 'fitted' may be regarded as in the middle voice (of the Greek verb), which implies action done by oneself...there is a suggestion, therefore, that the persons referred to as 'vessels of wrath' have fitted themselves for destruction."[10]

British Bible teacher C. H. Macintosh, the author of Notes on the Pentateuch, comments well on this point:

> "In Romans 9, speaking of 'vessels of wrath,' it says, 'fitted to destruction,' fitted not by God surely, but by themselves. On the other hand, when speaking of 'vessels of mercy,' it says, 'which He had afore prepared unto glory.'"[11]

God in his sovereignty would use even that part of Israel, which rebelled against Him to display His glory. He would use them to demonstrate His righteous judgment, and use their disobedience to enable the Gentiles by faith to become right with God.

THE CHOICE OF A BELIEVING JEWISH REMNANT

The inspired apostle continues his argument of the believing and unbelieving portions of the Jewish nation into this last section. Paul quotes from the Old Testament prophet Hosea (2:23) as support for his argument, "I will call them My people, who were not My people; and beloved, which were not beloved..." (v. 25) Those who were not "His people," and those who were not "beloved" were the unbelieving portion of the Jewish nation. He is not referring to the Gentiles at this point, although they are certainly included as vessels of mercy (v. 24). However, in the development of his argument he first addresses the issue of the Jewish remnant (vv. 25-29), and then picks up his discussion of the Gentiles in verse 30. Bible scholar Dr. Alva McClain, former president of Grace Theological Seminary, comments:

> "Many think that this passage refers to the Gentiles. It does not. They think that Paul made a mistake and quoted from the Old Testament something that belonged to the Jews and applied it to the Gentiles. He is talking about Israel. 'I will call her My people which was not My people.' God cast Israel off and then picked her up in mercy."[12]

Paul continues his theme, which runs all through Romans 9, that is, that God has a believing remnant, which He will not cast off. Paul demonstrates that the Jewish prophets clearly stated that only a remnant would be saved. This is part of God's sovereign plan, foretold by the Old Testament Scriptures. He makes liberal use of quotations from the Old Testament to show that this was exactly what the Scriptures teach. Paul quotes from two portions, both from the prophet Isaiah. The force of the first quotation (Isa. 10:22) is to show that although Israel would grow into a great nation, only a small portion of the nation would be saved. "Though the number of the children of Israel be as the sand of the sea, a remnant shall be saved" (v. 27). The second quotation lays stress upon the faithfulness of a sovereign God. Even though only a small portion are saved, God nonetheless, has shown Himself to be fully sovereign and gracious. "Except the Lord of Saboath had left us a seed, we had been as Sodom, and been made like unto Gomorrah" (v. 29). New Testament Greek authority, H. G. C. Moule, expresses the solemnity of this sovereign work of God:

> "The prophets who foretell that great ingathering indicate with equal solemnity the spiritual failure of all but a fraction of the lineal heirs of promise…A remnant, still a remnant, not the masses, entered upon an inheritance of such ample provision, and so sincerely offered."[13]

Indeed, God's ways with Israel have been just and gracious and in full accord with the Old Testament Scriptures. However, one question yet remains for the apostle to take up in this chapter: Why did the majority of Israel fail to attain to the righteousness of faith? Why did some Gentiles attain to the righteousness that is by faith? The apostle closes the chapter with his solemn and probing answer, "Because they sought it not by faith, but as it were, by the works of the law." Paul now moves from divine sovereignty to human responsibility. Israel sought to be justified before God by keeping the law, instead of by faith in the Lord Jesus Christ. They rejected the righteousness according to grace and tried to please God with a righteousness according to works. God sent His Son into the world, Who was the embodiment of perfection, who fulfilled the law perfectly. Yet the Jewish nation did not receive Him, but stumbled over the stumbling stone of a lowly Christ, when they were expecting a triumphant King. By rejecting Him, they fulfilled the prophetic Scriptures, " 'Behold, I lay in Sion a stumbling stone and rock of offense: and whosoever believes on Him shall not be ashamed' " (v. 32-33). Even though the nation of Israel has stumbled and fallen, God is still saving individual Jews who receive Him by faith. Finally, no one will deny that this chapter presents its share of difficulties to the interpreter of Scripture. The weighty subjects of the sovereignty of God and the free will of man are presented equally. Nowhere does God ask us to choose between the sovereignty of God and the free will of man. They are both from God and are both part of God's divine plan. The main thrust of this chapter, however, is to present the faithfulness of a sovereign God. God is faithful, just, righteous, and good, and can be trusted to keep His promises and accomplish His eternal purposes. Moreover, may we humbly suggest that Romans chapter 9 does not teach that God sovereignly elects some to salvation and others to reprobation. The Calvinist view of election must look elsewhere for its biblical basis. Romans 9 sets forth God's sovereign plan with the nation of Israel concerning her role, privilege, and future upon earth. This plan is a part of His eternal purposes, once concealed in the mind of God, but now revealed, and in a day to come, to be fully manifested.

Endnotes

1. William Sanday, A. Headlam, *Romans, A Critical and Exegetical Commentary* (New York, NY: Scribner, 1910) p. 248-250
2. Erich Sauer, *Dawn of World Redemption*, (Grand Rapids, MI: Eerdmans, 1973), p. 148,149
3. William MacDonald, *Romans*, (Kansas City, KS: Walterick Publishers, 1981), p.103
4. W. H. Griffith Thomas, *Epistle to the Romans*, (Grand Rapids, MI: Eerdmans, 1946), p.255
5. Alexander Maclaren, *Exodus*, (Grand Rapids, MI: Baker Books, 1989), p. 36
6. Norman Geisler, *Chosen But Free*, (Minneapolis, MN: Bethany Books, 1999), p. 188
7. W. H. Griffith Thomas, *Epistle to the Romans*, (Grand Rapids, Mi: Eerdmans), 1946, p. 262
8. Josephus, *The Jewish War*, (New York, NY: Penguin Books, 1981), p. 371
9. Frederick L. Godet, *Romans*, (Grand Rapids, MI: Zondervan, 1956), p. 360
10. W. E. Vine, *Romans*, (London: Oliphants Limited, 1948), p. 147-148
11. C. H. Macintosh, *Treasury*, (New York, NY: Loizeaux, 1976), p. 606
12. Alva J. McClain, *Romans*, (Chicago, IL: Moody Press, 1973), p. 183
13. Handley G. C. Moule, *The Expositors Bible: Romans*, (London: Hodder & Stoughton, 1905), p. 256,257

- 11 -
Is Faith the Gift of God?

The evangelist D. L. Moody was once asked if he thought faith was a gift of God. He replied, "Some say that faith is the gift of God. So is the air, but you have to breathe it; so is bread, but you have to eat it; so is water, but you have to drink it. Some are wanting some miraculous kind of feeling. That is not faith. 'Faith cometh by hearing and hearing by the Word of God.' It is not for me to sit down and wait for faith to come stealing over me... it is for me to take God at his word."

The teaching that faith is a gift of God is a truth stated in Scripture. It is given by Him who gives every good gift and every perfect gift. Faith is not the only gift that comes from above from the father of lights. The Scriptures also teach that the salvation through our Lord Jesus Christ is an unspeakable gift (2 Cor. 9:15), and that our daily bread is a gift from God, along with the grace of God, and the Word of God, the Son of God, these all and many others are God's gracious gifts. Indeed, the gift of faith is one of God's most gracious and precious gifts for it is through faith by grace that we are saved. This gift is within the grasp of us all, for God desires all to be saved. All that was necessary for our salvation has been accomplished and so he charges us to receive this free gift of salvation through faith.

The question is not so much whether faith is a gift of God but rather is this gift given in a unique way exclusively to the elect. And thereby the elect will unconditionally and irresistibly be saved but concerning the non-elect, from them God will withold this gift and they will be eternally lost. For faith is a condition for salvation and without which none will be saved. What does the Bible teach? Is faith given exclusively to the elect for salvation and witheld from others? Is faith the gift of God referred to in Ephesians 2:8?

THE SCRIPTURES AND THE GIFT OF FAITH

There are a number of Scriptures that speak of faith as a gift of God. There are Scriptures such as Romans 12:3, "As God has dealt to every man a measure of faith," and in 1 Corinthians 12:9, "For to one is given...faith by the same Spirit." These Scriptures when carefully studied reveal that this gift of faith is not a condition for salvation but a requirement for effective Christian living and service. The gift of faith in this sense is the special ability given to members of the body of Christ to accomplish great things for God. George Mueller, of Bristol, England who established an orphanage of which thousands would call home, and the missionary Hudson Taylor who reached the previously unevangelized interior of China with the gospel are examples of this gift of faith. This may have been one of the gifts that Stephen possessed, for it speaks of him as being "full of faith." This gift may have been in the apostles mind when he wrote, "...if I have all faith, so as to remove mountains, but do not have love, I am nothing" (1 Cor. 13:2). But this gift is not the faith which saves but the gift of faith for service. This gift of faith for service is received after one comes to Christ by faith and not before.

But the question naturally arises but what does Ephesians 2:8 teach about the gift of faith? Does it not say, "For by grace are ye saved through faith; and that not of yourselves, it is the gift of God?" Many Calvinists would teach that this verse teaches that faith is the gift of God. And that the faith spoken of here is saving faith without which no one can be saved. Their argument runs, salvation is truly of God because faith cannot proceed from the flesh or the natural man it must be a gift of God. Many would also conclude that faith which flows out of the natural man cannot save, for his faith would be a "work." And no one is saved by the works of the law. Let us explore these and other questions as we examine further this subject.

Is Faith the Gift of God in Eph. 2:8?

Is faith the gift spoken of in Ephesians 2:8? The Greek construction of this verse seems to indicate that faith is not the gift but rather that salvation is the gift of God. New Testament Greek authorities contend that the key to understanding Ephesians 2:8 is to properly identify the antecedent of the pronoun "that"*(touto)*. A general rule of Greek grammar concerning identifying the antecedent is: Pronouns agree with their antecedent in gender and number. Their case is determined by their use in their own clause. The fact that the demonstrative pronoun "that" is neuter and the words "faith"*(pistis)* and "grace"*(charis)* are feminine in gender must rule out faith as the gift of God. If Paul wanted to say that "faith" was the gift of God he would of used the feminine form of the word "that" *(haute)*.

A number of respected evangelical Greek scholars have commented on the grammatical structure of this verse and have concluded that salvation and not faith is the gift of God. The word "That" seems to refer back to the verses 2:4-7 to God quickening, and raising us up together and in showing his grace towards us. None of this is of works but it is a gift of God.

British Bible commentator, and former professor at the University of Sheffield F. F. Bruce writes,

> "The fact that the demonstrative pronoun 'that' is neuter in Greek (tauto), whereas 'faith' is a feminine noun (pistis), combines with other considerations to suggest that it is the whole concept of salvation by grace through faith that is described as the gift of God."[1]

W. E. Vine, an respected authority on the Greek New Testament and author of *Expository Dictionary of New Testament Words*, concerning the word "gift" he writes:

> "...Doron, to give, is used of salvation by grace, as the gift of God in Ephesians 2:8."[2]

WHAT IS FAITH?

After considering whether or not faith is the gift of which leads to salvation, one will naturally ask what then is faith? We know that even demons believe and shudder (Jas. 2:19). But what is faith? And how does one obtain faith that leads to salvation. Hebrews 11:1 is often considered to be the biblical description of faith "Now faith is the substance of things hoped for, the evidence of things not seen." A proper description of faith must contain the three elements mentioned in Hebrews 11:1-3: Substance, Evidence, and Witness. But how might we define what faith is? A number of evangelical theologians have given us biblical definitions in answering the question; what is faith?

The biblical faith that leads to salvation, which is sometimes called "saving faith," consists of three primary elements:

1.) Knowledge of the object of faith; 2.) Mental assent; that which the Bible says about Christ, the object of our faith, is true and then; 3.) The use of the human will to place dependence or trust in him alone. It is noteworthy that this definition is accepted and taught by Calvinist teachers. The Reformed theologian and former Princeton Theological Seminary professor Charles Hodge writes,

> "That faith therefore, which is connected with salvation, includes knowledge, that is, a perception of the truth and its qualities; assent, or the persuasion of truth of the object of faith; and trust, or reliance…The exercise of faith is the reliance on the truth as revealed in the gospel."[3]

In a similar vein Calvinist theologian Louis Berkhof, in his *Systematic Theology* posits that faith has three elements: (1) an intellectual element *(notitia)* or knowledge; (2) an emotional element *(assensus)* or assent to the truth; and (3) a volitional element *(fiducia)* or the involvement of the human will. Concerning the involvement of the human will he writes:

> "The third element consists in a personal trust in Christ as Savior and Lord, including a surrender of the soul as guilty and defiled to Christ, and a reception and appropriation of Christ as the source of pardon."[4]

It is striking to note that these definitions of faith include the exercise of the human will. Both Calvinists and non-Calvinists will concede this point. The Calvinist unfortunately will go further in his theology and state that regeneration by the Spirit must be prior to the exercise of faith. For he insists that the will is in bondage to a corrupt sinful nature and without regeneration, or "new birth" faith will never be placed in Christ for salvation. The Non-Calvinist believes that man through the fall, as the Scriptures describe, is "dead," "lost," "perishing," "condemned," "in darkness." The fall includes all of this and more besides, however, the fall has not brought to pass an inability to believe in Christ unto salvation. For the boundless grace of God and penetrating power of the word of God and the convicting of the Holy Spirit is more than sufficient and has provided all that is necessary to enable a man to exercise faith as an act of the human will.

What is the source of faith? The Word of God tells us that from the divine side the Scriptures, the Spirit of God and the grace of God working in concert to produce faith. But there is the human side, which is the exercise of human will in response to these divine promptings. The word of God tells us that "So then faith cometh by hearing, and hearing by the word of God" (Rom. 10:17) and "being born again, not of corruptible seed, but of incorruptible, by the Word of God, which liveth forever and ever" (1 Pt. 1:23). Again concerning the Spirit's work in new birth we read, "Verily, verily, I say unto thee, except a man be born of water and of the Spirit, he cannot enter the kingdom of God" (Jn. 3:5). Although God enables us to believe through divine promptings the responsibility to believe is ours. God has done all that is necessary for salvation. Our responsibility is to receive the gift of salvation by faith. Concerning the inter-working of the divine and human aspects that together produce faith which ultimately leads to regeneration, respected Bible commentator and former professor of Bible Exposition at Dallas Theological Seminary, in Texas, Dr. J. Dwight Pentecost comments,

"The Word of God, convicts, reproves, enlightens, exhorts, and reveals, not only our need but also the Lord Jesus Christ who can meet that need. The instrument that convicts is the Word of God, but it is the Spirit that produces the new birth. The word of God, energized by the Spirit of God, produces new birth."[5]

Another respected author, C. H. Mackintosh, commenting on the formation of saving faith that leads to new birth writes,

"New birth is not a change of man's fallen nature, but the imparting of a new, divine nature. How is this new nature produced? This is a point of immense importance, inasmuch as it places the Word of God before us as the grand instrument that the Holy Ghost uses in quickening dead souls…All who place their trust in Christ have gotten new life—are regenerated."[6]

Faith is indeed a gift of God. God has provided the One who paid a price that we could not pay, the Lord Jesus Christ, the object of our faith. Faith is an important condition for salvation. But the Lord Jesus Christ is the cause of our salvation.

IS FAITH A WORK?

The Calvinist argues that unless faith is given irresistibly by God then salvation is a "works salvation." It is said that this defective salvation is not of God, for it is partly of God and partly of man. Is this view in accordance with Scripture? Does this view stand upon sound logic?

Firstly, the very nature of faith is an admission that man is unable to earn or merit salvation but rest upon God alone and his grace. It is an act of the will prompted by the moving of God's abundant grace. Faith is not the act of doing something but rather receiving something. Does a downtrodden beggar who receives a handout receive the credit for the gracious deed? Or the one who graciously gave? The act of receiving God's unconditional gift of salvation is of no merit to the receiver. However, all praise and glory goes to the Giver of "every good and perfect gift" (Jas. 1:17). One of Calvinism staunchest defenders and most able theologians has readily admitted that faith cannot be a work or meritorious deed in regard to salvation. J. Gresham Machen, the first president and the founder of Westminster Theological Seminary, in Philadelphia writes:

> "The faith of man, rightly conceived can never stand in opposition to the completeness with which salvation depends upon God: it can never mean that man does part while God merely does the rest; for the simple reason that faith consists not in doing something but in receiving something."[7]

Faith may rightly considered to be a gift of God. In the sense that all good things come from God. Faith is of God, who has inscrutably given fallen man the ability to respond to the drawing power of God, through the promptings of divine grace of God, the Word of God and Spirit of God working together to form faith in a willing heart. Yet the responsibility to believe is all of man and not God. The charge from God to the lost is believe on the Lord Jesus Christ and you will be saved. We are not to pray to receive the gift of faith so we can believe. No. We are to believe, as an act of the human will in the finished work of the Lord Jesus Christ unto salvation.

Endnotes

[1] F. F. Bruce, *Ephesians,* (London: Pickering & Inglis, 1961), p. 51
[2] W. E. Vine, *Dictionary of N. T. Words,* (Old Tappan: Revell, 1981), p. 146
[3] Charles Hodge, *Romans,* (Grand Rapids, MI: Eerdmans, 1976), p. 29
[4] Louis Berkhof, *Systematic Theology,* (Grand Rapids, MI: Eerdmans, 1941), p. 505
[5] J. D. Pentecost, *The Divine Comforter,* (Westwood: Revell, 1963), p. 131
[6] C. H. Mackintosh, *Treasury,* (Neptune, NJ: Loizeaux, 1976), p. 618
[7] J. Gresham Machen, in J. I. Packer, *Fundamentalism and the Word of God,* (Grand Rapids, MI: Eerdmans, 1958), p. 172

- 12 -
Reformed Theology, the Mosaic Law and the Rule of Life

Reformed theology has long given great significance to the term "the believer's rule of life." By this term they are referring to the "moral" law given to Moses on Mount Sinai. Reformed teachers acknowledge that this phrase does not occur in the Bible; nevertheless, they argue that it is an indispensable principle in the life of a Christian. These teachers fully concede that the ceremonial law, civil ordinances, and statutes have been done away by Christ on the cross of Calvary. However, they contend that the moral law is God's method of leading a Christian into a life of holiness. Representative of this perspective, Reformed preacher D. Martyn-Lloyd Jones writes:

> "The Christian has been delivered from the curse of the law. But that does not release him from the law as a rule of life. Holiness means being righteous and righteous means keeping the law. The Ten Commandments and the moral law have never been abrogated."[1]

Similarly, Anthony Hoekema, a former professor at Calvin Theological Seminary, in Michigan writes:

> "The Christian life must be a law-formed life. Though believers must not try to keep God's law as a means of earning their salvation, they are nevertheless enjoined to

do their best to keep the law...the law is one of the most important means whereby God sanctifies us."[2]

The question naturally arises: What was the purpose of the Mosaic Law? And what does the New Testament teach concerning God's way to a holy life? Let's take a closer look at these questions.

THE PURPOSE OF THE LAW

The Mosaic Law gave unambiguous clarity and authority to God's timeless moral standards. God's holy principles had already been revealed in part from the time of Noah (Gen. 9:4-6). Naturally what was revealed in the law was in harmony with what God had said to the patriarchs. God's principles do not change. But now these rules would regulate all moral, civil, and ceremonial life in the nation of Israel. These standards were "holy, righteous, and good" (Rom. 7:12). God's ethical standards were incorporated in the Law of Moses that "every mouth may be closed, and all the world may become accountable to God" (Rom. 3:19). The ultimate purpose of the law was to demonstrate the exceeding sinfulness of sin and to be our tutor to lead us to faith in Christ.

Nevertheless, the cross of Christ brought an end to the obligation of the believer to the Mosaic Law in its entirety. Paul tells us that; "Christ is the end of the law for righteousness to everyone that believeth" (Rom. 10:4). The believer in Christ is no longer under the law, but under grace (Rom. 6:13), because the law only has power over a person when he is alive. Since the Christian has died and is risen in Christ, then the law has no more power over him. In the language of the New Testament, "Wherefore, my brethren, ye also are become dead to the law by the body of Christ and married to another, even to him who is raised from the dead, that we should bring forth fruit unto God" (Rom. 7:4). Although the Christian is no longer under the law, this does not mean he does not have a responsibility to meet the righteousness contained in the law.

Dispensationalists have long recognized that, except for the commandment to keep the Sabbath, all of the Ten Commandments are included in the New Testament instructions for believers. As a result, dispensationalists are concerned about following this biblical standard of morality. However, the New Testament never charges the believer to return to the Old Testament Mosaic system of law. The Holy Spirit's power is God's method of liberating and energizing the Christian to meet His holy standards. The Holy Spirit's controlling work in the Christian enables him not only to fulfill the righteousness of the law, but also to produce the fruit of the Spirit. Nevertheless, the righteousness of the law must be and is expected to be kept. How is this to be done if Christians are not under the Mosaic system? The New Testament teaches that, "...what the law could not do, in that it was weak through the flesh, God sending his own Son, in the likeness of sinful flesh, condemned sin in the flesh, that the righteousness of the law might be fulfilled in us, who walk not after the flesh but after the Spirit (Rom. 8:3-4). Of course, when the believer's actions and attitudes transgress the standards of the law, the Holy Spirit also condemns those actions and attitudes as sin. In this way, God's eternal moral standards of the Mosaic Law are repeated in the New Testament. This, however, does not make the Mosaic Law the believer's rule of life. This leads us to the issue of the Ten Commandments and the eternal moral law of God.

THE MORAL LAW AND THE TEN COMMANDMENTS

Reformed leaders, almost universally, contend that the Ten Commandments and the moral law of God are one and the same. They teach that the civil, ceremonial components of the Mosaic Law have passed away, but not the Ten Commandments. They suggest that the Ten Commandments are based upon the moral law of God. While it is true that the Ten Commandments, and indeed all of the Mosaic Law, are based upon the moral law of God, we must not make the mistake of equating the Ten Commandments with the moral law of God. Lake Superior, in Michigan, is a great body of water, but pales in comparison to the vastness of the Pacific Ocean, the greatest body of water on the earth. Likewise, we cannot compare the Ten Commandments with the moral law. God's law is eternal, higher, more glorious, and a fuller reflection of His nature than the Ten Commandments. This is seen in our Lord's teaching in the Sermon on the Mount when He said, "You have heard it said of old...but I say to you"... (Matt. 5:33-48) We may well ask what is the moral law of God? We may describe the Moral Law as the eternal principles of righteousness, reflecting the mind and heart of God. This law has always existed and is the essence of the will of God for all believers in every dispensation. Its standards are as high as the glory and character of God. This truth is seen in Paul's definition of sin when he writes, "For all have sinned and fall short of the glory of God" (Rom. 3:23).

Reformed leaders suggest that the Ten Commandments apply to Christians as fully as they ever did to Israel, and are still binding upon them. However, if the laws of the Ten Commandments are still binding, then all of the penalties must also be in force. The penalty of death was imposed for adultery, idolatry, Sabbath-breaking, and disobedience to parents. The death penalty was imposed on the first four of the Ten Commandments. To change a law's penalty is to change the law. A law without its penalty is only good advice. This is not merely theological hairsplitting, but is the very point of the Apostle Paul when he describes the Ten Commandments as "the ministration of death, written and engraved in stones" (2 Cor. 3:7). Strikingly, it is declared three times in 2 Corinthians 3:6-16 that the Mosaic system, including the Ten Commandments, is done away with or abolished (vv. 7, 11, 13). The participle used in each of these three verses is from the verb *katargeo*, which means to abrogate, to cancel, and to bring to an end. No stronger term could be used to describe the abolishing of the Mosaic Law. This word is also used to describe the destruction of the Antichrist in 2 Thessalonians 2:8. Since the day of Pentecost, the spiritual walk of the believer is no longer under any part of the Mosaic Law, but is to be in accord with the character of the Spirit of God. The negative precepts of the Ten Commandments have been replaced with the positive requirements of the ethics of heaven. The Christian is to "bring into captivity every thought to the obedience of Christ" (2 Cor. 10:5). Every step of his walk is to be by faith, "…for whatsoever is not of faith is sin" (Rom. 14:23), "for we walk by faith, not by sight" (2 Cor. 5:7).

Such a standard of life is as high as heaven itself and has never been perfectly attained, except by the Lord Jesus Christ Himself. Yet the failure to meet these requirements does not change or lower God's high standard. The ability to reach, in some measure, God's standard is only through the power and ministry of the Holy Spirit of God. We read, "…walk in the Spirit, and you shall not fulfill the lust of the flesh" (Gal. 5:16), and "but if you are led by the Spirit you are not under the law" (Gal. 5:18).

Laws are not identical simply because they are based upon the same moral principles. The passing away of the Mosaic Law does not mean the end of the eternal law of God. Only a divinely instituted theocracy could enforce the ten Mosaic laws with their death penalties, and no such government exists today. The moral law of God belongs to all ages and its authority extends to all. The infinitely high and holy demands of the moral law are more clearly seen in the New Testament than in the Old. The believer's standard of conduct is the standard of heaven (Col. 3:1). He is not without the law but under the "law of Christ" (1 Cor. 9:21), the "royal law" of love, and "the law of liberty" (Jas. 2:8).

THE LAW AND THE WESTMINSTER CONFESSION

The Mosaic Law is important to all, especially when we understand its purpose and place in biblical history. However, Calvinistic theology, due to its failure to see distinctions between Israel and the church and between law and grace, has sought to place the Christian back under the Mosaic Law. Calvinist leaders reason that if it can be proven that the Mosaic Law was in full force prior to the giving of the law then it follows that the Mosaic Law must be applied in every age. It has been suggested that the Mosaic Law, in the exact form as given to Moses, was also given to Adam in the Garden of Eden. This idea finds itself fully developed in the Westminster Confession, which was completed in 1649. In section 19, under the heading *The Law of God* we read the following statement:

"God gave to Adam a law, as a covenant of works by which He bound him and all his posterity to personal, entire, exact, and perpetual obedience, promised life upon the fulfilling, and threatened death upon the breach of it: and endued him with power and ability to keep it. This law, after the fall, continued to be a perfect rule of righteousness, and, as such, was delivered by God upon Mount Sinai..."3

Doctrinal words have doctrinal consequences, and these consequences can have far reaching implications. We would humbly suggest that there is neither Scripture nor any theological basis for such a dogmatic statement. Furthermore, such an interpretation will have broad theological and important practical consequences. The Mosaic system would detract from clear statements in the New Testament concerning the role of the Holy Spirit in the believer. It would touch on instruction in the New Testament concerning Christian liberty and the principle of grace.

Why would the 151 members of the Westminster Assembly, among which were 121 Calvinist scholars and theologians, include such an idea in this confession for believers? One important reason, among others, was the improper translation of 1 John 3:4, in the *1611 Authorized Translation,* which reads as follows: "Whosoever committeth sin transgresseth the law; for sin is the transgression of the law." Allow us to quote the words of Greek scholar and theologian John Nelson Darby on the translation of this verse:

"'Sin is the transgression of the law'. This is really, I must say, a wicked subjection of the Word to theology;

the word anomia is never used for 'transgression of the law' anywhere else in the English translation of the Holy Scriptures; another expression is parabasis nomou. I call it 'wicked,' because by it a human system denies what the Word of God carefully insists on. Not only so, but the word is rightly translated elsewhere 'without law'. Sin is not transgression of the law, to say so, universal as it may be, is a wicked anti-scriptural perversion. Sin is the evil nature, which produces lust, the enmity of the heart against God. It is written, 'sin by the commandment became exceeding sinful,' which could not be, if sin was not there before the commandment...It is a false theological perversion, and nothing else, and it is time that false theology gave way to the Word of God; for this affects the whole nature and character of Christianity."[4]

Calvinism reasons that if sin is the transgression of the law, and the law is the Mosaic Law, then when Adam sinned, it was the transgression of the Mosaic Law. If the Mosaic Law was in force in the Edenic time period, then should it not be also in force in the Church Age? However, can we build doctrine upon such reasoning? According to the wording of Scripture, the law was not given until the days of Moses. Paul writes, "As by one man sin entered the world, and death through sin, and thus death has spread to all men for all have sinned. For until the law, sin was in the world; but it is not imputed when there is no law. Nevertheless, death reigned from Adam to Moses..." (Rom. 5:12-14). Certainly, sin and its consequences were in the world prior to the giving of Mosaic Law. We must therefore conclude, based upon Scripture, that sin must not be solely defined as the transgression of the Mosaic law, but rather as the will of man in rebellion to God, as the outflow of a sinful nature.

However, we must return to 1 John 3:4 for a moment. If the translation of this verse is accurate, then we have Scripture in disagreement. On the other hand if there is a mistranslation, then Scripture is in complete harmony. Some suggest that this rendering may have been an accommodation to the leading Puritan politicians and theologians, who exercised great sway in that day.[5] A more literal and accurate translation of this verse is given to us by Dr. Alfred Marshall in his Greek-English Interlinear of the New Testament, "Everyone doing sin also does lawlessness, and sin is lawlessness." There is a broad theological gulf between the phrases "transgresseth the law," as given in the KJV, and the word "lawlessness," as given by the more literal versions. We would suggest that this verse has no reference to the law breaking of Adam in the Garden at all, but rather the self-will, enmity, and rebellion of man to God. This view seems to best harmonize both Scripture and doctrine. This now brings us to the subject of the law as the "rule of life" and sanctification of the believer.

THE LAW OF MOSES AND SANCTIFICATION

The New Testament makes it clear that a Christian is not under the law in regard to his salvation or sanctification. The law in its entirety, moral, civil and ceremonial, has been done away (Rom. 6:14, 15). Time and again the New Testament states that we "are not under law but grace." This truth includes our justification, sanctification, and the rule of life. What then, was the purpose of the law? The law was given to reveal sin. "What shall we say then? Is the law sin? God forbid. Nay, I had not known sin but by the law…" (Rom. 7:7). The law can "show sin to be exceeding sinful" (Rom. 7:13)! The law can condemn, penalize, and punish, but never make a Christian more holy. Just as our nation's system of law does not empower men to live moral lives, but punishes transgressors, so too, God's law cannot make a believer more holy, but reveals him to be a sinner. Paul states, in this same passage, that the law was designed for unregenerate man, that is, man "in the flesh," and not for a child of God (1 Tim. 1:9). The law awakens sin in sinful man. The law may be rightfully considered to be a rule of life for unregenerate man. Romans 7:5 sets forth this principle vividly, "For when we were in the flesh, the sinful passions, which were by the law, did work to bring forth fruit unto death." Commenting on this passage, John Nelson Darby gives needed insight to the rule of life for the Christian:

> "But we are not in the flesh, but in the Spirit, because the Spirit of God dwells in us. Hence, it does not look for a rule of life in the law, because that was a rule of life for a man in the flesh, a child of Adam (Rom. 7:5). And we have died to the law (Rom. 7:4) are delivered from it…we are partakers of the divine nature, and this has its full force by the Holy Spirit dwelling in us; by Him we know that we are in Christ…the rule of life then is Christ."[6]

The believer is not under the law for his salvation or for his sanctification. The book of Romans makes this principle exceedingly clear. The apostle Paul first presents the doctrine of justification in Chapters 3:21-5:11; and then in chapters 5:12-8:4 the doctrine of sanctification is expounded. Concerning the doctrine of justification, the apostle writes, "...a man is justified by faith apart from the deeds of the law" (Rom. 3:28). The law has no part in the justification of man. Then as he takes up the doctrine of sanctification in chapter six, he writes, "...for ye are not under the law but under grace" (Rom. 6:14). Here the law has no part in the sanctification of a believer. He is making it clear that the Christian is not under the law, including the Ten Commandments, for his sanctification. The way to be free from sin's power and dominion is through the grace of God and the cross of Calvary (Rom. 6:1-13), not through the law given to Moses at Sinai. In another place the apostle Paul writes, "I through the law died unto the law that I might live unto God" (Gal. 2:19). The believer is delivered from the law and its bondage through the death of the old life, as a man in Adam, under the dominion of sin, and is free and empowered to live for Christ. The Bedford prison's preacher-poet John Bunyan has written:

> "Run, run and do, the law commands.
> But gives me neither feet nor hands.
> Better news the grace-gospel brings.
> It bids me fly and gives me wings."

THE BELIEVER'S RULE OF LIFE

What then is the "rule of life" for a Christian? Where can he find the power to live a holy life? The Christian life is a dynamic, living relationship with the resurrected Christ. It is this power and life flowing out of the indwelling Christ that transforms the believer. The Spirit of God in the souls of men does not set the believer's affections upon ordinances, statutes and regulations, but rather fills him with a vital, living relationship with Christ. This love relationship so completely empowers the Christian that, with a holy desire, finds himself yielding to the holy and righteous requirements of God. The apostle Paul describes this spiritual phenomenon when he writes, "...that the righteousness of the law might be fulfilled in us, who walk not after the flesh, but after the Spirit" (Rom. 8:4). This powerful reality is surely the New Testament's teaching concerning our "rule of life." Listen to the apostle: "...for me to live is Christ" (Phil. 1:21); "looking unto Christ the author and finisher of our faith..." (Heb. 12:1-2); "the life I now live in the flesh I live by the faith of the Son of God..." (Gal. 2:20). We may conclude from these verses that our rule of life is not the law, but Christ and His death. Interestingly, the word "rule" in respect to living the Christian life only occurs once in the New Testament. In Galatians 6:16 we read, "as many as walk according to this rule." What is this "rule?" Just two verses earlier we read, "But God forbid that I should glory except in the cross of our Lord Jesus Christ, by whom the world is crucified unto me, and I unto the world" (Gal. 6:14). It is our focus upon Christ that is the "rule of life" for the believer. As a Christian is taken up with Him, he is transformed "from glory to glory" by the power of the Spirit of the Lord" (2 Cor. 3:18). This is the secret to power and holiness in the Christian's life.

C. H. SPURGEON AND THE RULE OF LIFE

It is noteworthy that this principle is recognized in reality, though not doctrinally, even by Reformed and Calvinist leaders to be God's way to power and effectiveness in the Christian life. Following the death of the Calvinist preacher Charles Haddon Spurgeon, Mr. William Olney, deacon for many years at the Metropolitan Tabernacle and a close friend of Spurgeon's, was asked, "What was the secret of Spurgeon's power?" Mr. Olney almost leaped out of his chair and with deep emotion said, "It was his personal love for Christ."[7] Was Mr. Olney familiar with the Reformed doctrine of the "rule of life?" Undoubtedly, he was. How forcefully, then, does this illustrate the reality of the New Testament doctrine of Christ, not the law, as the believer's "rule of life"!

ANTINOMIANISM AND THE BELIEVER'S RULE OF LIFE

Dispensationalists, who teach that Christ is the believer's rule of life, have been branded as unorthodox and unjustly accused of antinomianism. Reformed writers have incorrectly concluded that if dispensationalists have set aside the Mosaic Law as the rule of life, then they must be lawless in Christian life and conduct. Moreover, they charge that the standard of holiness has been lowered, thus corrupting the church of God. Certainly, nothing could be further from the truth; instead of debasing the standard of holiness in the church, this teaching has elevated it to a level higher than the law, to Christ Himself. In 1907, respected author and then president of Rochester Theological Seminary, Dr. Augustus Hopkins Strong, unjustly accused the so-called "Plymouth Brethren" of antinomianism in his book *Systematic Theology*.[8] Mr. H. A. Ironside, in the spirit of Christian love, silenced this unfounded criticism. Regarding this charge he wrote:

> "We are neither saved by the law, nor under it, as a rule of life; we are not lawless, but 'under law (enlawed) to Christ'. Is Christ Himself a lower standard than the law given at Sinai? This is not antinomianism, but it is the very opposite. It is subjection to Christ as Lord of the new dispensation and mediator of the New Covenant."[9]

How can obedience to Christ be a lower standard than the Mosaic Law? For Christ is the very source of the law. Is the moon a greater light than the sun, whose light it reflects? The Scriptures speak eloquently concerning this point. The Law of Moses commanded, "…thou shalt love thy neighbor as thyself" (Lev. 19:18); but the Lord says, "A new commandment I give unto you, that ye love one another; as I have loved you, that ye love one another"(Jn. 13:34). The New Testament urges, "He that saith he abideth in Him, ought himself also to walk even as He walked"(1 Jn. 2:6); and in another place we read, "Hereby perceive we the love of God, because He laid down His life for us: and we ought to lay down our lives for the brethren"(1 Jn. 3:16). Is this teaching lowering Christian character or enhancing it? How can this emphasis laid upon the imitation of Christ ever be considered a vice and not a virtue?

Conformity to the image of Christ, who is the highest measure of holiness, is God's way to a godly life. When He is our heart's desire and our love is upon Him, we will find our lives and character being daily transformed into His likeness. This is not a one-time crisis event, but a daily discipline; this is not holiness attained or perfectionism sought after; on the contrary, it is a humble heart and mind looking away from self unto Christ. W. E. Vine, Bible commentator and respected authority on the Greek New Testament, may have described the believer's rule of life best when he wrote:

> "'Sanctify in your hearts Christ as Lord' (1 Pt. 3:15). This is not an attainment to be reached by the Christian of mature experience; it is the daily, joyous rule of life for every believer."[10]

Endnotes

[1] D. Martyn Lloyd-Jones, *Sermon on the Mount*, (Grand Rapids, MI, Eerdmans Publishing, 1979), p. 179
[2] Anthony Hoekema, *Five Views of Sanctification*, (Grand Rapids, MI, Zondervan Publishing, 1987), p. 88
[3] Westminister Confession of Faith, Article 19 The Law of God, Westminster Presbyterian Church, Pittsburgh, PA, 2001
[4] J. N. Darby, *Collected Writings Vol. 23*, (Kingston-on-the-Thames, GB: Stow Hill Bible and Tract Depot), p. 307
[5] David Neff, "A Translation Fit for a King," Christianity Today, Oct. 22, 2001, p. 36)
[6] John N. Darby, *Collected Writings, Doctrinal, vol. 3*, (Kingston-on-Thames, GB: Stow Hill Bible and Tract Depot,), p. 176
[7] Richard Day, *The Shadow of the Broad Brim: The Life of C. H. Spurgeon*, (Chicago, IL, Judson Press, 1934), p. 227
[8] A. H. Strong, Systematic Theology, (Chicago, IL, Judson Press, 1907), p. 895-896
[9] H. A. Ironside, *The Teaching of the So-called Plymouth Brethren: Is it Scriptural?*, (NY, Loizeaux Brothers, 1930), p. 13
[10] Percy O. Ruoff, *W. E. Vine; His Life and Ministry*, (London, Oliphants LTD, 1951), p. 146

- 13 -
Reformed Theology and the Christian's Standing

There can be no greater joy for a believer than to know that through the work of Christ his standing with God is settled. He who was once an enemy of God is now a child of God. He, who at one time was at war with God, now has peace with God. The apostle explains, "Therefore, being justified by faith, we have peace with God through our Lord Jesus Christ, by whom also we have access by faith into this grace in which we stand" (Rom. 5:1-2). Our immutable standing with God is the position in which God now views us because of the finished work of Christ. We are justified, holy, children of God, kings and priests of God, we have unfettered access to God. All this and more is ours because of our standing in Christ. Deliverance from sinful conduct does not enhance our standing in Christ. And our standing in Christ should never be used in such a way as to excuse sin. Our standing is what we are in Christ, secured by the very power of God; therefore it can never suffer damage or loss. This standing, however, must be seen in distinction from our state, which changes day by day. Our state is the practical side of Christian life; it is the "living out" of the Christian life. Our standing is perfect, but our state is imperfect; this state is what we are in ourselves. Spiritual failure, sin, and disobedience are all common to our state. We must not be satisfied with our state, but we should seek to rise to the level of our standing in Christ. Yet at the same time, we should not condemn ourselves and engage in self-flagellation because of guilt of sin. For our salvation is never in doubt, and it is eternally secure because of our standing in Christ. This truth is extremely important in striking the proper balance in our spiritual life. Careless thinking in regard to this truth will have far-reaching spiritual consequences. Throughout the history of the church there have been those who have not fully appreciated the difference between a believer's state and standing.

REFORMED THEOLOGY AND SPIRITUAL CONSEQUENCES

Reformed theology has never clearly acknowledged the biblical truth of a believer's standing in Christ. The late professor of theology at Pittsburgh Theological Seminary and Reformed author Dr. John Gerstner illustrates this position when he writes,

> "The classic dispensational distinction is evidence of a persistent misunderstanding of the doctrines of justification and sanctification."

In another place Gerstner says,

> "...A man's standing is perfect before God, though his state may not be. This might seem to be the only traditional distinction between justification and sanctification, but it is not. In Reformed teaching this difference is one of fact...that is, according to the Reformed view, the justified person is not perfectly (positionally) sanctified."[1]

The Reformed view does not place an emphasis on the fact that a believer has a perfect position or standing in Christ. Rather, it teaches a striving after, a working for, and an achieving of a right position with God. Reformed doctrine stresses that a believer must not view his position before God as based upon what God has done (justification), but rather, by what one has demonstrated in his Christian life (sanctification). In this view, justification and sanctification seem to be so closely linked together as to make our standing in Christ fully dependent upon self-effort. The sad result is that the believer becomes increasingly more conscious of the indwelling sin nature and his personal failures, and has less confidence in the finished work of Christ. In time, this perspective often leads to somber introspection, doubt, and spiritual restlessness. Instead of affirming that a believer in Christ has an unshakable standing, Reformers sought to attain this standing through fasting, asceticism, and a rigorous discipline of the flesh. They soon discovered, however, that the flesh is incorrigible; it can never be improved. A prolonged focus upon the flesh in the believer's life can never lead to spiritual victory. The biblical focus is to yield to the sanctifying work of the Spirit in the believer's life. The Scriptures exhort us, "Walk in the Spirit and you shall not fulfill the lusts of the flesh" (Gal. 5:16). However, leaders of this doctrinal perspective from the 1700's down to the present day have suffered spiritually because of this crucial misunderstanding. This suffering arose out of the guilt from indwelling sin, which, in turn, cast doubt on one's eternal salvation. This resulted, in some cases, in heart-wrenching despair, and the unnatural desire for death, as a means of deliverance from the corruption of the sin nature. Listen to the voices of spiritual anguish, which were the result of setting aside the importance of our standing in Christ. One year before his death, in 1769, George Whitefield (1714-1770), the renowned eighteenth century evangelist wrote concerning an earlier time of great difficulty in his life:

> "I began to fast twice a week for thirty-six hours together, pray many times a day and received the sacrament every Lord's Day. I fasted myself almost to death all the forty days of Lent, during which I made it a point of duty never to go less than three times a day to public worship, besides seven times a day to my private prayers. Yet I knew no more that I was to be born a new creature in Christ Jesus than if I had never been born at all." On another occasion he writes, "The searcher of hearts alone knows what agonies my poor soul has undergone...the Lord has withdrawn Himself from me...I have sunk into deep despair, and like Elijah, I wish for death."[2]

Some Reformed leaders have laid such stress upon the elimination of all sin that it became the determining factor in whether one was a Christian at all. The clear distinction between standing and state, law and grace became hopelessly blurred. Representative of this perspective is William Law (1686-1761), the famed author of A *Call to a Devout and Holy Life* who writes:

> "Unless our heart and passions are eagerly bent upon the work of our salvation; unless holy fears lead our endeavors, and keep our consciences strict and tender about every part of our duty, constantly examining how

we live, and how fit are we to die, we shall in all probability fall into a state of negligence, and sit down in such a course of life as will never carry us to the rewards of heaven."[3]

This practice of excessive self-introspection often led the sincere believer to self-condemnation for the guilt of sin. Instead of a focus upon Christ and His finished work, the focus was directed toward self, sin, and personal failure. In time this practice became the source of an incurable spiritual plague withering the souls and spirits of men in the front lines for the cause of Christ. David Brainerd (1718-1747), a missionary to the Indians in New Jersey, wrote of this plague in his journal. He mourns:

> "My heart seemed like a nest of vipers, or a cage of unclean and hateful birds; and therefore I wanted to be cleansed of all sin...my sinfulness, the plague of my own heart...which often drove me to an impatient desire of death, a despair of doing any good in life: I would rather choose death than a life spent for nothing."[4]

Reformed theology lays such little stress on the finished work of Christ in a believer's life that the joy of our position in Christ is all but lost. There is a strange silence concerning the guilt of our sins blotted out forever, and condemnation ended forever. Reformed theology seems to almost encourage spiritual misery, dread and fear in the believer's life. The New Testament teaching that a believer is secure and his sins are removed completely, by virtue of his standing in Christ, is a truth that seems to be all but forgotten. This point is well illustrated in *Bunyan's Characters* by the Scottish Reformed preacher Alexander Whyte (1837-1921), of St. Georges West, Edinburgh, when he writes of the plague of the guilt of sin:

> "Our guilt is so great that we dare not think of it...It crushes our minds with a perfect stupor of horror, when for a moment we try to imagine a day of judgment when we shall be judged for all the deeds that we have done in the body. Heart-beat after heart-beat, breath after breath, hour after hour, day after day, year after year, and all full of sin; all nothing but sin from our mother's womb to our grave."[5]

Is this the hope of the believer in Christ? Are not all our sins forgiven? Is not our standing in Christ sufficient and able for every sin? Is this "miserable sinner Christianity" the Christianity of the Bible? We must in the strongest terms protest that it is not! Reformed theology seeks to establish the believer's standing in grace by the progress he has made in his state. The result in the lives of the most illustrative saints is misery, guilt, and despair. The word of God is clear we grow in grace not into grace (Rom. 5:1-2). C. H. Macintosh, author of *Notes on the Pentateuch*, carefully sets forth the inherent dangers regarding the Reformed point of view, when he writes:

> "We must not measure our standing by our state, but ever judge our state by our standing. Many err in reference to this, and their error leads to disastrous results. Hence, if a Christian set about measuring his standing by his state, he must be miserable, and his mental mis-

ery must be commensurate with his honesty and intelligence...there must be mental anguish if the standing is measured by the state."[6]

The Adversary of our souls longs to turn our eyes from all that Christ has wrought to that which we are in the flesh, from an immovable standing in Christ to a standing of shifting sand.

DISPENSATIONAL TRUTH AND THE BELIEVER'S STANDING

The believer's standing in Christ was first clearly taught by early dispensationalists as an important pillar in the foundation of biblical truth. Leaders of the so-called Plymouth Brethren were among the first to provide clarity in this area. Many were pleased to see biblical balance struck in this area at a time when Reformed theology was dominant. Leaders among the Church of England, Presbyterians, Baptists, and other denominations began to express their appreciation of this teaching. Watchman Nee, the Chinese church leader, looking back to this time in church history sums up the theological impact of this teaching when he writes:

> "They showed us how the blood of Christ satisfies the righteousness of God, our standing in Christ, the assurance of salvation...since church history began, there never was a period when the gospel was clearer than in that time."[7]

However, leaders from the Puritan and Reformed churches began to circulate papers largely critical of this teaching. Criticism came from such notable reformed leaders as C. H. Spurgeon, and later from theologians Dr. A. H. Strong and B. B.

Warfield, and in our own day from Reformed Baptist radio preacher John MacArthur, Dr. R. C. Sproul, and the late John Gerstner. Much of this criticism rises from a commendable zeal to stem the rising tide of antinomianism in the church. The critics charge that Dispensational theology fosters and advances antinomianism. Some opponents have accused dispensational leaders of not being true evangelicals and called the teaching of Dispensationalism a heresy. John MacArthur points to Dispensationalism as the primary reason for a growing permissiveness in the carnal living among Christians today. He writes:

> "It is undoubtedly also true that this idea of two classes of believers (carnal and spiritual, 1 Cor. 2:14-3:4) was an unfortunate extension of Chafer's dispensational perspective, a classic example of how Dispensationalism's methodology is carried too far."[8]

Leading dispensationalists such as J. N. Darby, D. L. Moody, Reuben Archer Torrey, Louis Sperry Chafer, and John Walvoord spent much of their lives vigorously fighting against every inroad of antinomianism. Those who knew them well would testify that they would never condone sin nor promote a worldly Christianity. Moreover, how can the work of Christ, which affords the believer a righteous position ever, be the cause of unrighteousness? Clearly, disobedience in Christians must never be ascribed to the work of Christ, but rather to the failure of the believer to avail himself of his rich spiritual resources in Christ. Is our standing in Christ a case of aberrant Dispensationalism carried too far or a gracious provision as taught in the word of God?

THE BELIEVER'S STANDING AND THE FLESH

The word of God tells us that the moment one trusts in the finished work of Christ, he is a child of God, a new creature in Christ (2 Cor. 5:17). The moment one places his trust in Christ, his standing is secure. Even as the moment a child is born in the family of a king, he becomes a prince; he may not yet behave in a princely manner, yet his standing is never in doubt because of his royal birth. In the same way, the Christian's standing in Christ is secure through regal birth. At his new birth, the Christian receives a new nature, a new relationship, and a new power. The new nature enables him to enter fully into his new relationship with Christ. Out of this vital, living relationship comes the strength to live a godly life.

THE CHRISTIAN'S STANDING AND THE FLESH

Our standing is not based upon a process of improving the flesh. It will never do to take the material of the "old man" and, through fastings, vigils, and religious discipline, attempt to make the corrupt flesh acceptable to God. Consider for a moment, the surprise of the owner of an old and dilapidated house who, on asking the builder how much it will cost to put it in shape, is told, "Oh, it won't cost very much at all," the builder explains, "because we can use all the old material." Similarly, in the things of God that just will not do. There must be a new start with altogether new material. The apostle explains further the purpose of God, "For what the law could not do, in that it was weak through the flesh, God sending His own Son, in the likeness of sinful flesh and for sin, condemned sin in the flesh" (Rom. 8:3). The flesh was disqualified and set aside as unusable, worthless for the purpose of God. Our standing is founded upon our new life in Christ. The believer's standing in Christ is based upon grace. The true estimate of a believer is not what we are in the flesh, but rather what we are in Christ by virtue of His grace. It is not what we are doing now, but rather what Christ has done on Calvary's cross. It is not what we think of ourselves, but what Christ thinks of us, that is of eternal consequence.

The apostle John counsels believers that the condemnation of our heart is a faulty compass and it is not to be trusted. He writes, "Beloved if our hearts condemn us, God is greater than our hearts, and knoweth all things" (1 Jn. 3:20). We may be like the thief on the cross, sentenced to be unfit to live on earth, but through His boundless grace, we are accepted in the Beloved (Eph. 1:6).

IS THE CHRISTIAN'S STANDING A PRESENT POSSESSION?

Reformed teachers have so stressed the guilt, the horror and plague of sin that it has inadequately emphasized the believer's standing as a present possession in Christ. This is one of the great shortcomings of Reformed theology. However, it is one thing for a non-Calvinist to make such a statement but it is a powerful indictment for one from their own camp to pointedly address this issue. J. Sidlow Baxter, the Reformed Baptist pastor and author writes,

> "Also, the more I reflect upon it, the surer I become that we cannot have a true disposition toward the New Testament teaching on holiness unless we have a discerning appreciation of our standing and privilege in Christ. Nobody thanks God more than I for the Protestant Reformation. Nobody glories more than I in its triumphal arch of the 'doctrines of grace,' with it

shining keystone, 'justification by faith.' Nobody marches more positively than I under the aegis of Luther and Calvin. Yet just because I march beneath the same banner I claim the same right to differ...the "miserable sinner" emphasis of the Reformers may be overdone to the point where it actually incapacitates our response...All the New Testament epistles were written to Christian recipients, and they all alike assume that the new Christian standing has fundamentally changed all the relationship of those who are "in Christ." The standpoint is not that we are seeking forgiveness but that we are already forgiven...we are not just seeking peace with God but we "have peace with God." May we never forget the New Testament emphasis that the Christian belongs to the new, in Christ, rather than the old, in Adam. It says that we already are saints, positionally, in Christ, and that we are to become saints of His in our character."[9]

A proper understanding of our standing in Christ will on one hand preserve us from legalism, and on the other from spiritual laxity. Christ, in His infinite grace, came and died in our place, paying the eternal punishment for our sins, and thereby satisfying perfectly the righteous demands of a holy God. Now God sees every believer in Christ; He has accepted them all because of the Beloved One; no one and nothing can ever touch this high and glorious position, which is ours through and because of Christ.

Endnotes

[1] John Gerstner, *Wrongly Dividing the Word of Truth*, (Brentwood, TN: Wolgemuth & Hyatt, 1991), 213, 240

[2] Arnold Dallimore, *George Whitefield*, (London, Banner of Truth, 1970,) 60, 401

[3] William Law, *A Serious Call to a Devout and Holy Life*, (Grand Rapids, MI, Eerdmans, 1977), p. 21

[4] Jonathan Edwards, *Life of David Brainerd*, (Grand Rapids, MI, Baker Books, 1978), 117

[5] Alexander Whyte, *Bunyan Characters, vol. 3*, (Edinburgh: Scotland,) p.136

[6] C. H. Macintosh, *Treasury: The True Workman*, (Neptune, NJ: Loizeaux, 1976), 490

[7] Dana Roberts, *Understanding Watchman Nee*, (Plainfield, NJ, Haven Books, 1980), p.16, 17

[8] John MacArthur, *The Gospel According to Jesus*, (Grand Rapids, MI: Zondervan, 1988), p. 25

[9] J. Sidlow Baxter, *A New Call To Holiness*, (London: Marshall, Morgan & Scott, 1967), 35-36

- 14 -
Reformed Theology and "One-Naturism"

Five days after the young Charles H. Spurgeon trusted Christ for salvation, and knew the blessing of the assurance of salvation, he also came to clearly see that he still possessed a sin nature. On the Sunday of his conversion he was filled with the joy and excitement of new life in Christ. But, on Friday he realized that he had some of the same sinful desires as he had before he was saved. He knew he was saved for eternity but the reality of the sin nature disturbed him.

On Sunday, he went back to the same little chapel where he was saved, eager to find an answer. The preacher that morning turned to Romans 7, and preached upon Paul's inner conflict with sin. Spurgeon felt that this message was surely for him. But then the preacher proceeded to say that this portion in Romans 7 referred to Paul before he was saved. Then he went on to say with great emphasis that, "no child of God ever felt any inner conflict." Young Spurgeon was so sure this was wrong that he left in the middle of the message never to return.

Some years later Spurgeon attended a conference, at which another preacher proclaimed that a Christian could reach the place of sinful perfection, where he no longer struggled with sin. The preacher went on to say this was true in his life. Spurgeon decided that he would see for himself, if this was, indeed, true. The next morning at breakfast, he quietly crept up behind this preacher while he was eating and poured an entire jug of cold milk on his head. It was quickly discovered by all that this man did indeed still possess a sinful nature.[1]

It is, indeed, true that we all possess the sin nature. This inner plague with its unholy urges and unrelenting power to draw into sin is not to be underestimated, for it is truly a formidable foe. Paul confesses, "I find then a law that, when I would do good, evil is present with me...O wretched man that I am! Who shall deliver me from this body of death?" (Rom. 7:21, 24). Scripture speaks carefully and in great detail about the conflict between our sinful nature and the new nature. However, some theological traditions have not always fully acknowledged the biblical distinction between the new nature and the sinful nature in the believer.

Reformed theology differs greatly from Dispensational theology in many respects, not the least of which is whether the believer possesses a sin nature. When an unbeliever trusts in the Lord Jesus Christ, God imparts His very life and moral nature within that individual. Despite a corrupt sin nature, Christians are enabled to experience a dynamic life for Christ through the indwelling new nature. This new nature cannot sin because it is born of God (1 Jn. 3:9). However, current Reformed theology argues vigorously that the believer cannot have both a new nature and the sin nature simultaneously. This, it is assumed, introduces an untenable spiritual contradiction within the believer, which causes confusion in the Christian life. This view, called "One-Naturism," is rapidly gaining adherents in Reformed circles and is also making inroads among those in other theological traditions. Two of the most notable non-reformed teachers to espouse this view are David C. Needham, of Multnomah School of the Bible, and popular author Neil Anderson.

IS THERE NO NEW NATURE IN THE BELIEVER?

Moreover, a growing number within current Reformed theology maintain that, at regeneration, the believer does not receive a new, divine nature, but simply a new human nature, which replaces the sin nature. According to this view, the believer does not have an old sin nature, nor does he have a new divine nature from God. This leads many to wonder how spiritual change can ever be wrought in man without a nature that is the expression of the moral, holy and spiritual nature of God. A popular Reformed author, Keith Mathison, explains this perspective:

> "It is therefore important to stress that God does not give us a divine nature when He regenerates us. He gives new life to our spiritually dead human nature. The result is a spiritually alive human nature, but not a divine nature. That cannot be overemphasized. If you have a divine nature, you are God. We must fight against any doctrine that teaches that man becomes divine."[2]

The Calvinist R. C. Sproul agrees that the new nature is no more than simply a new human nature. He writes:

> "Of course reformed theology agrees that regeneration is creative and that it results in a fundamental change in the individual. It involves a new nature. But this new nature is a new *human nature;* it is not a divine nature..."[3] (italics mine)

This growing minority of Reformed teachers mistakenly infer that the indwelling divine nature defies the believer; that is, the believer becomes a little god. The believer does not become God by partaking of the divine new nature; but rather, he shares in the spiritual or moral nature of God. Christians partake of the divine nature in the sense that they receive a disposition that is an expression of the holy nature of God. To espouse the view that a believer does not share in the divine nature is certainly foreign to Scripture. This is an unusual position, especially in light of the statement of Peter, "According as His divine power hath given unto us all things that pertain to life and godliness...Whereby are given unto us exceeding great and precious promises: that ye might be partakers of the divine nature" (2 Pt. 1:3-4). How is it then that we can possess the divine nature of God and not become gods? Dr. D. Edmond Hiebert, a commentator and authority on New Testament Greek, gives needed clarity to this issue when he writes:

> "In regeneration the believer does not cease being a human being; he does not become a little god. Through the implantation of a new nature by the indwelling Holy Spirit believers become partakers or sharers in the moral nature of God, enabling spiritual communion with God. This new life with its new attitudes and dispositions is none other than 'Christ in you, the hope of glory.'"[4]

What is the root cause of this misinterpretation of the Christian's spiritual nature? Some within the Reformed movement have failed to acknowledge the biblical distinction between the new nature received through new birth and the new man, that is regenerate man. At the moment of new birth

Don't Give Up The Day Job (Yet)!

Are you from a management, team leading, recruitment, sales, teaching, nursing or business background; honest, with complete integrity, looking for long term security, flexible working hours and to be paid what you are worth?

Are you looking for some or all of the following?

- **More time**
- **More money**
- **Financial freedom**
- **Good pension**
- **New Car**
- **To be successful**
- **To help others**
- **Be debt free**
- **Self development**
- **Meet new people**

I am from a professional background and looking for like minded people who wish to start their own home based business, initially 5 - 10hrs/wk, to achieve some or all of the above.

For FREE Information, please Call: 01908 520 377

(Serious Enquiries Only)

in Christ, a believer begins to enjoy new life in Christ and receives a new nature from God. The new man is the saved man, who is freed from the position of a slave to sin. However, the new nature is the moral character and nature of God, written in the heart of regenerate man. The new nature is in the new man, but it is not the new man; the two are vital, but yet distinct.

THE ONE-NATURE VIEW DEFINED

Among Reformed Bible teachers, the view that a believer does not possess a divine new nature is admittedly a minority view. In contrast, the Reformed view that a Christian does not possess an old nature has rapidly become the majority view. During the last fifty years, Reformed teachers have stepped forward, ardently stressing that believers do not possess an old sinful nature. They teach that the "old self," or, the "flesh" at regeneration ceases to be present in the body of the believer. The believer does not possess two natures, the old sinful nature and the new divine nature, but rather one nature received at conversion. Reformed Baptist author and preacher John MacArthur, from Panorama City, California, writes:

> "I believe it is a serious misunderstanding to think of the believer as having both an old and new nature. Believers do not have dual personalities...there is no such thing as an old nature in the believer."[5]

In another place he explains:

> "At new birth a person becomes a new creature; old things have passed away; behold, new things have come

(2 Cor. 5:17). It is not simply that he receives something new, but that he becomes someone new...The new nature is not added to the old nature, but replaces it. The transformed person is a completely new "I." Biblical terminology, then, does not say that a Christian has two different natures. He has but one nature, the new nature in Christ. The old self dies and the new self lives, they do not coexist."[6]

Most current Reformed teachers and theologians have embraced this unorthodox view. However, it must be noted that this view is of recent origin, and was not the view of the majority of Reformers from the time of the 1500's to our present century. In our present era Reformed professor Robert Dabney taught this view in the late 1800's and Reformed theologian B. B. Warfield espoused this view in his work *Christ Is Lord*. However, many observers trace this view's rise in popularity back to the 1940's to the teaching and writings of Professor John Murray (1898-1975), who was associated for many years with Westminster Seminary in Philadelphia. His writings were instrumental in influencing and molding the thinking of many of his contemporaries and of those who today are leading voices within the Reformed movement. It is noteworthy that many current writers, when defending this view often refer back to the writings of John Murray. Yet we must reiterate that this view is a new view; a view that was not held by the majority of the early Reformers, nor does leading Dispensational theologians hold it. Anthony Hoekema, a respected Calvinist theologian, who holds the one-nature view, candidly concedes that this view is new and was not held by the Reformers. He writes:

"On the question of these two selves, Reformed theologians differ. Most of them, particularly those who taught and wrote some years ago, hold that the old self and the new self are distinguishable aspects of the believer. Before conversion believers had an old self; at the time of conversion, however, they put on the new self-without totally losing the old self. Older Reformed teachers, such as Calvin, Herman Bavinck, Charles Hodge, and William Hendriksen, held the dual nature view."[7]

This issue is not merely an academic exercise, but one in which clear biblical thinking is needed. Right thinking in this issue will help to establish the believer concerning the doctrines of sin, sanctification of the believer, and the appropriation of our rich spiritual resources in Christ.

THE REFORMED DEFENSE OF THE ONE-NATURE VIEW

Current Reformed writers are convinced that this new view is rooted in New Testament teaching concerning the nature and spiritual constitution of the believer. The teaching found in the letters of the Apostle Paul is often used to buttress this view. The much-debated Chapter six of Romans, verses 1 through 12, is set forth as the foundation for "one-naturism." Again Anthony Hoekema, a leading proponent of this view, explains:

> "'For we know that our old self was crucified with Him, so that the body of sin might be rendered powerless, that we should no longer be slaves to sin' (Rom. 6:6 NASB). What does Paul mean here by the 'old self?' John Murray suggests that this expression designates

'the person in his unity as talking about a totality: the total person enslaved by sin-what we all are by nature.' That 'person enslaved by sin,' he is saying, was crucified with Christ. When Christ died on the cross, He dealt a deathblow to the old self we once were. Given the meaning of 'crucified,' Romans 6:6 states with unmistakable clarity that we who are in Christ, who are one with Him in His death, are no longer the old selves we once were."[8]

This view causes important questions to arise in our minds. Is the old nature or the old self now in some way removed from the believer by the work of Christ on the cross of Calvary? Do we now have but one nature? When we were crucified with Christ, what was it that took place in what the Bible calls our "old self?" Does the Bible teach that our old self, that is, our old nature, has been dealt such a death blow that this nature no longer exists? Or, on the other hand, should we understand our crucifixion with Christ to be a legal judgment upon our old manner of life? These and other questions need to be asked and thoughtfully considered as we look into this important issue. In the past, able Bible teachers have understood this "old self" that was put to death in Romans 6 to be our old manner of life, that is, all we were before we came to Christ by faith. The British commentator W. H. Griffith Thomas, a careful Bible expositor and one of the co-founders of Dallas Theological Seminary, gives added clarity to Romans 6:6 when he writes:

> "This is an important verse, and we must clearly distinguish between our 'old man', the 'body of sin' and 'we.' The first of these, 'our old man,' means 'our old self,'

what we were as unregenerate sons of Adam. It must not be identified with 'the flesh,' or 'our sinful nature.' The phrase occurs in Romans 6:6, Ephesians 4:22, and Colossians 3:9. The 'old man' ceased to exist at our regeneration, when it was 'put off.' We are never exhorted to 'put off' the 'old man.' A careful study of the three passages shows that it is regarded as in the past. An exhortation to 'put off the old man' would be tantamount to an exhortation to become regenerate."[9]

Traditionally, the understanding of the term "old man" has been the old manner of life. Bible teachers have expressed that this is the suitable view when all aspects of Bible interpretation are taken into account. Dr. John Walvoord, the former President of Dallas Theological Seminary, explaining the traditional meaning of the phrase "that our old man is crucified," writes:

"There is some confusion with the terms 'old man' and 'new man.' This problem can be resolved if it is understood that 'old man' and 'new' man are references not to the old or new nature, or self, but rather to the old manner of life, which is an expression of the old nature, and the new manner of life, which is an expression of the new nature. The NIV's translation of 'old man' as 'old self' in Colossians 3:9 can be questioned. As the subsequent context of this verse indicates, Paul is talking about our manner of life after being saved rather than our essential nature."[10]

In addition to Romans 6, current Reformed writers point also to Ephesians 4:22 and Colossians 3:9 in defense of their "one-nature" position. These two texts convey similar ideas, both speaking of "putting off" the old man and "putting on" the new man. Ephesians 4:22 says, "That you put off concerning the former conversation the old man…" and Colossians 3:9 says, "Seeing that you have put off the old man with his deeds." Reformed writers press the point that the Greek participle in Col. 3:9 is in the aorist tense, indicating past completed action; thus the putting off of the old man is something that occurred once for all in the past. They conclude that the old nature was done away with at the cross in the death of Christ; therefore, the believer does not possess an old sinful nature, but only a new nature in Christ. Anthony Hoekema writes:

> "Passages in Paul's epistles confirm this understanding of the death of the old self. Colossians 3:9-10, for example, teaches us also about the old and the new self. Paul here tells the Colossian believers not that they now should take off the old self and put on the new self, but that they have already done so! They made this change, then, at the time of conversion. The Greek participles are in the aorist tense, which describes snapshot action; Paul is referring to something these believers have done in the past."[11]

This reasoning may at first glance appear to be the proper approach to these passages. However, upon closer study, this view's weaker aspects become exposed. It is noteworthy that in the parallel passage, Ephesians 4:22, the verb "put off" is not in the aorist tense. Here Paul urgently charges believers to put off the deeds of the old man. This fact undermines the position that the sin nature in totality has been put away at the cross.

Anthony Hoekema himself admits this to be a powerful argument against his own view, writing:

> "Ephesians 4:20-24 is closely parallel but seems to offer some difficulty. The Greek text has three main infinitives translated in many versions as imperatives. Following this rendering, that passage would convey a command, which would indeed be inconsistent with the view just defended."[12]

Secondly, the verb "putting off" is seen by many New Testament Greek authorities as being in the imperative mood, indicating a command to urgency (Alford, Hendriksen). Therefore, according to Paul, Christians should be earnest about putting off the deeds that spring from the old man. Thirdly, it may not be accurate to conclude that because the verb "putting off" is in the aorist tense, this necessarily indicates snapshot, once-for-all action. The majority of Bible interpreters would agree that to lay all the weight of a view upon our understanding of the verb tense of a Greek participle in one particular passage alone is, at the least, unwise. The use of a word, the overall theology of the New Testament, and the context should determine the meaning. Respected Greek authority, W. E. Vine, takes a careful look at the New Testament usage and the aorist tense and concludes that the verb "putting off" (Col. 3:9) indicates continual action. He writes:

> "'Seeing that you have put off' is a translation of one word *apekdusamenoi,* an aorist participle, 'to put off.' Another, and likely, rendering of this one form is 'putting off.' This is the construction in Ephesians 4:22, 25.

That the tense is the aorist, of complete and decisive action, provides no reason for rejecting such a rendering, as even when there is a necessity for repeated action, the act should be complete on each occasion."[13]

Some have seen an apparent contradiction in these verses. If our old manner of life was put off at the point of conversion, why then does Colossians 3:9 instruct us to continually put off the old manner of life? Often times apparent contradictions can serve as choice opportunities to point out biblical truth. In this case, the answer is to be found in a clear understanding of the distinctions between the believer's position and his experience. It may be helpful to state it as follows: Positionally, our old man, our old manner of life was put off at the moment of conversion. But in our Christian experience, we should continually be putting off the old man and its deeds. This truth may have been stated best by C. I. Scofield:

> "It is at once evident that here in Ephesians 4:22 the phrase 'old man' occurs in relation to the believer's state; in Romans 6:6 it occurs in relation to the believer's standing. Positionally, therefore, the 'old man" is crucified; but experientially, the believer is to put off the "old man" and his ways."[14]

WHY DO BELIEVERS SIN?

Why do believers sin? This is the most difficult question for proponents of the "one-nature" view. However, for opponents of this one-naturism, it is one of their strongest arguments. If, as Reformed writers tell us, the old sinful nature no longer exists in a Christian and if believers have only one nature, our new nature in Christ which is not subject to sin and can't sin—then the logical question arises in our minds: why does a believer sin? Reformed teachers explain that, although the old sinful nature no longer exists in the Christian, the ingrained patterns and habits of the old life are, nonetheless, deeply imbedded into our minds; and it is these sinful patterns that cause sin in our lives. Popular author and conference speaker Neil Anderson, a former professor at Talbot Seminary in California, who, in the area of the believer's nature, has taken the Reformed position, explains why believers sin:

> "Where does sin mount its attack to keep me from doing what I really want to do? My flesh, my learned independence...residual effect of who I was in Adam, is no longer part of my true identity in Christ...Your flesh, that part of you which was trained to live independently of God...memories, habits, conditioned responses, and thought patterns ingrained in you. It is your responsibility to crucify the flesh by repatterning your old thoughts by allowing your mind to be renewed (Rom. 12:2)."[15]

With all due respect, we must differ and suggest that this novel view as to why a Christian sins strains logic and more importantly, is at odds with Holy Scripture. Firstly, allow us to consider the unreasonableness of this view. The ingrained patterns, habits, and responses of sin that are formed in a believer may account for sin in the lives of those who come to Christ at an older age, adults who have had time for sin to form deep-seated patterns in their lives. But how do we explain the sin in the lives of those who come to faith in Christ as young children.

Certainly, they have not had the same deeply ingrained sin patterns as older adults. Yet, by their own admission, they sin just as often, and in the same ways, as believers who come to Christ at a much older age. Furthermore, how does it explain new sins in the life of a believer as he becomes older? A person who has come to Christ at age ten, for example, does not have the ingrained patterns of drug abuse, adultery, fornication, and sexual immorality, yet in the lives of many believers who come to Christ at a young age, these sins do appear in their lives as adults. This view fails to logically explain the cause of sin in believers.

Also this view contradicts the testimony of Holy Scripture. What does the Bible say concerning why a believer sins? In addressing this very point, the Bible sets forth vividly the source of sin. James tells us, "But every man is tempted, when he is drawn away of his own lust, and enticed. Then when lust hath conceived, it brings forth sin: and sin when it is finished, brings forth death" (Jas. 1:14-15). Jeremiah adds, "The heart is deceitful above all things, and desperately wicked who can know it?" (Jer. 17:9). Then, Isaiah laments, "All we like sheep have gone astray, we have turned each one to his own way"… (Isa. 53:6) Paul, the apostle, confesses the reason for his sin, "…sin that dwells in me. For I know that in me (that is, in my flesh) dwells no good thing" (Rom. 7:17-18). Paul further explains, "I find then a law, that, when I would do good, evil is present with me" (Rom. 7:21). What, then, is the biblical reason for the cause of sin? The cause of sin is our old nature, that the Bible variously calls the "heart." or "his own lust," or "his own way," "sin that dwells in me," or "evil is present with me." We must, therefore, conclude that our sinful disposition, that is our sin nature, is the reason for our sin. We sin because we are sinners possessing a sin nature. We must not deceive ourselves into thinking that sinful living is the result of mere habits and ingrained thought patterns, and thereby miss appropriating to ourselves God's infinite resources for holy living.

THE CONSEQUENCES OF "REMNANT" VIEW

As we have seen, current Reformed theology states that believers do not possess a sin nature. However, they teach that the believer possesses merely the "remnants of original sin." These remnants are old memories, thought patterns, and ingrained habits. When one changes the focus of the cause of sin from the old sinful nature to the memories and ingrained patterns of our mind, the spiritual consequences will be significant. The emphasis for victory over sin will not be upon the Word of God, prayer, and yielding to the infinite power of the Holy Spirit. The new emphasis will be upon the "mind," "old thinking," "memories," and "conditioning." It is taught that as the Christian controls his thoughts and re-conditions his old thinking, the result will be victory over sin. Popular author Neil Anderson explains,

> "When individuals come to Christ, their minds are still programmed to live independent of God. There is no "delete" or "clear" button that can be pushed to get rid of old thinking patterns; hence, the need to renew (reprogram) their minds. If the strongholds in your mind are the result of conditioning, then you can be reconditioned by the renewing of your mind. Anything that has been learned can be unlearned. Certainly this is the major path in the New Testament."[16]

According to this new view, victory over sin is now predominantly mental and not spiritual. Godliness, we are told, is to be, for the most part, the result of self-discipline and self-control. Reformed writer Jay Adams has written about this approach in the book *Godliness Through Discipline*. The emphasis is upon the "psyche" and old habits, leading the Christian to look inward instead of looking upward at the finished work and spiritual resources of Christ. The full and sufficient spiritual resources are set aside and the principles of mind control, behavior modification, and psychology are set in its place. The Christian is offered the empty promises of re-conditioning and re-programming of the mind. These techniques of mind control, albeit couched in evangelical terminology, are more similar to the new age philosophies than to the sound doctrines of the Word of God. This view also gravely underestimates the unyielding conflict of the flesh against the spirit. Spiritual warfare is not a series of special Christianized psychological techniques, but rather the Christian's daily battle to die to self and live for Christ. This new system of spiritual victory exchanges the spiritual resources in Christ for resources of mind control, re-programming, and re-conditioning.

OUR SIN NATURE WILL BECOME PROGRESSIVELY WEAKER

Reformed theology teaches that although the sin nature is no longer present within the believer, the "remnants of original sin" are present. These remnants are the former patterns of thinking and old sinful habits. Therefore, it is taught that as the Christian matures in Christ, the grip of these fleshly habits will become less and less. Reformed theologian John Gerstner explains,

> "The Spirit of God continues to work faith in the regenerate and they therein persevere in good works, always struggling against the remnants of their original sin whose guilt is pardoned but whose power is decreasingly felt until destroyed at death."[17]

In like manner, Robert L. Dabney, the Reformed theologian and former professor of Systematic Theology at Princeton, writes,

> "...And if the old nature never loses any of its strength until death...if then any professed believer finds the 'old man' in undiminished strength, this is proof that he has never put on the new man."[18]

Is this true? This again may at first glance appear to be innocent Christian teaching. However, under closer examination, this too fails to meet the requirements of Scripture. One of the best ways to examine this teaching is to examine the life of the Apostle Paul. All Christians would agree that the Apostle Paul should be held up as an example of a mature believer, one who has certainly progressed in the faith. If this doctrine of a lessening of the pull of the flesh in the experience of mature believers were true, then we would see it evident in the life of the apostle. However, the very opposite is seen, for we read in Romans:

> "For I know that in me (that is, in my flesh,) dwelleth no good thing: for to will is present with me, but how to perform that which is good I find not. For the good that I would I do not: but the evil that I would not, that I do. Now if I do that I would not, it is no more I that do it,

but sin that dwelleth in me. I find then a law, that, when I would do good, evil is present with me (Rom. 7:18-21)."

The Apostle Paul clearly expresses the working of the flesh as an integral part of his Christian experience; and instead of a lessening and diminishing of the power of the sinful nature, it is seen in all its evil strength. It is pulling, tearing, and striking at the apostle in its attempts to bring him to sin. Instead of language that would indicate the simple workings of the "remnants of original sin," old habits, and thought patterns that are lessening in this mature saint of God, we read:

> "But I see another law in my members, warring against the law of my mind, and bringing me into captivity to the law of sin that is in my members. O wretched man that I am! Who shall deliver me from the body of this death?" (Rom. 7:23-24)

We see that as a Christian progresses in maturity and spiritual growth, his old nature continues to assail him with sinful desires. The old nature can never be reformed or changed. However, by yielding to the indwelling Spirit of God, and taking up the weapons of prayer and the Word of God, the urges and temptations of the old nature can and will be resisted. This is the biblical path to victory over sin.

However, victory over sin does not mean the elimination of the tenacious pull of our sin nature. In fact, the very opposite will be discovered to be true. How can this be? Men and women of God through the centuries of the church have testified that the closer we walk with God and the further we mature in holiness, the more sensitive we become to the power and pull of the flesh and the more grieved we are because of it. This is the experience of the apostle in Romans 7, and it is the experience of all men and women of God. To teach otherwise is to offer an empty and false hope, which will certainly lead to discouragement and despair. Such self-deception concerning our sin nature will leave us unprepared in resisting, through the power of the Spirit, the grip and urgings of our sinful flesh. The flesh is incorrigible, it cannot be improved and it cannot be reformed. John Nelson Darby (1800-1882) was once asked in a debate with theologian Thomas Steele, of Boston, if he felt that since he became a Christian he had progressed in conquering the flesh. The biographer of Darby, Mr. W. G. Turner, comments on Darby's reply during the debate, writing,

> "In response to the question that was once put to Mr. Darby, he said his nature, or old man, had been growing worse and worse ever since he believed in Christ."[19]

This candid answer, at first glance, may surprise us. However, as we look closely at Darby's response, it surely illustrates the experience of every sincere believer in Christ. Does our old sinful nature grow worse and worse? Of course not. But to the saints of God who follow hard after God and linger long in His holy presence, it seems as if it has grown worse. Doubtless, it is an arrogant Christian who is able to say that he has made progress in eliminating the desires of his sinful old nature. Do we struggle against only the "remnants of our original sin?" The clear testimony of Scripture argues to the contrary. Do mature saints of God experience a lessening of the firm grip of the old sinful nature? Again, the Scripture and the testimony of men and women of God would certainly deny this unequivocally. The believer in the Lord Jesus Christ has both an old and new nature, and within these two natures there is a spiritual struggle. There are divine resources that supernaturally enable the believer to live a victorious life in Christ. The apostle Paul knew something of these resources, for he wrote, "...who shall deliver me from the body of this death? I thank God through Jesus Christ our Lord" (Rom. 7:24-25). May we, like the apostle, begin to appropriate the fullness of our spiritual resources in living victoriously and joyously for Jesus Christ, our Lord.

Endnotes

[1] Charles H. Spurgeon, *Autobiography: The Early Years 1834-1859, Vol. 1.*, (Edinburgh: Banner Of Truth Trust, 1962), p. 100
[2] Keith Mathison, *Dispensationalism, Wrongly Dividing The People of God*, (Phillipsburg, NJ: P & R Publishers., 1995) p. 82
[3] R. C. Sproul, *Willing to Believe*, (Grand Rapids, MI: Baker Books, 1997), p. 198
[4] D. Edmond Hiebert, *Second Peter and Jude*, (Greenville, SC: Unusual Publications, 1989) p. 48
[5] John MacArthur, *Freedom from Sin—Rom. 6-7*, (Chicago, IL: Moody Press, 1991), pp. 31-32
[6] John MacArthur, *Ephesians*, (Chicago, IL: Moody Press, 1987) p. 164
[7] Anthony Hoekema, *Five Views on Sanctification*, (Grand Rapids, MI: Zondervan, 1987), p.78
[8] Anthony Hoekema, *Five Views on Sanctification*, (Grand Rapids, MI: Zondervan, 1987), p.79
[9] W. H. Griffth Thomas, *Romans*, (Grand Rapids, MI: Eerdmans Publishing Company, 1946), p. 167-168.
[10] John Walvoord, *Five Views on Sanctification*, (Grand Rapids, MI: Zondervan, 1987), p.100-101
[11] Anthony Hoekema, *Five Views on Sanctification*, (Grand Rapids, MI: Zondervan, 1987), p.79

[12] Anthony Hoekema, *Five Views on Sanctification,* (Grand Rapids, MI: Zondervan, 1987), p. 80
[13] W. E. Vine, *Philippians and Colossians,* (London: Oliphants Limited, 1955), p. 179
[14] C. I. Scofield, *Scofield Correspondence Course,* (Chicago: Bible Institute Colportage Association, ND), p. 1222
[15] Neil Anderson, *Victory over Darkness,* (Ventura, CA: Regal Books, 1990), p. 83-84, 75, 45-4
[16] Neil Anderson, *Common Made Holy,* (Eugene, OR: Harvest House Publishers, 1997, 150-151, Neil Anderson, *Victory over Darkness,* (Ventura, CA: Regal Books, 1990), p. 167-168
[17] John Gerstner, Dispensationalism, Wrongly Dividing the Word of Truth, (Wolgemuth & Wyatt, Brentwood, TN, 1991), p. 147
[18] Robert L. Dabney, quoted in John MacArthur, *Vanishing Conscience,* (Waco, TX, Word, 1995), p. 219
[19] W. G. Turner, *John Nelson Darby,* (London: C. A. Hammond, 1951), p. 15

- 15 -
Reformed Theology and the Righteousness of Christ

In the late 18th century a group of intrepid British Dispensational leaders began to raise their voices in uncompromising opposition to, what seemed to many, an established doctrine of the church. This doctrine was called the "Imputation of the Active Obedience of Christ." This doctrine was so accepted at the time that few imagined that it could be challenged. It was a doctrine that grew out of the Reformation period and was first articulated in the writings of Reformers John Calvin and Martin Luther. But when British Dispensationalists such as J. N. Darby and William Kelly opposed this doctrine on biblical grounds, they were bitterly denounced as unorthodox and even heretical. At that time, a book by William Reid called *Heresies of the Plymouth Brethren* was issued as an attack on these Dispensationalists; and Dr. Robert Dabney set forth a similar attack in a work called *Theology of the Plymouth Brethren* in 1891. However, in the years to follow and up to the present day, leading evangelicals have concluded that this Reformed doctrine of imputation was not based upon the bedrock of the Word of God, but rather on the shifting sand of human reason. Today, this doctrine is not generally accepted among evangelicals; in fact, there are few serious-minded Christians who would even be familiar with it. Reformed writer Dr. R. C. Sproul laments that among present-day evangelicalism this doctrine is largely unknown and overlooked.[1] However, in recent years there has been a growing interest in this doctrine due to the popularity of Reformed theology.

WHAT IS SALVATION BY THE "OBEDIENCE" OF CHRIST?

Reformed theology, since the time of the Reformers, has taught that Christ provided a two-fold foundation for justification. It has been asserted that our Lord's sufferings from His birth until His death were His "active obedience" and His sufferings and death on the cross set forth Christ's "passive obedience." These two aspects combine to form the basis for the believer's justification. All evangelical Christians affirm that Christ's death on the cross is the biblical foundation for justification. However, Reform theology insists that the obedience and sufferings of Christ prior to the cross are essential for our salvation. Calvinism affirms that the death of Christ, His "passive obedience," dealt with our guilt, while the merits in the life of Christ, his "active obedience" provides for our justification. Reformer John Calvin, in his most important theological work, *The Institutes of Christian Religion,* sets forth this view:

> "...When it is asked how Christ, by abolishing sin, removed the enmity between God and us, and purchased a righteousness which made him favorable and kind to us, it may be answered generally, that he accomplished this by the whole course of his obedience. This is proved by the testimony of the Paul, 'As by one man's disobedience many were made sinners, so by the obedience of one shall many be made righteous' (Rom. 5:19). And indeed he elsewhere extends the ground of pardon which exempts from the curse of the law to the whole

life of Christ, 'When the fullness of the time was come, God sent forth his son, made of a woman, made unto the law, to redeem them that were under the law' (Gal. 4:4-5). Thus even at his baptism he declared that a part of righteousness was fulfilled by his yielding obedience to the command of the Father. In short, from the moment when he assumed the form of a servant, he began, in order to redeem us, to pay the price of deliverance..."[2]

The implication of what Calvin is saying must not be lost on us. It is not the death of Christ alone that redeems and justifies; it is also the sufferings and obedience that Christ endured during His life prior to the cross. Every act of obedience, as a child, was redeeming, every drop of blood shed, in early manhood, was atoning, in every act of obedience from the time He assumed the form of a servant, from the time of His birth, he was "paying the price of deliverance." At times, so much weight is given to the redemptive work in the life of Christ by Reformed authors, that one wonders why the death of Christ was necessary at all. Some Reformed writers press this issue so much so that they attribute a redemptive quality to specific events in the life of Christ. The hymn writer and Reformed theologian Horatius Bonar details events in Christ's life that he considers to be redemptive sufferings prior to the cross. He writes:

> "Christ's vicarious life began in the manger...there his sin-bearing had begun...when He was circumcised and baptized it was as a substitute...and He was always the sinless One bearing our sins..."[3]

As alarming as this may seem to many serious Bible students, this Reformed position of justification persists to our present day. The popular Reformed theologian R. C. Sproul has set forth this view in the most extreme terms. He asserts that the cross alone was insufficient, for the death and the life of Christ are on equal footing in the work of justification and redemption. Therefore, without the redemptive work in the life of Christ, the death of Christ could not justify the believer. He writes:

> "The cross alone, however, does not justify us...We are justified not only by the death of Christ, but also by the life of Christ. Christ's mission of redemption was not limited to the cross. To save us He had to live a life of perfect righteousness. His perfect, active obedience was necessary for His and our salvation...We are constituted as righteous by the obedience of Christ which is imputed to us by faith."[4]

Christ's holy and spotless life is of great interest to those who are spiritually minded. Contemplation of His perfections displayed prior to the cross evokes true worship, for worship does not arise from our appreciation of His death alone but also from consideration of all that He was in Himself and for the pleasure of God (Matt. 17:5). This is not to say that His life contributes directly to our redemption. Rather His Holy character was something essential to His own nature as well as qualifying Him to become the sacrificial Lamb. For God made it clear in the establishment of the Passover that "your lamb shall be without blemish and without spot" (Ex. 12:15) and Peter confirms that He fulfilled this divine requirement (1 Pt. 1:19). His holiness was, as we have said, essential to Him personally but it is not vicarious or made over to us in some way. The Gospel is not that Christ lived His life for our benefit but that He "died for our sins...was buried and rose again" (1 Cor. 15:3, 4).

Rreformed Arguments Examined

Reformed theologians struggle to find clear and unambiguous biblical support for this view of justification. However, one verse that is consistently quoted by Reformed writers is Romans 5:18, "Therefore, as by the offense of one judgment came upon all men to condemnation, even so by the righteousness of one the free gift came upon all men unto justification of life." Reformed writers understand the phrase "by the righteousness of one" to mean the righteous, obedient, and law-keeping acts in the life of Christ prior to the cross. This righteousness, it is theorized, becomes imputed to us by faith. However, is this what Romans 5:18 teaches? Does the phrase "righteousness of one" refer to His life or to His once for all death on the cross? William MacDonald provides needed clarity on this point when he writes:

> "The righteousness of Christ mentioned in Romans 5:18 does not mean His righteousness as a Man on earth or His perfect keeping of the law. These are never said to be imputed to us. If they were, then it would not have been necessary for Christ to die. The *New American Standard Bible* is on target when it translates: 'So then as through one transgression there resulted condemnation to all men, even so through one act of righteousness there resulted justification of life to all men.' The 'one act of righteousness' was not the Savior's life or His

keeping of the law, but rather His substitutionary death on Calvary's cross."[5]

A careful reading and study of this verse shows that the word "righteousness" (Gr. *dikaioma*) should be rightly rendered "act of righteousness." It refers to that which was accomplished at His death, and stands in contrast to righteousness as a quality. The discussion in verses 8-10 of the same chapter cast further light on the fact that it is a reference to the death of Christ. Moreover, the Word of God never teaches that we are justified by the righteous life of Christ, but rather by the righteous act of Christ on the cross, which permitted God to pour out His wrath against sin.

WHAT ARE THE BIBLICAL IMPLICATIONS?

Every careful student of the Scriptures should be concerned about this teaching. At the very outset, this Reformed view of justification opposes the very tenor of New Testament teaching on justification. The New Testament repeatedly states that the basis of justification is found, not in the life of Christ, but in His death; and that justification was not through numerous events in the life of Christ, but by one event, namely, the death of Christ. The sheer weight of the biblical record should make us pause. We read, "For Christ once suffered for sins, the Just for the unjust, that He might bring us to God, being put to death in the flesh..." (1 Pt. 3:18); "...being justified by His blood we shall be saved from wrath through Him" (Rom.5:9); "So Christ was once offered to bear the sin of many..."(Heb. 9:28). Moreover, the gospel writers make it very clear that up to the time of the suffering of Christ on the cross, our Lord did not "drink the cup" of God's wrath and become the sin-bearer. The righteous

God did not forsake the Son prior to the cross. The Son, prior to the cross, never uttered the awful lament, "My God, my God why has thou forsaken Me." (Mk. 15:34) The cross of Christ was the only place where the holy God poured out His unreserved and righteous judgment against sin. There the Holy God poured out His unmitigated wrath without mercy, that we might receive the infinite mercy of God without wrath. In this regard our Lord states, "Now is my soul troubled; and what shall I say? Father save Me from this hour. But for this cause came I unto this hour " (Jn. 12:27). Is not Scripture exceedingly clear that it was upon the cross that our Lord suffered for our sins and bore the wrath of God against sin?

There is yet another serious consequence of this Reformed doctrine of justification. This doctrinal perspective turns the salvation through the grace of God into a works-salvation through a focus on the keeping of the Mosaic Law. The Scripture is very clear on this point; no one shall ever be saved by keeping the law. Paul unequivocally proclaims, "...to him that worketh not, but believeth on Him that justifieth the ungodly" (Rom. 4:5); "...no man is justified by the law in the sight of God" (Gal. 3:11); "knowing that a man is not justified by the works of the law, but by the faith of Jesus Christ..."(Gal. 2:16). Nevertheless, in the Reformed view of justification, we are instructed that we are reckoned righteous by the keeping of the law. However, there is an unusual twist; it is not our individual law-keeping that justifies, us but that of Christ who kept the law representatively for us, so His merits of keeping the law are imputed to us. Notice the words of respected author and Reformed theologian Dr. J. I. Packer:

"In classical (Reformed) Protestant theology the phrase 'the imputation of Christ's righteousness,' means, namely, that believers are righteous and have righteousness before God for no other reason than that Christ, their head, was righteous before God, and they are one with Him, sharers of His status and acceptance. God justifies them by passing on them, for Christ's sake, the verdict that Christ obedience merited. God declares them to be righteous because He reckons them to be righteous; and He reckons righteousness to them, not because He accounts them to have kept His law personally, but because He accounts them to be united to the one who kept it representatively."[6]

Christian righteousness begins with the death and resurrection of Christ. The risen Christ Himself is our righteousness, not Christ fulfilling the law in our place. The Christian's connection to the law is broken through the death and resurrection of Christ. The apostle Paul in Romans 7 expands upon this important theme. The law's power is only in force as long as a person is alive, or in the words of the apostle, "Law has dominion over a man as long as he liveth" (Rom. 7:1). Paul then sets forth our complete deliverance from under the law when he says that those who were under the law were made dead to the law by the death of Christ, that they might be joined to another, to Him that was raised from the dead (Rom. 7:1-6). A dead man is not subject to civil or religious law; in like manner, the believer is not subject to the Law of Moses because he is dead and risen in Christ. Therefore, to those who believe on Christ, the law has lost its authority to bring either condemnation or righteousness through the obedience of Christ. Paul finally concludes this argument in Romans by writing, "For Christ is the end of the law for righteousness to every one that believes" (Rom. 10:4). If the law is powerless to make righteous, what then is the true character of justification? Justification is the declaration by God unto us of a high and measureless righteousness, in that the whole value of the death of Christ was credited to the believer by faith, irrespective of the law, according to grace. Through the resurrection of Christ the believer now has a new standing in the risen Christ in glory (Rom 4:25). Dispensational scholar William Kelly beautifully describes the basis and character of the righteousness of God through Christ when he writes:

> "Had Christ only kept the law, neither your soul nor mine could have been saved much less be blessed as we are. Whoever kept the law; it would have been a righteousness of the law, and not God's righteousness, which has not the smallest connection with obeying the law. Because Christ obeyed unto death, God brought in a new kind of righteousness—not ours, but His own favor. Christ has been made a curse upon the tree; God has made Him sin for us that we might be the righteousness of God in Him."[7]

John Nelson Darby sets forth the important connection between the resurrection of Christ and our new standing in Him. He writes:

> "What I deny is the doctrine that, while the death of Christ cleanses us from sin, His keeping the law is our positive righteousness; and that His keeping the law is imputed to us as ourselves under it, and that law keep-

ing is positive righteousness. I believe that Christ perfectly glorified God by obedience even unto death, and that it is to our profit, in that, while His death has canceled all our sins, we are accepted according to His present acceptance in God's sight...being held to be risen with Him, our position before God is not legal righteousness, or measured by Christ's keeping the law, but His present acceptance, as risen...and we accounted righteous according to the value of His resurrection."[8]

THE IMPORTANCE OF THE CROSS OF CHRIST

Moreover, the death of Christ must never be trivialized. If Christ's keeping the law could justify, if it was truly vicarious, then why did Christ die? Understandably, the Reformed Christian would raise his vigorous objection. He would strongly argue that the death of Christ was truly needful and essential for our salvation. This sincere objection is noted and respected. However, the most serious question still remains unanswered. If, as the Reformed view suggests, justification comes through the law, since Christ was fully obedient to the law in every respect, and if the merits of Christ's righteous life were as truly redemptive as the death of Christ, then why did Christ die? Reformed theology strongly asserts that the obedience and righteous merits of the life of Christ are as truly redemptive as the death of Christ. The respected Reformed theologian Archibald Alexander Hodge explains:

> "The Scriptures teach us plainly that Christ's obedience was as truly vicarious as was his suffering, and that he reconciled us to the Father by the one as well as by the other."[9]

If this is all true, why did Christ have to die? Why do Old Testament prophetic passages such as Isaiah 53 and Psalm 22 speak of the necessity of the death of the Messiah? Reformed theology has never given a satisfying answer to this important question. Reformed writers, due to the influence of Covenant theology, do not see a distinction between righteousness through the law in the Old Testament and righteousness through Christ death alone in the New Testament. Covenant theology fails to see significant distinctions between earthly Israel under the law and the New Testament church. Therefore, it suggests a doctrine of righteousness through the co-mingling of both law and grace. This will never do. God has set aside righteousness according to the law and has brought in something altogether new. The law came by Moses, but grace and truth through our Lord Jesus Christ. The cross of Christ must stand at the forefront and alone in any theology of righteousness. Therefore, it must be stated with great earnest that the death of Christ, without dispute, was necessary. Any attempt to minimize or lessen its importance and its efficacy must be vigorously resisted. Respected Bible commentator John Ritchie has well summarized the Reformed view of justification and the phrase "the righteousness of Christ." He writes:

> "The theological phrase, 'The righteousness of Christ,' so much used, is not a scriptural term. The meaning usually read into it is, that the sinner having failed to keep the law, Christ has kept it for him, that His obedience is counted man's righteousness, and put on all that believe as a 'robe.' But this would not be 'righteousness apart from law' (Rom. 3:21). If God reckons the sinner to have kept the law because Christ kept the law for him,

then righteousness surely comes by law, and the death of Christ was 'in vain' (Gal. 2:21). In all this, justification by grace through redemption has no place. The gospel is not that a sinner is made righteous by the imputation of Christ's legal obedience on earth, and saved by His death, but rather that 'being now justified by His blood, we shall be saved from wrath through Him.'" [10]

We must reject the conclusions of otherwise biblically sound believers that the law keeping of Christ justifies, redeems, and reconciles. We must set aside the recent statements of Reformed theologian R. C. Sproul who states that "the cross alone, however, does not justify us..."(*Faith Alone,* p. 103) and that of Dr. D. James Kennedy who commented, "We are clothed in His righteousness alone...his perfect obedience provides our righteousness. This is all that is needed, and nothing less will suffice" (*Is Jesus the Only Way to God,* Coral Ridge Ministries, p. 8-9 undated). The Scriptures are clear and definitive on this point that no one is partially redeemed or justified in any degree by keeping the law.

However, this is not to say that the New Testament is silent concerning the glories and perfections of the life of Christ. Without question, our beloved Lord fully and completely satisfied the demands of God's holy law during His earthy life. His obedient life was necessary to manifest the glories of God in Christ to the world and to His disciples. The Lord Jesus Christ lived a life of obedience as none other had ever lived, or will ever live. He always did that which pleased His Father (Rom. 15:3). No word that He spoke ever needed to be withdrawn, for he never spoke rashly or in exaggeration. No action of our Lord ever required apology, for our Lord never wronged another man. No thought or deed of our Lord's ever needed confession, for He never sinned or transgressed the law of God. Our Lord never asked advice of another during His earthly ministry, for He was ever the all-wise and omniscient God. However, none of these perfections and glories of our Lord ever justified or redeemed man from a single sin. For it was only the matchless and infinite work of our Lord upon the cross of Christ that can redeem. New Testament scholar W. E. Vine summarizes the relationship of the earthly life of our Lord and His death upon the cross when he writes:

> "Neither the incarnation of the Son of God, nor His keeping of the law in the days of His flesh availed, in whole or in part, for the redemption of men... His redemptive work proper began and ended on the cross; ...Hence it is nowhere said in the New Testament that Christ kept the law for us. Only His death is vicarious, or substitutionary. He is not said to have borne sin during any part of His life; it was at the cross that He became the sin-bearer."[11]

Endnotes

[1] R. C. Sproul, *Faith Alone,* (Grand Rapids, MI: Baker Books, 1997), p. 103
[2] John Calvin, *Calvin's Institutes, vol. 2,* (Grand Rapids, MI: Eerdmans Publishing Company, 1962), p. 437
[3] Horatius Bonar, *The Everlasting Righteousness,* (London: J. Nisbet & Co., 1879), p. 26, 27, 29, 32
[4] R. C. Sproul, *Faith Alone,* (Grand Rapids, MI: Baker Book House, 1995), p. 104
[5] William MacDonald, *Justification by Faith* (Romans), (Kansas City, KS: Walterick Publishers, 1981), p. 62

[6] J. I. Packer, Justification, in *Wycliffe Dictionary of Theology*, (Ed.) Harrison, Bromiley, Henry, (Peabody, MA: Hendrickson Publishers, 1999), p. 306

[7] William Kelly, *Lectures on the Epistle to the Ephesians*, (Addison, IL: Bible Truth Publishers, 1979), p. 104-105

[8] J. N. Darby, *Collected Writings, vol. 14*, (Kingston-on-Thames, GB: Stow Hill Bible and Tract Depot, ND), p. 250

[9] Archibald Alexander Hodge, *The Atonement*, (Grand Rapids, MI: Eerdmans Publishing, 1953), pp.248, 249

[10] John Ritchie, *Romans*, (Charlotte, NC: The Serious Christian, 1987), p. 161

[11] C. F. Hogg, W. E. Vine, *The Epistle of the Galatians*, (London; GB: Pickering and Inglis, LTD.), 1959, p.186

- 16 -
Reformed Theology and Antinomianism

In the March 1887, issue of the Calvinist magazine, The Sword and the Trowel, the first of a series of articles appeared, entitled "The Down Grade", which gripped evangelical England. The author carefully outlined his deep concern. His heart ached over what he was seeing among Reformed churches in his own day. The articles unfolded a trend within Calvinist churches from the 1600's to the late 1800's. The Calvinist movement throughout history has tended to move from orthodoxy to theological error, and eventually, to antinomianism. He began his historical portrait by describing how hundreds of Puritan churches in the late 1600's abandoned sound doctrine in favor of Arianism (denial of the deity of Christ), Socinianism (denial of original sin), Unitarianism, and many other tenets of modernism. He went on to explain how in the 1740's Calvinist leader Phillip Doddridge opened the doors to modernism and antinomianism through his toleration of error. Even the church where Matthew Henry labored in the gospel for many years had given way to full-blown Socinianism. The "Down Grade", he warned, proceeded ever so slowly and was almost imperceptible in the early stages, but eventually gave way to full and complete error. Calvinistic churches soon became lax, granting membership, and later even leadership positions to unbelievers. The preaching was cold, dry, listless, and unfaithful to Scripture. Those churches that remained faithful to Christ were, nevertheless, reluctant to fight for holiness, godliness, and biblical truth. The sad consequence of all of this was an antinomian haze that soon covered Calvinistic and Reformed churches throughout England and America.[1] We may be getting a bit ahead of ourselves in our examination of this topic. Permit us to first examine the question: What is antinomianism?

WHAT IS ANTINOMIANISM?

The word antinomianism comes from the Greek *anti*, meaning against, and *nomos*, meaning law, and signifies lawlessness. The word, it is believed, was first coined by the Reformer Martin Luther in regard to his old friend John Agricola (1492-1566), who taught that Christ's death was the end of the law (Rom. 10:4). Luther initially feared that this doctrine, though biblical, would lead to unrighteousness in the lives of believers. He later came to understand and teach that the Mosaic Law in its entirety was ended; however, this truth should never hinder a believer's zeal to live a life of holiness. This unfounded and exaggerated fear still lingers today. Moreover, this term has come to mean moral permissiveness, worldliness, and a lax Christian lifestyle. Dispensationalists are the primary object of this criticism because of their teaching concerning law and grace, the two natures of the believer, and the believer's position in Christ (i.e. state and standing). Reformed theology has leveled this charge against Dispensationalism so often that today Dispensational theology, in some quarters, is almost synonymous with antinomianism. Listen to the unflattering words of leading Reformed author R. C. Sproul:

"Dispensational Theology is 'dubious' evangelicalism ...there is an inherent antinomianism built into the dispensational view of grace and law."[2]

Another Reformed writer, the late John Gerstner, states:

"Probably the most pernicious error to spring from this dispensational view of sanctification is its Antinomianism. It is most pernicious because it affects a person's behavior...Dispensationalism views the Christian as not under the law in any sense at all—even as a rule of life."[3]

ANTINOMIANISM AND MARTIN LUTHER

Despite the fact that Calvinist authors never miss an opportunity to label Dispensationalists as antinomian, we must question whether this is a fair charge. A number of questions need to be posed. Firstly, does Dispensational teaching produce Christians that are weak, lax, and ungodly in conduct? Is it biblical to teach that the believer is no longer under the law, even as a rule of life? Are Dispensationalists the only ones to espouse this view of the law? Let us take up these last two questions. Who, if any, of the church's leading theologians of past generations were known to hold the believer's freedom from the Mosaic Law? It is striking to discover that one of the chief architects of Reformed theology, Reformer Martin Luther (1483-1551), held and taught this very same view. Martin Luther, in his commentary *Paul's letter to the Galatians*, wrote:

"And here Paul speaks not of the ceremonial law only, but of the whole law, whether ceremonial or moral, which to a Christian is utterly abrogate, for he is dead unto it: not that the law is utterly taken away; nay, it remaineth, liveth, and reigneth still in the wicked. But a godly man is dead unto the law, like he is dead unto sin, the devil, death and hell: which notwithstanding do still remain, and the world with all the wicked shall still abide in them. Wherefore when the Papist understandeth that the ceremonial law only is abolished, understand thou that Paul and every Christian is dead to the law, and yet the whole law remaineth still. As for example: Christ rising from death is free from the grave, and yet the grave remaineth still. Wherefore these words, 'I am dead to the law,' are very effectual. For he saith not: 'I am free from the law for a time,' or 'I am lord over the law;' but simply, 'I am dead to the law,' that is, I have nothing to do with the law…Now to die to the law is not to be bound to the law, but to be free from the law, and not to know it. Therefore let him that will live to God endeavor that he may be found without the law, and let him come out of the grave with Christ."[4]

In this quotation the intrepid Reformer makes a number of points that are at odds with modern Reformed theology, but in surprising agreement with Dispensationalism. First of all, he states that the Mosaic Law cannot be divided into sections, some of which are for the believer, and others that have been done away with at the death of Christ. He writes, "Paul speaks not of the ceremonial law only, but of the whole law…" Secondly, he sets forth the idea that the law has no more power over a Christian, not even as a rule of life, because a Christian is in Christ and thus dead to the law. Luther writes, "…the whole law, whether ceremonial or moral, which to a Christian is utterly abrogate, for he is dead unto it: not that the law is utterly taken away; nay, it remaineth, liveth, and reigneth still in the wicked. But a godly man is dead unto the law, like he is dead unto sin, the devil, death and hell..." Luther appeals to Romans chapters six and seven for his position concerning the Christian and the law. He argues that his view is contextual, supported by good theology, and is in opposition to Catholicism ("Papist"). If Calvinist leaders persist in their view that Dispensationalists are antinomian, they must likewise, also label the great Reformation leader Martin Luther, to be antinomian as well.

ARE DISPENSATIONALISTS ANTINOMIAN?

Calvinist writers suggest that Dispensationalists are truly antinomian because they do not teach that Christians must live holy, consecrated, and devoted lives. They charge that Dispensationalists teach that Christians should, or may live for Christ, but not that they must live holy lives. Keith Mathison is representative of those who bring this accusation:

> "Reformed doctrine of perseverance says that all who... are eternally saved...they must and will persevere in holiness to the end. The Dispensational view is not that believers must, but that they may, persevere in holiness to the end. In fact, according to some Dispensationalists, not only is perseverance in holiness unnecessary, even remaining a believer is unnecessary"[5]

Calvinist leaders teach that Dispensationalism promotes worldliness, spiritual slackness, and carnal living. They suggest that Dispensationalism contains an inherent, pervasive, and widespread antinomianism. The Calvinist charge of

Dispensational antinomianism is doubtless a baseless attempt to undermine the influence and validity of this theological system. May we suggest that Dispensationalism, far from being antinomian, is a sound and God exalting system of biblical theology. Dispensationalism, as a theology, has generated more devoted missionaries, evangelists, sound theologians, and Bible teachers than any other theological perspective over the last 150 years. The list of those who considered themselves to be committed dispensationalists reads like a hall of fame of Christian devotion: hymn writer Isaac Watts, John Nelson Darby, evangelist D. L. Moody, R. A. Torry, Lewis Sperry Chafer, C. I. Scofield, Greek scholar W. E. Vine, Bible teacher Sidlow Baxter, Harry Ironside, Charles Ryrie, John Walvoord, missionary martyr Jim Elliot, Nate Saint, Billy Graham, W. A. Criswell, the list is endless. It is beyond belief that these men could be considered by some to be antinomian or to foster antinomianism. It staggers the imagination that some would impugn the character and richness of the ministry of these men. What did these men teach? Did they spurn the truths of Christian holiness and devotion? Permit us to list a number of quotations of Dispensational teachers from the past and present concerning their commitment to holiness and faith:

J. N. Darby (1800-1882), one of the early dispensational theologians:

"Many persons think that the full and unwavering assurance of our salvation tends to make us careless as to the state of our souls; but this is a mistake. The Holy Spirit has set His throne in our hearts, and if we will judge ourselves, we shall not be judged. It is He, who makes us fully enjoy God, and who makes us judge what is not of God in us; who alone sets us in the truth, and gives us the assurance of what is accomplished for us."[6]

William Kelly, an early British Dispensational theologian:

"Holiness, we all agree, is so imperative that without it no one shall see the Lord; and the professing Christian who does not pursue it only deceives himself. It is false and misleading to let people fancy that they may be real saints, yet unholy...those who do the wicked works of the flesh, and abide impenitent and indifferent have no part or lot with Christ, shall not inherit the kingdom of God, and in no way share the portion of saints in light."[7]

Lewis Sperry Chafer, one of the founders of Dallas Theological Seminary:

"After a soul has been saved there is a normal experience. There are new and blessed emotions and desires. Old things do pass away, and behold all things do become new...True salvation must result in just such realities. It is inconceivable that Christ should come to live in a human heart and its experiences remain unchanged. There must be, under such conditions, a new and vital relationship to God the Father, to fellow-Christians and to Christ Himself, a new attitude toward prayer, toward the Word, toward sin and toward the unsaved. This is the viewpoint of the Apostle James when he contends so earnestly for works that justify (to the outside world)."[8]

H. A. Ironside, Bible expositor, writer, visiting lecturer at Dallas Theological Seminary:

"To the haughty, self-righteous leaders, John said 'O, generation of vipers, who hath warned you to flee from the wrath to come? Bring forth therefore fruits meet for repentance.' 'Fruits meet for repentance'—that is, the changed life must evidence the changed attitude; otherwise there is no true repentance at all."[9]

Charles C. Ryrie, author of *Dispensationalism Today* (1966), and former professor at Dallas Theological Seminary:

"Every Christian will bear spiritual fruit. Somewhere, sometime, somehow. Otherwise that person is not a believer. Every born-again individual will be fruitful. Not to be fruitful is to be faithless, without faith, and therefore without salvation."[10]

Dr. Timothy Weber, a church historian at Yale University, has noted that the Dispensational system of theology has been a great incentive in world missions since the rise of Dispensational Pre-millennial teaching in the 1840's:

"By the 1920's (Dispensational) premillennialists were claiming that they made up 'an overwhelming majority' of the missions movement. Others estimated that believers in the imminent second coming made up from 75 to 80 percent of the missionary force world-wide... American premillennialists were better represented on the mission fields than in the home churches...Instead of cutting missionary involvement, premillennialism increased it."[11]

Every attempt at portraying Dispensationalism as inherently antinomian quickly unravels under the light of closer examination. Dispensationalism's missionary zeal, its evangelistic fervor, the godly character of its leaders, and the thoughtfulness of its theologians together show it to be a faithful and sound system of theology. However, allow us to turn the tables and ask the question of Calvinism: Is Calvinism antinomian? If one were to closely examine the history and fruits of Calvinism, what would one uncover? One historian has suggested that although Calvinists are quick to charge their opponents with antinomianism, it is the Calvinists themselves who have historically been identified with this malady, not their opponents.[12]

ANTINOMIANISM AND CALVINISM

Antinomianism and unfaithfulness to biblical truth has been a dark blot upon the historical legacy of Calvinism. Having said this, we must be quick to add that there have been many fine Calvinist believers throughout the history of the church. We are not speaking of individuals, but of the Calvinist movement as a whole. Calvinism has been a disappointment historically, even to Calvinists. Calvinist leaders have traced its spiritual and moral decline from the Calvinist churches that embraced Arianism and Socinianism in the 1600's, to Calvinist churches that denied the work of Christ and the plenary-verbal inspiration of Scripture in the 1700's. To the "Down Grade" controversy exposed by the ministry of Charles Spurgeon in the late 1800's. Historians have looked in vain to find any spiritual longevity in Calvinist churches in England or the United States or in Western Europe. Today, nearly all major Calvinist denominations are laced through with modernism and antinomianism. To name just a few: The Dutch Reformed Church, The Christian Reformed Church in America, The United Presbyterian Church, Presbyterian Church USA, The Church of England.

There are many reasons that could be given for the spiritual decline in Calvinist churches. We must resist the tendency to be too general or overly simplistic. However, one factor that stands out is Calvinism's weakness in the area of Bible interpretation. Calvinism, as a whole, struggles to discern dispensational distinctions in its interpretation of the "kingdom parables" in chapter thirteen of Matthew. As a result Reformed theology consistently teaches that the kingdom and the church are the same, and must be interpreted as such. Dispensationalism on the other hand distinguishes between the kingdom, the church, and Israel. What difference does proper theology make? The difference has tremendous ramifications on the purity of the church and antinomianism. Allow me to explain. Calvinism teaches that the parable of the "wheat and tares" refers not only to the kingdom but to the church also, since the kingdom and the church are one and the same. This parable causes great difficulty to the Calvinist, for it tells us that at the end of the age the "tares"(unbelievers) will be separated from the "wheat"(true believers) (Mt. 13:36-42). Where does the difficulty lie? If separation or judgment in the kingdom-church takes place at the end of the age, what then of the correction of sin and doctrinal error today in the local church? Must we conclude that God desires a church that consists not of believers only but also of unbelievers, false teachers, and immoral men and women? Sadly, this is exactly what Calvinism teaches.

According to Calvinist teachers, God desires to have an "impure church", rather than having a church that has put away from its fellowship sin, heresy, and immorality. Notice the carefully chosen words of the late Dr. James Boice, the Calvinist minister of the Tenth Presbyterian Church in Philadephia:

> "It must be acknowledged that the church on earth will always contain tares as well as wheat and that Christians must exercise utmost care in how they deal with them. The great temptation, particularly for those who are most serious about the church and its doctrine, is to root up the tares. But those who incline to this must remember that in Christ's parable (Matt. 13:24-30) it was precisely this course that was forbidden to the householder's servants...The time for separation was to be at the time of the final harvest when the wheat should be gathered into barns and the tares burned. The implication of Christ's parable is that some Christians are so much like non-Christians that it is impossible to tell the difference. In Christ's judgment the protection and nurture of all his followers within the church, regardless of outward appearance or degree of sanctification, are of such value that He would *rather tolerate an impure church than forfeit them.*"[13] (Italics mine)

Obviously, this cannot be the meaning of this parable. Holy Scripture nowhere implies or ever suggests that God desires an "impure" church. All true Christians must set aside such an interpretation as unbiblical and unworthy of Christ! What must we say of the Scriptures which state that our Lord desires the church to be as a "chaste virgin" (2 Cor. 11:2), or that Christ is washing the church with "the water of the Word that He might present it to himself a glorious church, not having spot, or wrinkle, or any such thing; but that it should be holy and without blemish" (Eph. 5:26-27). Can it be, that much of the antinomianism that has arisen in Calvinist churches historically is the result of a faulty interpretation of Scripture that tolerates and approves sin in the church of God? C. H. Spurgeon faced this same problem in the Calvinist churches in London in late 1800's.

ANTINOMIANISM AND C. H. SPURGEON

C. H. Spurgeon exerted, through his masterful expositions of Scripture, the greatest spiritual power and influence of any preacher of his day. Although Spurgeon came to London as a fresh-faced young preacher, he soon became a commanding figure among the Calvinist Baptist churches. At this particular time most of the Baptist churches in England were of a strong Calvinist persuasion, including those churches in London. Iain Murray, a biographer of Spurgeon, states that in 1851, 1,374 (88%) of the 1,553 Baptist churches in England, were strongly Calvinistic.[14] However, Spurgeon was a Calvinist of a much more moderate stripe than most of his contemporaries; indeed, he felt that many of the ministers had strayed much too far from the teaching of Scripture. During this time, he also became the object of much criticism from fellow Calvinists; but this did not hinder him from speaking out about unbiblical practices and teaching that he observed among his Calvinist colleagues. One of the main issues that stirred his heart had to do with the increasing tendency towards antinomianism. His love for all true believers, on one hand, and the devastating effect of antinomianism, on the other hand, weighed heavily upon his heart.

In 1889, he could contain himself no longer and wrote concerning these antinomian Calvinists in the magazine *The Sword and Trowel*:

> "They did not give up Calvinism, or in other words, renounce the Confession of 1689, but they overlaid it with an encrustation of something which approached Antinomianism, and ate out the life of the churches, and of the gospel as preached by many ministers…"[15]

He observed a growing permissiveness and carnality among many Calvinist churches throughout London and elsewhere. He saw the havoc that antinomian doctrine had wrought first hand. He stated from the pulpit:

> "My heart bleeds for many a family where Antinomianism has gained the sway. I could tell many a sad story of families dead in sin; whole consciences are seared as with a hot iron, by the fatal preaching to which they listen. I have known convictions stifled and desires quenched by the soul-destroying system which takes manhood from man and makes him no more responsible…"[16]

What was it that caused this shift towards antinomianism among the Baptist Calvinists in England? C. H. Spurgeon was quick to lay his finger upon the root of the problem. The problem, according to Spurgeon, was the rigid determinism inherent in Calvinism from its earliest days. By determinism, Spurgeon was referring to the Calvinist concept that all things that come to pass are caused or decreed by God alone.

Spurgeon saw clearly the dangers of such a doctrinal perspective. He proclaimed from the Metropolitan Tabernacle pulpit:

> "If I declare that God overrules all things, as that man is not free to be responsible, I am driven at once to Antinomianism or fatalism..."[17]

How was it that the poison of antinomianism had so infected the Calvinists in England? According to Spurgeon, it was their denial of the free will and responsibility of man. Spurgeon's reasoning in this was sound. If, as the Calvinists taught, God sovereignly determines and decrees all that comes to pass, then He also decrees and determines sin, not only sin in the unbeliever, but also sin in the believer. Furthermore, if God, directly or indirectly, causes every sin that comes to pass, then the free will of man is effectively eliminated. If man cannot resist sin, if it is God's sovereign will for sin to come to pass, why then should a Christian seek to live a holy life, for it is simply man resisting the will of God? Spurgeon saw this Calvinistic reasoning as an affront to the character and attributes of God. Such thinking was anti-Christian, and such reasoning was not fitting or worthy of a true Christian. Spurgeon forcefully charged his listeners at the Metropolitan Tabernacle:

> "The religion of a man who preaches divine sovereignty but neglects human responsibility. I believe it is a vicious, immoral, and corrupt manner of setting forth doctrine, and cannot be of God."[18]

Such thinking horrified Spurgeon, for he could see clearly where it would ultimately lead. It was the forerunner of the antinomian poison that would eventually devastate the

Calvinist Baptists in England. Within a relatively short period of time, the Calvinists in England and the circle of churches called the Baptist Union, with which Spurgeon was associated, became more and more infected with modernism, antinomianism, and unbelief. The Baptist Union was of particular concern to Spurgeon. Many of its churches denied the inspiration of Scripture, divine creation, the sinfulness of man (Socinianism), eternal punishment, gospel preaching, and bodily resurrection. The situation soon worsened, and C. H. Spurgeon could no longer bear to be associated with the error that had permeated this denomination. On October 28, 1887, Spurgeon officially withdrew from the Baptist Union. Soon after his departure, the Baptist Union passed a motion of censure condemning Spurgeon's actions, this motion passed the Council 95 votes to 5. The pattern had now repeated itself again; the Calvinist movement in England had declined from faith to unfaithfulness, from belief to unbelief, from devotion to antinomianism.

HOLINESS AND ITS IMPORTANCE

Holiness is mentioned in the Bible over 600 times, and is the great desire of God for His people. Sadly, holiness, for the most part, has been one of the most neglected areas of Christian living. This neglect of holiness was a problem in the early church, as well as in our own day. The apostle John urged his readers, "Everyone who has this hope (of eternal life) within him purifies himself even as He (Christ) is pure" (1 Jn. 3:3). The apostle Paul charged the believers at Thessalonica, "For this is the will of God, even your sanctification, that you abstain from fornication" (1 Thess. 4:3). Peter exhorted the followers of Christ, "As He who has called you is holy, so be ye holy in all manner of life, because as it is written, Be ye holy; for I am holy" (1 Pt. 1:15-

16). We must reject the current notion that suggests that one who lives an unholy and wicked life may nevertheless be a true Christian. The charge of the Scriptures to holy living is not optional but mandatory. Therefore, everyone then who professes salvation in Christ should ask himself, "Is there evidence of practical holiness in my life? Do I desire and strive after holiness? Do I grieve over my lack of holiness and earnestly seek God's help to be holy?" Christians should bow in soul-searching conviction at the Scripture, "...holiness, without which no man shall see the Lord" (Heb. 12:14). However, God has not commanded us to be holy without providing the means to be holy. The indwelling Spirit of God, the given resources to empower the believer. The privilege of being holy is ours, and the responsibility to live holy lives is ours. Therefore, those who take up this charge of holy living will experience the fullness of joy and the power of God that is promised to all who walk in obedience to Him.

Endnotes

[1] Robert Shindler, "The Down Grade", <u>The Sword and the Trowel</u> (March 1887), p, 122
[2] R. C. Sproul, *Grace Unknown,* (Grand Rapids, MI: Baker, 1997), p. 192
[3] John Gerstner, *Wrongly Dividing The Word of Truth,* (Brentwood, TN: Wolgemuth and Wyatt, 1993), p. 248-249
[4] Martin Luther, *Commentary on Paul's Epistle to the Galatians,* (Westwood, NJ: Fleming H. Revell, 1947), p. 158-159
[5] Keith Mathison, *Dispensationalism: Rightly Dividing the People of God,* (Phillipsburg, NJ: P & R Publishing, 1995), 76
[6] J. N. Darby, *Ephesians,* (Oak Park, IL: Bible Truth Pub, ND), p. 12
[7] William Kelly, *Bible Treasury, New Series, vol. 5,* (H. L. Heijkoop Verlag, Winscoten, Netherlands, 1986), p. 162

[8] Lewis Sperry Chafer, *Salvation*, (Philadelphia, PA: Sunday School Times Company, 1917,) p. 12

[9] H. A. Ironside, *Unless You Repent*, (Grand Rapids, MI: Gospel Folio Press, 1994,) p. 28

[10] C. Ryrie, *So Great Salvation*, (Wheaton, IL:Victor, 1989), p. 45

[11] Timothy Weber, *Living in the Shadow of the Second Coming*, 1875-1982, (Grand Rapids, MI: Zondervan, 1983), p. 81

[12] Laurence Vance, *The Other Side of Calvinism*, (Pensacola, FL: Vance Publications, 1999), 590

[13] James Montgomery Boice, *The Epistles of John*, (Grand Rapids, MI: Zondervan, 1994), p. 87

[14] Iain Murray, *C. H. Spurgeon and Hyper-Calvinism*, (Carlisle, PA: Banner of Truth, 2000), p. 41

[15] Sword and Trowel, 1889, p. 600, quoted in Iain Murray, *Spurgeon v. Hyper-Calvinism*, (Carlisle, PA: Banner of Truth, 2000), p.126-127

New Park Street Pulpit, vol. 6, (London: Passmore and Alabaster), p. 28, quoted in Iain Murray, *Spurgeon v. Hyper-Calvinism*, (Carlisle, PA: Banner of Truth, 2000), p.155

[17] *New Park Street Pulpit, vol. 4*, (London: Passmore and Alabaster), p. 343 quoted in Iain Murray, *Spurgeon v. Hyper-Calvinism*, (Carlisle, PA: Banner of Truth, 2000), p.82

[18] *Metropolitian Tabernacle Pulpit, vol. 9*, (London: Passmore and Alabaster), p. 190

Bibliography

Sir Robert Anderson, *Redemption Truths,* (Kilmarnock, Scotland: Ritchie, 1940)

Roland H. Bainton, *Here I Stand,* (New York, NY : Meridian Books, 1995)

David & Randall Basinger, (ed), *Predestination and Free Will,* (Downers Grove, IL: Intervarsity, 1986)

J. Sidlow Baxter, *New Call to Holiness,* (London, GB: Marshall, Morgan & Scott, 1967)

Louis Berkhof, *Systematic Theology,* (Grand Rapids, MI: Eerdmans, 1941)

G. C. Berkhower, *Divine Election,* (Grand Rapids, MI: Eerdmans, 1975)

James Montgomery Boice, *The Epistles of John,* (Grand Rapids, MI: Zondervan, 1994)

F. F. Bruce, *Ephesians,* (London : Pickering & Inglis, 1961)

George Bryson, *The Five Points of Calvinism,* (Costa Mesa, CA: The Word For Today, 1996)

John Calvin, *Institutes, Vol. 1, 2,* (Grand Rapids, MI, : Eerdmans, 1952)

John Calvin, *Concerning Eternal Predestination,* (London, GB: Clarke, 1961)

Lewis Sperry Chafer, *Salvation,* (Philadelphia, PA: Sunday School Times Company, 1917)

Lewis Sperry Chafer, *Systematic Theology,* (Dallas, TX : Dallas Seminary Press, 1948)

James Daane, *The Freedom of God,* (Grand Rapids, MI: Eerdmans, 1973)
Arnold Dallimore, *George Whitfield, vol. 1,* (London, GB: Banner of Truth Trust, 1970)
John Nelson Darby, *Collected Writings, vol. 3,* (Kingston on the Thames, GB: Stow Hill Bible and Tract Depot, ND)
John Nelson Darby, *Ephesians,* (Oak Park, IL: Bible Truth Publishers, ND)
Dieter, Hoekema, Horton, McQuilkin, Walvoord, *Five Views on Sanctification,* (Grand Rapids, MI : Zondervan, 1987)
Jonathan Edwards, *Life of David Brainerd,* (Grand Rapids, MI: Baker, 1978)
Samuel Fisk, *Divine Sovereignty and Human Responsibility,* (Neptune, NJ : Loizeaux, 1981)
Samuel Fisk, *Calvinistic Paths Retraced,* (Murfreeboro, TN: Biblical Evangelism Press, 1985)
Roger Forster, V. Paul Marston, *God's Strategy in Human History,* (Bromley, GB : STL Books, 1981)
John Gerstner, *Dispensationalism: Wrongly Dividing the Word of God,* (Wolgemuth & Wyatt , Brentwood, TN, 1991)
John Gerstner, *Jonathan Edwards, Evangelist,* (Morgan, PA:Soli Deo Gloria Publications, 1995)
Norman Geisler, *Chosen But Free,* (Minneapolis, MN, Bethany House, 1999)
Fredrick Godet, *Romans,* (Grand Rapids, MI : Zondervan, 1956)
F. W. Grant, *Sovereignty of God in Salvation,* (NY, NY: Loizeaux)
Everett Harrison (ed.) *Wycliffe Dictionary of Theology,* (Peabody, MA: Hendrikson Publishers, 1999)
Matthew Henry, *Commentary on the Whole Bible,* (Peabody, MA: Hendrikson Publishers, 1991)
D. E. Hiebert, *1 Peter,* (Chicago, IL : Moody Press, 1992)

D. E. Hiebert, *2 Peter & Jude,* (Greenville, SC: Unusual Publications, 1989)
D. E. Hiebert, *Titus,* (Chicago, IL:Moody Press, 1957)
A. A. Hodge, *The Atonement,* (Grand Rapids, MI : Eerdmans, 1962)
Charles Hodge, *Romans,* (Grand Rapids, MI : Eerdmans, 1976)
Charles Hodge, *1 & 2 Corinthians,* (Carlisle, PA: Banner of Truth, 1974)
H. A. Ironside, *The Teaching of the So-Called Plymouth Brethren: Is It Scriptural?,* (New York, NY: Loizeaux, 1930)
H. A. Ironside, *What's the Answer,* (Grand Rapids, MI: Zondervan, 1944)
H. A. Ironside, *Unless You Repent,* (Port Colborne, ON: Gospel Folio Press, 1994)
Josephus, *The Jewish War,* (New York, NY: Penguin Books, 1981)
William Kelly, *John,* (Denver, CO: Wilson Foundation, 1966)
William Kelly, *Bible Treasury, New Series, vol. 5*
R. T. Kendall, *Once Saved, Always Saved,* (Chicago, IL: Moody Press, 1983)
G. H. Lang, *World Chaos,* (London, Paternoster Press, 1950)
Robert P. Lightner, *The Death Christ Died,* (Grand Rapids, MI: Kregel Publications, 1998)
R. C. H. Lenski, *1st & 2nd Epistles to the Corinthians,* (Minneapolis, MN:Augsburg Publishing House, 1963)
John MacArthur, *Ephesians,* (Chicago, IL: Moody Press, 1987)
John MacArthur, *Freedom From Sin-Rom. 6-7,* (Chicago, IL: Moody Press, 1991)
John MacArthur, *Gospel According to Jesus,* (Grand Rapids, MI: Zondervan, 1988)
John MacArthur, *Vanishing Conscience,* (Waco, TX, Word Publishing, 1995)

William MacDonald, *Matthew,* (Kansas City, KS: Walterick, 1974)
William MacDonald, *Romans,* (Kansas City, KS: Walterick, 1981)
C. H. Macintosh, *Macintosh Treasury,* (Neptune, NJ : Loizeaux, 1976)
C. H. Macintosh, *Short Papers, vol. 2,* (Sunbury, PA : Believer's Bookshelf, 1975)
Harold Mackay, *Biblical Balance,* (Port Colborne, ON, Everyday Publications, 1978)
Alexander Maclaren, *Exodus,* (Grand Rapids, MI : Baker, 1989)
John T. McNeill, *The History and Character of Calvinism,* (New York, NY: Oxford University Press, 1967)
James Moffat, *Predestination,* (NY, NY: Loizeaux, ND)
D. Martyn Lloyd-Jones, *Romans 8:5-17, Sons of God,* (Grand Rapids, MI: Zondervan, 1979)
D. Martyn Lloyd-Jones, *Sermon on the Mount,* (Grand Rapids, MI:Eerdmans, 1979)
Martin Luther, *Commentary on Paul's Epistle to the Galatians,* (Westwood, NJ: Fleming H. Revell, 1947)
Keith Mathison, *Dispensationalism: Wrongly Dividing the People of God,* (Phillipsburg, NJ : P & R Publishers, 1995)
Alva McClain, *Romans,* (Chicago, IL : Moody Press, 1973)
Iain Murray, *Spurgeon vs Hyper-Calvinism,* (Carlisle, PA : Banner of Truth, 1995)
J. B. Nicholson, Sr., *1 Peter,* (Kilmarnock, Scotland: Ritchie, 1986)
James Orr, *The Progress of Dogma,* (Grand Rapids, MI: Eerdmans, 1952)
Willem Ouweneel, *What is Election,* (Sunbury, PA: Believer's Bookshelf, ND)

J. I. Packer, *Fundamentalism and the Word of God,* (Grand Rapids, MI: Eerdmans, 1958)

Edwin H. Palmer, *The Five Points of Calvinism,* (Grand Rapids, MI, Baker Books, 1979)

John Parkinson, *The Faith of God's Elect,* (Glasgow, Scotland: Gospel Tract Publications, 1999)

A. W. Pink, *The Attributes of God,* (Swengel, PA: Reiner Publications, 1964)

A. W. Pink, *Gleanings from the Scriptures,* (Chicago, IL, Moody Press, 1964)

A. W. Pink, *The Sovereignty of God,* (Grand Rapids, MI : Baker, 1992)

A. W. Pink, *Practical Christianity,* (Grand Rapids, MI : Guardian Press, 1974)

William Sanday, A. Headlam, *Romans, A Critical and Exegetical Commentary,* (NY, NY:Scribner, 1910)

Erich Sauer, *Dawn of World Redemption,* (Grand Rapids, MI: Eerdmans, 1973)

C. I. Scofield, *Scofield Correspondence Course,* (Chicago, IL : Bible Institute Colportage Association, ND)

W. G. T. Shedd, *Dogmatic Theology,* (Grand Rapids, MI: Zondervan,)

R. C. Sproul, Jr. *Almighty Over All,* (Grand Rapids, MI , Baker Books, 1999)

R. C. Sproul, *Chosen By God,* (Wheaton, IL : Tyndale Publishers, 1986)

R. C. Sproul, *Faith Alone,* (Grand Rapids, MI : Baker, 1995)

R. C. Sproul, *Grace Unknown,* (Grand Rapids, MI: Baker, 1997)

C. H. Spurgeon, *Autobiography: The Early Years 1834-1859, vol. 1.,* (Edinburgh, Scotland: Banner of Truth Trust, 1962)

C. H. Spurgeon, *Metropolitan Tabernacle Pulpit, vol. 16,* (London: Passmore & Alabaster, 1907)

Steele, Thomas, *Five Points of Calvinism,* (Phillipsburg, NJ: Presbyterian and Reformed Pub., 1963)
A. H. Strong, *Systematic Theology,* (Philadelphia, PA: Judson, 1907)
Samuel Ridout (editor), *Numerical Bible, vol. 6,* (NewYork, NY: Loizeaux, 1903)
John Ritchie, *Romans,* (Charlotte, NC: The Serious Christian, 1987)
Charles Ryrie, *So Great Salvation,* (Wheaton, IL: Victor Books, 1989)
Henry Theissen, *Lectures in Systematic Theology,* (Grand Rapids, MI: Eerdmans , 1975)
W. H. Griffin Thomas, *Romans,* (Grand Rapids, MI: Eerdmans, 1946)
W. G. Turner, *John Nelson Darby,* (London, GB: Hammond, 1951)
A. W. Tozer, *The Knowledge of the Holy,* (New York, NY: Harpers and Row Publishers, 1961)
Laurance Vance, *The Other Side of Calvinism,* (Pensacola, FL: Vance Publications, 1998)
W. E. Vine, *Expository Dictionary of New Testament Words,* (Old Tappan, NJ: Revell, 1992)
W. E. Vine, *Philippians and Colossians,* (London, GB: Oliphants, LTD, 1955)
W. E. Vine, *Romans,* (London: Oliphants Limited, 1948)
Timothy Weber, *Living in the Shadow of the Second Coming, 1875-1982,* (Grand Rapids, MI: Zondervan, 1983)
M. B. Wynkoop, *Foundations of Wesleyan Arminian Theology,* (Kansas City, MO: Beacon Hill, 1967)